Brace yourself... this is one powerhouse book!

In a knowledgeable and gracious way, Dr. Dan Tomlinson carefully explains the parallels between the conception through the birth of a child and God's plan for the ages according to the Scriptures.

This is a must read for all who desire to know the greatness of our God who has revealed Himself through His Word as well as His creation.

Through the strength of his analysis and the lens of his experience, Dr. Dan will inspire us to reconsider the miracle of life and how God has a hand in even the finest details of life.

As you read this book, you will be changed. The content of which points us to our Creator and His sovereign hand in forming every detail of our lives.

I love this book and am deeply grateful to Dan for the gift he offers in its clear and compelling message. This is more than another book of inspiration although it is packed full of facts and truths and ideas that are gripping... *A Woman's Silent Testimony* is a work of art.

—Pastor Jim Wright
Mountain Christian Fellowship

In his book, *A Woman's Silent Testimony,* Dr. Dan Tomlinson has captured in a unique and insightful way the ability to challenge the reader to think outside the box of traditional ideology and view life through the lens of Scripture from his viewpoint as an experienced obstetrician. As you embark on this wonderful journey with Dr. Dan as your tour guide, be prepared to be intellectually challenged and encouraged to focus the light of God's Word onto the reality of everyday life issues as seen through the eyes of a caring physician, friend, and co-laborer in Christ.

—Pastor Abner Sumrall
Applegate Christian Fellowship

A WOMAN'S SILENT ✝ESTIMONY

A Woman's Silent ✝ Estimony

How Pregnancy

Enlivens Biblical Truths

by Daniel A. Tomlinson, M.D.

Tate Publishing *& Enterprises*

Published by Tate Publishing & Enterprises, LLC
127 E. Trade Center Terrace | Mustang, Oklahoma 73064 USA
1.888.361.9473 | www.tatepublishing.com

Tate Publishing is committed to excellence in the publishing industry. The company reflects the philosophy established by the founders, based on Psalm 68:11,
"The Lord gave the word and great was the company of those who published it."

Book design copyright © 2009 by Tate Publishing, LLC. All rights reserved.
Cover design by Kandi Evans
Interior design by Stefanie Rooney

Published in the United States of America

ISBN: 978-1-61566-692-8
1. Religion, Biblical Commentary, General
2. Religion, Christian Theology, Eschatology
09.12.10

ACKNOWLEDGMENTS

First and foremost, to my Lord and Savior, my big brother, my bridegroom and dearest friend, Jesus of Nazareth, born in Bethlehem and also known as the Christ: He, through his Spirit and his Word, has inspired me countless times. I am so thankful for his grace and mercy to me as well as for the calling he has given me as a physician and as a lay minister. I look forward to spending eternity with him!

To my wonderful wife, Julie: I thank her for her continued support, as well as to my two delightful children, Alexandra (Alex) and Zach.

To Pastor Jim Wright: Pastor Jim, the senior pastor of Mountain Christian Fellowship in Medford Oregon, was one of the first people I told of my vision to write a book dealing with obstetrics and spirituality. We were snowboarding on a beautiful winter day in southern Oregon when Pastor Jim encouraged me to "go for it." He had been studying in the Gospel of Mark at the time and had noted the sense of immediacy and urgency that is seen in that account. I took it as a word from God and started the outline for this book later that day. The first words of the narrative were begun on Easter later that spring.

To Pastor Jim Feeney, pastor of the Medford Christian Center and the man who inspired me to start reading through the Bible sequentially in a day-by-day type of format: I can't put into words how that has changed my life!

To the late Victor Paul Wierwille: Some of his unique perspectives upon the Word and especially his emphasis upon "the *Word* of God being the *Will* of God" have made a difference in my life.

To Pastor Jon Courson, founding pastor of the Applegate Christian Fellowship in Ruch, Oregon. Pastor Jon's distinctive gift from God in teaching the Word and especially in revealing the countless pictures found in the Old Testament, which reveal New Testament truths, have been nothing short of inspirational to me! His teaching has opened my eyes to see allegories everywhere in the Bible.

TABLE OF CONTENTS

BOOK ONE: *Parallels of Fetal and Earthly Life* 15

Introduction 17
Conception and the New Birth 17
Life in Utero and All My Days 19
Labor and Delivery: Death to Life Eternal 25

BOOK TWO: *Death, Burial, and Resurrection* 29

Introduction 31
Childbearing 33
Creation 34
The Story of Jonah 36
Baptism 42
The Story of Noah 45
The Baptism of the Children of Israel 48
The Story of Lazarus 50
The Order of the Resurrection 51
The Story of Manasseh 55
The Story of Isaac 57
Moses and the Ark 70
Moses and Mount Nebo 73
A Leper's Two Birds 83
Paul's Shipwreck 89
Crucified with Christ 94
Traditions of Spring 101
Application: The Death, Burial,
and Resurrection of Self 105

BOOK THREE: *SORROW TO JOY* 109

   The Labor 111
   The Delivery 117
   God is Faithful 120

BOOK FOUR: *The Price of Idolatry:*
The Babylonian Conquest of the Judeans 125

   Judah's Adulterous Affair 127
   Her Pregnancy 132
   Her Labor 134
   Her Delivery 136

BOOK FIVE: *Paul's Travail* 141

   Paul's Calling 143
   Paul's Conversion 147
   Paul's Quiet Time with the Lord 149
   Paul's First Missionary Journey 152
   Paul's Second Missionary Journey 154
   The Word of God Prevails 158
   Sincerity Is No Guarantee for Truth 159
   Paul's Jerusalem Trial and Travail 162
   Paul's Reality 164
   Paul's Thorn in the Flesh 166
   The Crown of Rejoicing 170
   Children Walking in Truth 171

BOOK SIX: *Of Blood and Water* 175

   The Second Adam 177
   Scripture Buildup 181
   The Garden Arrest 183
   Appearance Before Annas 191
   The Night Trial 194
   The Day Trial 200
   Jesus' First Appearance Before Pilate 201
   Jesus Before Herod 205

Jesus' Second Appearance Before Pilate 207
The Praetorium 216
Jesus' Death March 218
The Crucifixion of the Christ 224
The Death of the Christ 234
Blood and Water 245
Conclusions: Humility Before Honor 246

BOOK SEVEN: *The Valley Between the Mountains* 253
Introduction 255
Spiritual Treatments for Depression 266
Conclusions and Applications from Depression ... 273

BOOK EIGHT: *She Shall Be Saved in
Childbearing* 281

NOTE FROM THE AUTHOR

At the outset of this book, I want to make the distinction between ideas and truth. Ideas can be plagiarized; truth cannot! The reason I make this point is because the Bible is about truth. Also, when one sits under a man's teaching ministry, he or she will begin to take on the flavor of that teacher. Certainly this has happened here. I thank my mentors in advance, especially Pastor Jon, for their indulgence and understanding.

BOOK ONE

Parallels of Fetal and Earthly Life

Introduction

It's human nature to resist change. It is also natural to fear the unknown or unfamiliar. Thus, many people hold on to the belief that this life is "all that there is." They refuse to believe that the next life is as certain as their present life in spite of scriptural evidence to the contrary. Yet right in front of our noses whenever we see a pregnant woman or a newborn baby, we should be reminded that our lives have *already* gone through a transformation as radical as belief in the next life! When we were each conceived, formed in our mother's womb, and delivered, we all went through a metamorphosis that is now paralleled in our present life and death. In other words, there are numerous similarities between our fetal and earthly lives that picture spiritual truths. Let's look at some of them together.

Conception and the New Birth

Conception is a wonderful picture of the "new birth." Just as we were all conceived physically, Jesus said to Nicodemus (and by extension, he said to you and me) speaking of the spiritual, "Ye must be born again" (John 3:7b).

Let's look at the parallels.

At the moment of conception, the egg from the mother and the sperm from the father unite to form a new human being.

Likewise, before I was born again, the Bible teaches that I was a "natural man."

> But the natural man receiveth not the things of the Spirit of God: For they are foolishness unto him: Neither can he know them, because they are spiritually discerned.
>
> 1 Corinthians 2:14

I was a person of body and soul without the Spirit of God dwelling within. I was incomplete.

James says it this way: "The body without the spirit is dead" (James 2:26b).

Until I get the spirit, I'm not really alive!

But when a man or a woman or a boy or a girl puts his or her faith in Jesus Christ, he or she now becomes a person of body, soul, and spirit. He or she is complete. Paul's prayer for the Thessalonican believers illustrates this point. "And the very God of peace sanctify you wholly; and I pray God your whole *spirit* and *soul* and *body* be preserved blameless unto the coming of our Lord Jesus Christ" (1 Thessalonians 5:23).

You see, the egg and sperm coming together is analogous to the new birth. Before salvation, we are typified by the egg. The Spirit of God, delivered via the Word of God, is represented by the sperm. They come together to form a new creation, what the Bible calls the "spiritual man." This is the new birth!

> Being born again, not of corruptible seed, but of incorruptible, by the word of God, which liveth and abideth forever.
>
> 1 Peter 1:23

So in summary, we see conception as a picture of the new birth. The egg of the natural man and the incorruptible seed of the Word of God (having the Spirit embedded within) come together beautifully to start a new person.

Jesus told his disciples that the kingdom of heaven can be compared to a mustard seed. It starts out small but will grow into a large and beautiful plant. I think of this parable when thinking of the seed of life, the new conceptus, starting out so very small and yet growing into a mature and beautiful creation of God.

Life in Utero and All My Days

The time that a fetus spends in the womb I find to be a very interesting picture of our days here on earth. We here on this planet are like a baby inside the uterus of its mother. In fact, the world intuitively recognizes this as we hear often the term *Mother Earth* in relation to the nurturing we all receive from our home.

First of all, in utero it's dark. I mean it's *very* dark. It's a place devoid of light. So too is our world! The Bible states in Genesis, "And the earth was without form and void and darkness was over the face of the deep" (Genesis 1:2).

We here on earth grope around in darkness as the Bible illustrates in picture after picture. We see Jesus leaving heaven where he was in the presence of the Father of lights in order to come to the dark earth and be the light of man (John 1:9). We also note in Genesis 37, Joseph (who is a wonderful picture in the Old Testament of Jesus) leaving his father in Hebron (*Hebron* means fellowship) to bring bread (the Word of God) to his brothers. He found his brothers in Dothan, which means *double sickness* or *double darkness!* Do you see this marvelous type? Jesus left the place of fellowship with his Father to bring the light of God's Word to mankind!

Yes, the womb is a dark place, but consider how the fetus perceives his environment. He has never been in the light and, thus, has no real concept of what he is missing! He thinks the darkness is just fine. He has no thought or understanding of things we experience in our world. He does not comprehend mathematics, history, or language. Computer technology, aviation, love, and war are not a concern or an interest. I would go so far as to speculate that an ant on a baseball diamond could comprehend the rules of the game being played on the field more than the fetus could relate to the life ahead for him in just a few short months. Hopefully now you are beginning to understand what is in store for *us* when we are born out of this dark world and into the light!

The fetus feels as if he has everything he needs. The placenta delivers oxygen, that essential element necessary for survival. So too the Lord has sent the Comforter, the Holy Spirit. In English, our word *inspired* is derived from the phrase *in spirit,* which in Greek literally means "God breathed." Truly God has given us the air we breathe, which is the Holy Spirit.

It is also interesting to consider what happens when the fetus is deprived of oxygen. And likewise to reflect upon what happens to a man or woman deprived of the Spirit. The fetus will switch to anaerobic metabolism. That is, he will use another, very weak pathway to generate energy for his body to function. This type of metabolism will only maintain the fetus for a short time. Then fetal distress will set in and ultimately death will occur. So it is in our lives now. A man or woman without the Spirit of God dwelling within—without oxygen, if you will—is able to function for a short time. For indeed a lifetime is but a moment when compared to eternity. But ultimately, life without the Spirit will lead to distress and finally to death. Life with the Spirit will lead to peace and to life eternal!

The developing fetus also receives nutrition from the placenta in the form of amino acids. These are the building blocks of proteins that are needed for life to continue. Likewise, the Word of God is our food as we develop here "in utero." Jeremiah states, "Thy words were found, and I did eat them; and thy word was to me the joy and rejoicing of mine heart" (Jeremiah 15:16).

Peter tells us, "Desire the sincere milk of the word, that ye may grow thereby" (1 Peter 2:2a).

Yet again, though, there is a flip side both to the fetus and to those of us in our present terrestrial bodies. If the developing human being does not get amino acids to form proteins, he will be severely runted. We call this IUGR, or intrauterine growth retardation. That fetus may be getting oxygen, and thus survive, but will be limited after birth by the lack of complete development during his time in-utero. Likewise, the believer in Christ who does not take in spiritual food will also be growth retarded. Oh, he or she will be saved. They are getting oxygen; they have the Spirit, if you will. But I can't help but think that they will have a decreased capacity to enjoy the next life because of the lack of nutrition they took in during this life.

In utero, we know the fetus must have a minimal awareness of the outside world. She can feel her mother's heartbeat and can hear muffled sounds. We believe that the fetus has fearful fits of crying and kicking as well as times of rest and warmth. It's not hard when thinking of these things to see the parallels to life, is it? We too have a sense of the hereafter, of the "outside world," if you will. People of all cultures and of all times have felt the presence of a creator. Mankind has always sensed God or an essence more powerful and intelligent. Of course, without God's revelation to us of his nature, we have fallen woefully short in our understanding of him. Man has worshipped four-footed creatures and gods in our own image (Romans 1:23). We really have no comprehension of God without his light.

In these "last days," we still really do not have a clue! Indeed we are told that knowledge is doubling exponentially. But where is the *wisdom?* The book of Job states it well:

> Then the Lord answered Job out of the whirlwind, and said, Who is this that darkeneth counsel by words without knowledge? Where wast thou when I laid the foundations of the earth? Declare, if thou hast understanding... Hast thou commanded the morning since thy days; and caused the dayspring to know his place? Have the gates of death been opened unto thee? Or have thou seen the doors of the shadow of death? Have thou entered into the treasures of the snow? Or hast thou seen the treasures of the hail?
>
> Job 38:1–2, 12, 17, 22

The answer is a resounding no! Paul states it in these terms, "Ever learning, and never able to come to the knowledge of the truth" (2 Timothy 3:7).

The Bible makes it clear that one day we will indeed understand in ways that are not being comprehended now. We are told that on that day every knee shall bow and every tongue confess that Jesus is Lord (Philippians 2:10–11).

We have learned, "Eye has not seen, nor ear heard, neither have entered into the heart of man, the things which God hath prepared for them that love Him" (1 Corinthians 2:9).

Indeed our comprehension in this life is but a shadow of our future insights. But when we see him, then we will know him even as we are known.

> For now we see through a glass, darkly; but then face to face: Now I know in part; but then shall I know even as also I am known.
>
> 1 Corinthians 13:12

I don't remember anything of my life while my mother was carrying me. I suspect that you do not either. In my day-to-day life, I'm not really bothered by this, but I wonder what I experienced but no longer remember. The sensation I experienced when my mother was walking or exercising or with my father, was it pleasant or not? Was I cramped in the fetal position, or was it comfortable? I suggest to you that it really wasn't all that wonderful! As I mentioned earlier, we suspect from ultrasound observations that fetuses have bouts of crying and wild kicking in utero, which likely correlate to discomfort experienced. Likewise in this life, I feel like crying and kicking when I hit my thumb with a hammer or have a bad round of golf! Indeed, during our time in the uterus, just as in our lives now, things were and are not perfect!

Just as we don't remember our fetal lives, the Bible states that there is no remembrance of former things (Ecclesiastes 1:11a).

> For, behold, I create new heavens and a new earth: And the former shall not be remembered, nor come to mind.
>
> Isaiah 65:17

The Bible confirms that the things done in our lives will be tried as through fire and only those things of gold, silver, and precious stones will remain (1 Corinthians 3:12–15). We are told in 1 Corinthians 13:13, in speaking of our future life, that the things that will abide are faith, hope, and love.

These verses and others teach us that we will not have total recall of our earthly lives. Many are saying, "Praise the Lord for that," while others may be disappointed. For this second category, we have the words of Jesus to consider when he told his listeners to *remember Lot's wife* (Luke 17:32) in relation to the folly of looking back and longing for the worldly things of Sodom. Jesus says not to look back. So too in our next life we will not remember the things of wood, hay, and stubble (1 Corinthians 3:12–15). All tears will be wiped away.

> And God shall wipe away all tears from their eyes; and there shall be no more death, neither sorrow, nor crying, neither shall there be any more pain: For the former things are passed away. And he that sat on the throne said, Behold, I make all thing new.
>
> Revelation 21:4–5a

We won't remember those things that are not excellent, just as we do not remember our fetal existence.

Jesus told his disciples about our future homes and compared them to mansions.

> Let not your heart be troubled: Ye believe in God, believe also in me. In my Father's house are many mansions: If it were not so, I would have told you. I go to prepare a place for you. And if I go and prepare a place for you, I will come again, and receive you unto myself; that where I am, there ye may be also.
>
> John 14:1–3

Imagine that! It took God only six days to create the entire universe, but so far Jesus has been preparing our future homes for nearly two thousand years!

Now, just because we do not remember our fetal time does not mean it wasn't important to us. We were and are all strongly influenced by our fetal development. If my mother had taken poison or starved herself during her pregnancy, my potential for this life would have been impacted greatly. This may also be true for our next life. If we continually poison ourselves with worldly pleasures and lusts while starving ourselves of spiritual food, we may make it to heaven but I can't help but think that we may have a decreased potential to enjoy and appreciate the heavenly realm of our next lives.

So we see that our time on earth does parallel our fetal life. We don't remember any of it, but oh, how very important it was! It was dark and painful at times, and we didn't even comprehend what we were missing. We felt like we had it made in the shade and didn't want to leave. Please don't miss this perfect analogy that God wants us to consider.

Now let's look at the birth!

Labor and Delivery: Death to Life Eternal

The process we all undergo in arriving here as a newborn baby is remarkably revisited again upon our death. Labor and delivery is a wonderful picture of death from this life and birth into our next. The labor is analogous to our death, and the birth correlates to the start of our new life with God in his presence.

Paul states it this way in Philippians,

> For to me to live is Christ, and to die is gain. But if I live in the flesh, this is the fruit of my labor: Yet what shall I choose I know not. For I am in a strait betwixt the two, having a desire to depart, and be with Christ; which is far better.
>
> Philippians 1:21–23

Paul understood that dying would birth him into the presence of Christ.

Now, when mothers are asked how the birthing process went, most would agree that it was difficult. It seems like the baby just doesn't want to come. So too we cling to our lives here on earth with much vigor. It is estimated that over 80 percent of health care dollars are spent on care given in the last month of a person's life. We want to do just about anything to stay alive. So it shouldn't be so surprising that the baby also doesn't want to be born. We doctors have a saying in obstetrics that speaks to this: "Pregnancy is the only thing that makes labor look good!" Yes, we still haven't lost that notion of being resistant to change after a seventy-year life!

Labor can be a few hours, or it can be prolonged, taking even more than a day. In like manner, the death process can be quick, or it can be a long, painful process. Isaac, in Genesis 27, believed he was about to die at the age of 137 because that was the age his older half-brother Ishmael was when he died. Thus, Isaac called for his firstborn son, Esau, in order to bless him. We learn in Genesis 35 that Isaac lived another forty-three years! Indeed, dying can take a long time!

When we are born, we enter a world of light that we never could have imagined. That's what it will be like to enter into the presence of the Lord. We will be dumfounded with joy and wonder, which will cause us to cry out as that baby does when she takes her first breath.

Lastly, in heaven it will take us eternity and beyond to comprehend God, his grace, and the things of his realm. We see this in our lives now in the developmental stages a person experiences as he is learning and hopefully growing and maturing!

Truly, labor and delivery picture death and life anew! We leave one state for another in a process that can be short or long. Easy or hard. We try hard to cling to that of which we are familiar, but when the delivery occurs, we enter a world of light and wonder that we could never have imagined!

––––––––––––––––––

Now, the application to these parallels of fetal and earthly life is grand and wonderful. Just as the baby ultimately will be born the first time, we too will be born into heaven. And it will be sooner than we realize. This makes me want to live for heaven. To keep the main thing the main thing! It makes the reality of heaven the most important thing. As I can still hear Pastor Jon say, "Folks, if heaven is true, then that's all that matters, but if heaven isn't true, then nothing matters at all!"

Paul preaches to the Philippian believers that they are to learn contentment in life: "For I have learned, in whatsoever state I am, therewith to be content" (Philippians 4:11).

You see, God plans for us to be kings and priests with him for eternity. We have an inheritance reserved for us, which makes the birthright of a Rockefeller child pale in comparison.

So as we started, so shall we end. The next time you start thinking that this is all there is, tell your mind to pipe down and remember where you came from is analogous to where you are going!

God bless you as you consider these things.

BOOK TWO

Death, Burial, and Resurrection

Introduction

The resurrection of Jesus Christ *is* the focal point of history. In fact, the meaning of the word *history* can aptly be expanded into the phrase *his story*. The resurrection is not only important to the Christian faith; it's essential to our faith. Without it, really there is no Christian faith! It is the doctrine that separates our beliefs from all other dogmas and places Jesus Christ above every other spiritual leader and guru. Jesus alone had the power not only to die for the sins of mankind but also to take up his life again. He is utterly unique!

The resurrection of Jesus gives meaning and hope to life. The Bible declares, "For as in Adam all die, even so in Christ shall all be made alive" (1 Corinthians 15:22).

Without the resurrection, life is hopeless as only a sleep of death awaits. Paul states it this way,

> And if Christ be not raised, your faith is vain; ye are yet in your sins. Then they which are fallen asleep *(have died)* in Christ are perished. If in this life only we have hope in Christ, we are of all men most miserable
>
> 1 Corinthians 15:17–19

Irrefutable proof of the legitimacy of the resurrection of Jesus Christ has been fully documented elsewhere. There is abundant evidence that the resurrection of Jesus Christ is a historical fact. For our purposes in this book, though, we understand that the detractors of the resurrection of Jesus have no credible explanation that prove that the suffering and crucifixion of Christ did not indeed lead to his death. They have no explanation for the empty tomb. They cannot refute the accounts of the hundreds of eyewitnesses that saw the risen Lord. And they cannot explain away the transformation the once fearful disciples underwent after they saw the resurrected Jesus. It was indeed this transformation that led these men to die for their absolute knowledge of its truth. And it is this truth that has subsequently turned the world upside down.

But what we are looking at here in this book are pictures that God has painted in his Word which portray his plan of resurrection. Actually God has a sequence that he has used since the beginning of time, which demonstrates his plan of salvation. It's a sequence we see in childbearing as well as in all of life itself. It's called *death, burial,* and *resurrection.*

The gospel of Christ:

> For I delivered unto you first of all that which I also received, how that Christ *died* for our sins according to the scriptures; And that he was *buried,* and that he *rose again* the third day according to the scriptures.
>
> 1 Corinthians 15:3–4

In the gospel of Christ, we find our main text for this book.

You see, the Old Testament scriptures clearly reveal the death of a suffering servant. In Isaiah we read,

> He was oppressed, and he was afflicted, yet he opened not his mouth: He is brought as a lamb to the slaughter … For he was cut off out of the land of the living: For the transgression of my people was he stricken … Yet it pleased the Lord to bruise him; he hath put him to grief: When thou shalt make his soul an offering for sin.
>
> Isaiah 53:7a, 8b, 10a

And most importantly, we comprehend from the New Testament scriptures that the confession of Jesus as Lord and the belief in the resurrection, that Jesus rose from the dead, is the key to salvation.

> That if thou shalt confess with thy mouth the Lord Jesus, and shalt believe in thine heart that God hath raised him from the dead, thou shalt be saved.
>
> Romans 10:9

This truly is *good news!* Our Savior died for our sins, was buried, and rose again. God has placed this pattern everywhere for those who have eyes to see!

Childbearing

The birth of a child is a very poignant illustration of this principle. A person's birthday is a special day of the year. We celebrate birth and rightly so, as God uses it to portray the concept of resurrection. Thus, I will mention childbearing first as a springboard to the many other examples of death, burial, and resurrection.

The impartation of the sperm from a man into the egg of a woman is symbolic of death. The sperm dies, if you will, in the process of imparting new life. The chromosomes in the sperm leave its otherwise dying little body and become integrated into the egg. They then join with the corresponding chromosomes in the egg and a new creature is formed!

This principle of death to life is found throughout the Bible. Jesus told his disciples, "Whosoever shall seek to save his life shall lose it; and whosoever shall lose his life shall preserve it" (Luke 17:33).

And,

> Verily, verily, I say unto you, Except a corn of wheat fall into the ground and die, it abideth alone: But if it die, it bringeth forth much fruit. He that loveth his life shall lose it; and he that hateth his life in this world shall keep it unto life eternal.
>
> John 12:24–25

The application is obvious. As I die to self. As I die to my desires and agenda, I actually find life!

Burial in this analogy is typified as the time of pregnancy itself. The fetus is hidden away for nine months. She is out of sight or buried away. The type is then completed upon the birth of the baby. The baby arrives! She comes out of the grave! There has been a resurrection!

This example, though simplistic, we will see borne out time after time in God's Word. Let's look at some others.

Creation

In the beginning God created the heaven and the earth. And the earth was *(became)* without form and void; and darkness was upon the face of the deep. And the Spirit of God moved upon the face of the waters. And God said, Let there be light: And there was light.

Genesis 1:1–3

Some biblical scholars believe that there was a long interval of time between Genesis 1:1 and Genesis 1:2. For in verse 2 those same scholars teach that the best interpretation of the Hebrew phrase "and the Earth was without form and void" is "and the earth *became* without form and void." In other words, they suggest that the earth was not created that way.

Isaiah seems to confirm this idea: "For thus saith the Lord that created the heavens; God himself that formed the earth and made it; he hath established it, he created it *not in vain*" (Isaiah 45:18). The Hebrew phrase "not in vain" from Isaiah is the same as "without form and void" from Genesis.

The earth became without form and void; it was not created that way! Something died. There was a death and a burial in verse 2, followed by a resurrection in verse 3 and thereafter.

> And God *said,* Let there be light ...
> And God *said,* Let there be a firmament in the midst of the waters ...
> And God *said,* Let the waters under the heaven ...
> And God *said,* Let the earth bring forth grass ...
> And God *said,* Let there be lights in the firmament ...
> And God *said,* Let the waters bring forth abundantly ...
> And God *said,* Let the earth bring forth the living creature ...
> And God *said,* Let us make man in our image ... And God saw everything that he had made, and, behold it was very good.
>
> Genesis 1:3a, 6a, 9a, 11a, 14a, 20a, 24a, 26a, 31a

There we have it. The six days of creation, or of re-creation. This book won't solve that debate. But one thing we do know with certainty. When God says something, it comes to pass! For whatever God says *is!*

So we see a death of the earth, which God had created (*"the earth become without form and void"*). We learn of the burial of the earth (*"and darkness was on the face of the deep"*). And finally it's resurrection (*"And God said"*). Isn't God wonderful in majesty?

But what happened between verses 1 and 2 to lead to the death and burial of the earth? Postmodern scientists tell us that a meteor of terrible proportions struck the earth. Others propagate that the orbit of our planet changed drastically. But we suspect differently as we study the Word. Many interpret from Isaiah and Ezekiel, from Romans and Revelation (Isaiah 14:4–20, Ezekiel 28:12–19, Romans 8:22, Revelation 12:3–4, 7–9, 12) that there was a war in heaven of such a cataclysmic nature that the earth died and was buried. Satan, who was called Lucifer (the angel of light), exalted himself above God, the created over the Creator. The devil and one third of the angels who sided with him were defeated and cast down to earth. It is taught that this is the event that apparently caused the profound effect upon the earth, which is alluded to in verse 2 of Genesis.

But before we leave the creation story, let me make an application to my life and yours. When we die to self, when we die to our agendas, our worldly beliefs, our selfish desires, we will have resurrection in our souls. For as I follow Jesus and his agenda, his truth, his desires, then and only then will I have life. And since I've been a sinner since my youth, it is a resurrected life!

Jesus said, "I am come that they might have life, and that they might have it more abundantly" (John 10:10b).

Also, "And you shall know the truth and the truth shall set you free" (John 8:32).

Paul proclaimed in Colossians 1:16b, "All things were created by him (Jesus) and *for* him."

That's the secret of life, dear reader. All things were created by and for him! When we live for Jesus, we live for the one for whom we were created!

The Story of Jonah

Jonah, whose name means dove, was a prophet to the backsliding northern ten tribes of Israel from 785 to 775 BC while Jeroboam II reigned in Samaria. His story is the classic illustration of God's principle of death, burial, and resurrection. In fact, Jesus spoke of the Jonah experience when he pictured for the Pharisees the "sign of Jonah" in relationship to his own upcoming experience of death, burial, and resurrection. We will mention that statement in a moment. But first the story of Jonah!

Now the word of the Lord came to Jonah the son of Amittai, saying, Arise, go to Nineveh, that great city, and cry against it; for their wickedness is come up before me.

Jonah 1:1–2

Nineveh was the principle city of the Assyrians. They were *not* the people to whom Jonah was interested in bringing God's Word. In fact, earlier in Jonah's ministry to Israel, he had predicted the defeat of Syria by Jeroboam II (2 Kings 14:25). Jonah, as a prophet to Israel, was accustomed to bringing words of warning and deliverance to *his* people, not to their enemies!

With this background, we should not be too surprised at what Jonah did next. He indeed took on the characteristics of his name and tried to fly away!

But Jonah rose up to flee unto Tarshish from the presence of the Lord, and went down to Joppa; and he found a ship going to Tarshish: So he paid the fare thereof, and went down into it, to go from the presence of the Lord.

Jonah 1:3

Folks, it's never a good idea to try to flee the presence of the Lord! Thankfully, God will track his people down. But as we shall see, just as in Jonah's story, rebellion always costs more than one thinks. The Bible states, "He paid the fare thereof." Jonah didn't realize, though, the full cost he about to pay. The price was his life!

We read that the Lord sent a great wind, which imperiled the vessel. The mariners were fearful and cried out to their gods. Meanwhile, Jonah was asleep down in the bowels of the ship. He was in denial and was sleeping instead of repenting and praying! Thus we can surmise that God sent the shipmaster to Jonah, and he said, "What meanest thou, O sleeper? Arise, call upon thy God, if so be that God will think upon us, that we perish not" (Jonah 1:6).

It's interesting that this pagan ship captain intuitively

understood that there is a God and that he was behind their present circumstance!

We next learn that Jonah was the suspect as to the cause of their malady and he was called to the carpet, so to speak. The men of the ship asked Jonah about his business with them. They wanted to know were he was from. Who were his people? The Bible then tells us that when they learned Jonah was a Hebrew and that he feared the Lord God of heaven, they became exceedingly afraid.

Truly, since the days of God's judgment upon Sodom and Gomorrah, as well as the time of God's judgment upon Pharaoh and Egypt, the world has understood the potency of the God of Israel. This is yet another example of that respect!

Next the crew asked what should be done to calm the sea. What could they do to appease the God of Israel. Jonah took a page from the life of the one greater than Jonah, Jesus Christ, and laid down his life for the men. He said, "Take me up, and cast me forth into the sea; so shall the sea be calm unto you: For I know that for my sake this great tempest is upon you" (Jonah 1:12).

The men initially didn't want to kill Jonah, but after crying to God without relief, they cast Jonah into the deep. We learn that the men feared the Lord exceedingly and offered sacrifice to him (Jonah 1:16). They became believers in the one true God! It's wonderful to see how God will make lemonade out of a lemon! How he can bring some good out of things that inherently are bad!

After Jonah's terrible death, we next come to his burial.

> Now the Lord had prepared a great fish to swallow up Jonah. And Jonah was in the belly of the fish three days and three nights.
>
> Jonah 1:17

Three in the Bible is the number of completeness. Jonah was completely dead and buried. He was out of reach! Nothing short of resurrection would allow him to see the light of day again. It's interesting that the Hebrews felt a man was truly dead when he was in the grave for three days and three nights. The application to this is obvious both for the story of Lazarus and of Jesus!

The Bible clearly teaches in the next chapter of this story that even though Jonah was dead, he was able to pray to God. The idea of a godly man's spirit persisting after death is developed here in the Old Testament before being fully explained by Jesus in the New. Because of his affliction, Jonah repented and cried out to the Lord. He seemed to understand the resurrection, for he utters, "I am cast out of thy sight; yet I will look again toward thy holy temple" (Jonah 2:4).

Also Jonah proclaimed, "I went down to the bottom of the mountains; the earth with her bars was about me for ever: Yet hast thou brought up my life from corruption (death) O Lord my God" (Jonah 2:6).

Chapter 2 ends with the resurrection of Jonah.

> And the Lord spake unto the fish, and it vomited out Jonah upon dry land.
>
> Jonah 2:10

Wow! Jonah was going west to Tarshish, but God delivered him north to the coasts of Lebanon where he could go on to Nineveh. God will deliver you and me to where he wants us to be also!

Subsequently, the appearance of the death-warmed-over Jonah had the desired effect that God was looking for in Nineveh. Jonah entered the city and told the people that they had only forty days to repent of their evil ways before they were to be overthrown. The people from the least to the greatest did indeed believe God and repented. They put on sackcloth, and the king even sat in ashes! They proclaimed a fast, hoping that God would turn his wrath away. And guess what! That's exactly what God did.

And God saw their works, that they turned from their evil way; and God repented of the evil, that he had said that he would do unto them; and did it not.

Jonah 3:10

What a story! I love it! It illustrates the power of the resurrection of the one greater than Jonah, Jesus Christ, in bringing repentance unto salvation.

Undoubtedly, the people of Nineveh heard of Jonah's remarkable story, as news travels fast! They heard of his resurrection, and when they actually saw Jonah, their hearts were ready to repent and call upon the one true God for grace and mercy.

This also is what happens when people meet Jesus. They have heard of his resurrection, but when they see him in you and see him in me, *then* they will be ready to call upon him unto salvation. People don't care what you know until they know that you care! It's not about how much I know and preach to people but about how much I love them.

So we see in Jonah's story the death of his agenda (his running from the Lord resulting in his literal death), his burial in the great fish, and his resurrection to bring light to the Gentiles.

Now let me speak of the sign of Jonah described in the Gospels of Matthew and Luke.

"Then certain of the scribes and of the Pharisees answered, saying, 'Master, we would see a sign from thee'" (Matthew 12:38). These doubters wanted Jesus to back up his words with a miracle. As usual, Jesus didn't rise to the occasion but used their question as a springboard to deliver truth.

But he answered and said unto them, An evil and adulterous generation seeketh after a sign; and their shall no sign be given to it, but the sign of the prophet Jonah: For as Jonah was three days and three nights in the whale's belly; so shall

the Son of man be three days and three nights in the heart
of the earth.

Matthew 12:39–40

In this wonderful verse, Jesus told his detractors to look
for something fantastic. He straightly told them that he would
be dead for three days and three nights and then would come
back to life just as their prophet Jonah had done over seven
hundred years earlier! For indeed, the sign of Jonah illustrates
the Gospel of Christ. That is, the extraordinary story of Jonah
paints a powerful picture of the death, burial & resurrection of
Jesus Christ! I've always been a bit puzzled with the language
of the above verse though, and maybe you have been too. You
see, Good Friday to Easter Sunday is *not* three days and three
nights. But the Bible clearly makes the point in the book of
Jonah and here in Matthew that Jonah was in the belly of the
fish and Jesus was to be in the heart of the earth for three days
and three nights. I believe the key to unlocking this is found
in John's account of Jesus' passion.

> The Jews therefore, because it was the preparation, that the
> bodies should not remain upon the cross on the Sabbath day,
> *(for that Sabbath day was a high day,)* besought Pilate that their
> legs might be broken, and that they might be taken away.

John 19:31

The Jews did not want the Romans to have men on the
cross for their Sabbath. They understood the curse that God
pronounced on the land when a condemned man hung from a
tree over night (Deuteronomy 21:22–23). Thus, they requested
that Jesus and the others be killed more quickly so they could
be buried before the onset of the Sabbath at sunset.

We know from other scriptures of the passion that Jesus
was on the cross from the third to the ninth hour. From 9:00
a.m. to 3:00 p.m. So the Jews had about four hours to get
the men down and buried before sunset, which occurred about
7:00 p.m. at that time of the year.

Now the error in our understanding comes because we have

not discriminated before which Sabbath Jesus died. We followers of Jesus have assumed that Jesus died on Friday because Friday is the day before Saturday, the day of the Hebrew Sabbath. But Paul tells us that Christ *is* our Passover (1 Corinthians 5:7b), and John told us that the Sabbath in question was a high or special day.

You see, Jesus was killed at the same time the Passover lamb was sacrificed on the afternoon before the Passover. Jesus fulfilled Passover perfectly. He died outside of the city just as the priests were slaughtering the Passover lamb. Jesus died on the afternoon before the Passover. Passover started at sunset on the eve of the full moon, sunset on the fourteenth of Nisan. The day of the week was irrelevant. Passover could fall on any day of the week and was not determined by the Saturday Jewish Sabbath.

Now we know that Jesus was seen early on the first day of the week, on Sunday, in his resurrected body. Thus, for Jesus to be in the grave for three days and three nights, counting backwards, he must have died and been buried late on Wednesday afternoon and arose late Saturday just before the start of the new day of Sunday.

Thus the death, burial, and resurrection of Jonah did give the scribes and Pharisees the sign they were seeking. That being that Israel's Messiah would indeed be in the heart of the earth for three days and three nights!

Baptism

Baptism is a wonderful picture of death, burial, and resurrection. The Bible does not leave any guesswork in this area, as God's plan is plainly stated in Romans.

Know ye not, that so many of us as were baptized into Jesus Christ were baptized into his *death*. Therefore we are *buried* with him by baptism into death: That like as Christ was *raised* up from the dead by the glory of the Father, even so we also should walk in newness of life.

Romans 6:3–4

Also in Colossians:

Buried with him in baptism, wherein also ye are *risen* with him through the faith of the operation of God, who hath raised him from the dead. And you, being *dead* in your sins and the uncircumcision of your flesh, hath he quickened together with him, having forgiven you all trespasses.

Colossians 2:12–13

Marvelous! All trespasses. Not some, not a portion, but all trespasses! The doctrine of substitution is clear in these passages. Because he, taking our place, died, was buried, and rose again, we, in figure, through faith have died, were buried, and will rise again with him. Jesus received the punishment I deserved, and I receive the glory I don't deserve. It's all by God's grace! Grace is that unearned, unmerited, undeserved favor which God bestowed upon me through faith in his Son, Jesus Christ.

To corroborate the idea that baptism pictures Christ's death and resurrection, we need look no further than the words of our Lord himself.

But I have a baptism to be baptized with: And how am I straitened till it be accomplished!

Luke 12:50

Jesus spoke of the direction he was going, that being toward the cross in order to resurrect mankind.

Now the word *baptism* means to dip or immerse. In the New Testament, we see that there are two types of baptisms, or immersions, that a person is to undergo. The first is called the baptism of John. The second is termed the baptism of the Lord. One is a baptism of repentance, the other a baptism into the Spirit, into the new covenant life!

> John answered, saying unto them all, I indeed baptize you with water; but one mightier than I cometh, the latchet of whose shoes I am not worthy to unloose: He shall baptize you with the Holy Ghost and with fire.
>
> Luke 3:16

In the book of Acts, Paul explained to the men of Antioch in Pisidia of John's baptism, of that first baptism.

> When John had first preached before his (Jesus') coming, the baptism of repentance to all the people of Israel.
>
> Acts 13:24

Paul makes it clear that before Jesus, before salvation, comes John, comes repentance. This model is true for all time. I will not feel I need Jesus until I realize I am a doomed sinner, until I turn and repent.

Paul comments on the second baptism, the baptism in the spirit, in his letter to his disciple Titus.

> Not by works of righteousness which we have done, but according to his mercy he saved us, *by the washing of regeneration, and renewing of the Holy Ghost.*
>
> Titus 3:5

Jeremiah speaks of the regeneration and renewing of the Spirit in these well known verses;

> Behold, the days come, saith the Lord, that I will make a new covenant with the house of Israel, and with the house of Judah: Not according to the covenant that I made with their fathers *(the Law)* in the day that I took them by the hand to bring them out of the land of Egypt; which my covenant they brake, although I was an husband unto them,

saith the Lord: But this shall be the covenant that I will make with the house of Israel; After those days, saith the Lord, I will put may law in their inward parts, and write it in their hearts; and will be their God, and they shall be my people. And they shall teach no more every man his neighbor, and every man his brother, saying, Know the Lord: For they shall all know me, from the least of them unto the greatest of them, saith the Lord; for I will forgive their iniquity, and I will remember their sin no more.

Jeremiah 31:31–34

Lastly, Peter explains that the two baptisms do not have to occur separately but can both occur upon confession of Jesus as Lord.

Then Peter said unto them, "Repent, and be baptized every one of you in the name of Jesus Christ for the remission of sins, and ye shall receive the gift of the Holy Ghost."

Acts 3:38

Yes, baptism is a wonderful picture of our death through repentance of our sins, our burial in Christ, and our resurrection into the new covenant life, into the spirit-filled life!

Next, let's look at two other baptisms that picture these truths: the baptism of Noah and the baptism of the children of Israel.

The Story of Noah

When once the longsuffering of God waited in the days of Noah, while the ark was preparing, wherein few, that is, eight souls were saved by water. The like figure whereunto even baptism doth now save us (not the putting away of the filth of the flesh, but the answer of a good conscience toward God,) by the resurrection of Jesus Christ.

1 Peter 3:21

How do we have a good conscience toward God? By the resurrection of Jesus!

Now let's look at Noah's account and see what it has for us in our day as well as see how it pictures death, burial, and resurrection.

A study in Genesis 5 reveals that Noah, whose name means "rest and comfort," was the first son in the tenth generation after Adam. He was born 1,056 years after Adam, and the Bible tells us in Genesis 7:11 that he was six hundred years old when the judgment of the flood occurred. God discloses four characteristics of mankind's behavior at that time in chapter 6 that are important to be aware of. First, we note that during that time frame men were multiplying upon the face of the earth (Genesis 6:1). Next, we are told that the sons of God and the daughters of men bore children together (Genesis 6:4). (Scholars believe this is a reference to a type of aberrant sexual behavior.) Thirdly, we learn that "the wickedness of man was great in the earth, and that every imagination of the thoughts of his heart was only evil continually" (Genesis 6:5). Fourthly, we understand from verse 13 that the entire earth was filled with violence.

This is the background that led God to tell Noah in verse 13, "The end of all flesh is come before me … behold, I will destroy them with the earth" (Genesis 6:13b, d).

It's interesting that the description given in chapter 6 is eerily similar to the world today. We have seen a population explosion where the doubling time is exponential. The pornographic industry is rampant, and the wickedness of man's heart is displayed every night on the evening news as evil is called good and good called evil. Lastly, to say that the entire earth is filled with violence would be an understatement. With these comments, the warning Jesus gave his disciples is quite sobering.

> But as the days of Noah were, so shall also of the coming of the Son of man be.
>
> Matthew 24:37

Jesus plainly stated that at the time of his return the world will resemble the days of Noah!

Now, in this analogy of death, burial, and resurrection, it is the Lord calling Noah into the ark that illustrates death. He was called home, if you will.

> And the Lord said unto Noah, *Come* thou and all thy house into the ark; for thee have I seen righteous before me in this generation.
>
> Genesis 7:1

The floodgates of heaven subsequently opened, and Noah and his family were buried away safely in the ark. Verse 16 of chapter 7 states, "And the Lord *shut* him in" (Genesis 7:16b). They spent over a year in the ark in their buried state. The resurrection of Noah and his family is then seen in chapter 8.

> And God spake unto Noah, saying, *Go forth* of the ark, thou, and thy wife, and thy sons, and thy son's wives with thee.
>
> Genesis 8:15–16

A key to Christian living is seen here. God calls us to *come* unto him, we then spend time with him, we are *shut* in with him, if you will, and lastly we *go forth* to the world. I can't be effective in the world unless I spend time with him first!

The Baptism of the Children of Israel

> Moreover, brethren, I would not that ye should be ignorant, how that all our fathers were under the cloud, and all passed in the sea. And were all baptized unto Moses in the cloud and in the sea.
>
> 1 Corinthians 10:1–2

In Egypt, the children of Israel were in bondage to their task-masters. They were in bondage to the Egyptians. When God through Moses delivered Israel, they died to their lives under the provision of Egypt, were buried in the Red Sea, and were resurrected to a life with God as their provider and protector. Once again, we see death, burial, and resurrection in God's dealings with his children.

Here in chapter 10 of 1 Corinthians, Paul tells us that the story of Israel is an allegory for us (verses 1 through 5) and an example to us.

> Now these things were our examples ... Now all these things happened unto them for examples: And they were written for our admonition.
>
> 1 Corinthians 10:6, 11

Paul tells us that the meat and bread they ate, the rock that gave them water, and the serpents that bit them all picture spiritual truths bigger than the events themselves.

You see, the time Israel spent in Egypt represents the lives you and I had before we came to Christ. We were in bondage as were they. Their deliverance through Moses was a foreshadowing of the deliverance we receive upon salvation through faith in Jesus Christ. The baptism of repentance is the type seen here in their passage through the Red Sea. After this, the nation spent a year in the wilderness being tutored by God, if you will. They received the Law of God and were beginning to learn what he expected of them. This represents our time here on earth after salvation as we begin to fellowship with God and become more like Christ. We learn to transition from the milk of God's Word to the meat.

Unfortunately, the children of Israel did not initially enter into the promised land due their unbelief, as stated in Hebrews 3:19. But despite their frequent rebellions, God continued to provide for his children as the book of Numbers clearly documents. We as believers also have a choice to make, as did Israel. Will we believe God and move forward, or do we shrink back into unbelief and stay in a dry place? Stay in the wilderness?

Ultimately, the next generation under Joshua entered into the promised land. They entered into the land flowing with milk and honey, which God had promised. But first they needed to cross the Jordan River. That river, like the Red Sea, pictures a baptism. As the first crossing of the Red Sea is a type of the baptism of repentance, so the second crossing, the crossing of the Jordan River, typifies the baptism in the Holy Spirit! The promised land does not symbolize heaven as some have suggested, for there were battles still to be waged in the land. No, the promised land symbolizes the Spirit-filled life, the life where God puts his will into our hearts, the new covenant life! In this life we still have battles, just as did Israel under Joshua's leadership. But we have the spirit, so that indeed "we are more than conquerors through Christ who strengthens us" (Romans 8:37).

So we see a beautiful masterpiece when we study the exodus. It's a work of art by God the Father showing his plan for our lives. God sent his Son to rescue us from the bondage of Satan, our sinful flesh, and this world's evil systems just as he sent Moses to lead Israel out of Egypt. Out of bondage! We then grow and commune with God just as the people spent time with him in the wilderness. Lastly, we enter into the "promised land" of the Spirit-filled life just as Israel entered their promised land by crossing the Jordan River.

The Story of Lazarus

Jesus gave his disciples and the Jews a preview of his own death, burial, and resurrection with the events of his friend Lazarus's death.

The story is found in chapter 11 of John's gospel. There we learn that Lazarus lived in Bethany with his sisters, Martha and Mary. They were very close friends of Jesus. They loved him! In fact, Mary had earlier anointed the Lord with ointment and wiped his feet with her hair.

Now, when Jesus learned that Lazarus was sick, he tarried beyond the Jordan for two days. He then traveled up to Bethany were he found Lazarus to have been dead for four days. Martha first discovered Jesus upon his arrival and confessed the belief that whatever he would ask of God would come to pass. Jesus then told her that her brother would rise again. He went on to tell her, "I am the resurrection, and the life: He that believeth in me, though her were dead, yet shall he live" (John 11:25).

Later that day, Jesus wept when he came to the cave where Lazarus lay dead. Jesus told some men to take away the stone covering the entrance. Apparently Martha lost some of the faith she had earlier demonstrated as she blurted out without much insight,

> Lord, by this time he stinketh: For he hath been dead four days. Jesus said unto her, Said I not unto thee, that, if thou shouldest believe, thou should see the glory of God? Then they took away the stone where the dead was laid. And Jesus lifted up his eyes and said, Father, I thank thee that thou hast heard me. And I knew that thou hearest me always: But because of the people which stand by I said it, that they

may believe that thou hast sent me. And when he thus had spoken, he cried with a loud voice, Lazarus, come forth.

John 11:39b–43

Wonderfully, Lazarus did indeed come forth, and the result was that many of the Jews believed in Jesus as the Messiah.

The death, burial, and resurrection of Lazarus show us spiritual pictures bigger than the life of one man though. We learn in chapter 12 of John that Jesus was in Bethany six days before the Passover. That is six days before his death! He ate with Lazarus and we learn,

Much people of the Jews therefore knew that he was there: And they came not only for Jesus' sake only, but that they might see Lazarus whom he had raised from the dead.

John 12:9

People wanted to see Lazarus! They wanted to see a man who had been dead but was now alive! Do you see the analogy here?

People will want to see you and me also because we have been made alive by Jesus. Oh, maybe not so dramatically, but from death to life nonetheless. Additionally, because the people wanted to see Lazarus, the dead man who was now alive, they also got to see Jesus.

The Order of the Resurrection

For as in Adam all die, even so in Christ shall all be made alive. But every man in his own order: Christ the firstfruits; afterward they that are Christ's at his coming.

1 Corinthians 15:22–23

Indeed, the Bible states that it is appointed once for a man to die (Hebrews 9:27a). Everyone will die unless he or she is alive during the last generation when the Lord returns. No one can escape the grim reaper. Try as we do to extend our lives and to forget that we are mortal, we are *all* going to die!

But our verse in this section gives great hope as we see that just as Christ died, was buried, and rose again, so will we. It's a historical fact that Jesus rose from the dead, and it's our *hope* that history will repeat itself!

The word *hope* means the absolute expectation of coming good. When hope is used in the Bible, it's not the same as would be used today. It's not saying, "Well, maybe something good might happen." It's a sure thing! Only in the time-space continuum has it not yet happened. We absolutely expect that we will be resurrected as the Word of God promises.

But when will this happen? We see here and know from the gospel accounts that Jesus (who is the firstfruits) was resurrected after a relatively short interval in the grave, only three days. We, on the other hand, learn here that we will be buried until we are made alive at his coming, obviously a much longer interval of time!

To understand this, one needs to get a grasp on the Jewish concept of "firstfruits." The children of Israel were an agricultural nation that relied heavily upon the early and latter rains of the spring and late summer for their provision. Passover, which occurred in the spring at the beginning of the growing season, was immediately followed by a weeklong celebration called the Feast of Unleavened Bread, as we are told in Leviticus 23:6–14. This was the time that the first crop of the year, barley, would come to fruition. The high priest would offer up some barley to God, the firstfruits, as a token to God for his promise of provision and protection over the wheat harvest, which would come to fruition much later at the end of the agricultural season. This offering was to happen on the first day of the week, Sunday, during that weeklong celebration.

As an aside, recall that the Sunday when the firstfruits were offered in the year our Lord died was resurrection Sunday, fulfilling the picture perfectly!

In like manner, we who are God's children are a type of harvest. We are the wheat harvest and Jesus Christ, the Great High Priest, represents the barley harvest. He offered the first-fruits as the High Priest and *is* the firstfruits represented as the barley. As the barley came to fruition in the spring and the wheat in the fall, so did Christ resurrect first in the spring, and we who are the wheat will be resurrected second in autumn— in the end of this age as our verse indicates.

Now, it is interesting following this analogy that again the high priest would offer up a wheat offering to God in the fall at the Feast of Tabernacles. We see order to God's plan in another marvelous way. Jesus, upon his return as the High Priest, will offer us up to God as a wheat offering just as was done by the Jews in days of old!

Indeed, just as Christ died, was buried, and rose again, so will we.

But the question remains: when will this resurrection for us occur? The answer is given later in chapter 15 of 1 Corinthians. It will be at *the last trump!*

> Behold, I show you a mystery: We shall not all sleep *(die)*, but we shall all be changed. In a moment, in the twinkling of an eye, at the last trump: For the trumpet shall sound, and the dead shall be raised incorruptible, and we shall be changed. For this incorruptible must put on incorruption, and this mortal must put on immortality. So when this corruptible shall have put on incorruption, and this mortal shall have put on immortality, then shall be brought to pass the saying that is written, Death is swallowed up in victory. O death, where is thy sting? O grave, where is thy victory?
>
> 1 Corinthians 15:51–55

These verses clearly teach that we will be resurrected at the last trump. Also, as seen in our study text for this section, it will be "*afterward they that are Christ's at his coming*" (1 Corinthians 15:23b).

Now, am I saying that those who have died in the faith are not now presently with the Lord?

Not really. As Paul proclaimed in Philippians, "For to me to live is Christ and to die is gain" (Philippians 1:21). Also in 2 Corinthians, "To be absent from the body, and to be present with the Lord" (2 Corinthians 5:8).

But it would seem from our study here that the body is resurrected at the last trump. Apparently, our spirit must leave our corrupted bodies to be with the Lord upon our deaths. And our new bodies rejoin our spirits at the last trump.

Continuing, this last trump is also called the trump of God in 1 Thessalonians 4:13–17. This is the parallel text in the New Testament, which speaks of this resurrection.

Now if there is a last trump, it goes to reason that there must also be a first trump. We see this spoken of in Exodus 19 when God called the people together to receive the Law. He told Moses to tell the people to sanctify themselves and to prepare themselves to hear from him on the third day. He said,

> When the trumpet soundeth long, they shall come up to the mount. (Mount Sinai) And it came to pass on the third day in the morning, that there were thunders and lightnings, and a thick cloud upon the mount, and the voice of the trumpet exceeding loud; so that all the people in the camp trembled.
>
> 1 Corinthians 15:35–37

The earth quaked, and smoke ascended from the mount. We are told that the trumpet sounded long and waxed louder and louder (Exodus 19:19). Then the Lord came down upon the mount and spoke the Law. He thundered the Ten Commandments. This was the first trump!

Now, to complete the picture, we learn in the book of Numbers that "the Lord spake unto Moses, saying, make thee two trumpets of silver; of a whole piece shalt thou make them:

That thou mayest use them for the calling of the assembly" (Numbers 10:1–2)

There we have the key. In the Bible, silver is associated with redemption and trumpets for calling the people together. God uses the first trumpet to call his people to follow his commandments and the second to call his people home!

So in summary, we understand that after Adam's fall, all will die. Also in Jesus, all who die in Christ will live again. We see the order of death, burial, and resurrection once again in God's plan.

The Story of Manasseh

In the book of 2 Chronicles, chapter 33, we find a story that I find very intriguing. It's the story of the twelfth king of Judah, the infamous Manasseh.

You may recall that Manasseh was responsible for God's judgment that came upon the tribe of Judah. Jeremiah clearly states, "And I will cause them (Judah) to be removed into all kingdoms of the earth, because of Manasseh, the son of Hezekiah king of Judah, for that which he did in Jerusalem" (Jeremiah 15:4).

Just what did Manasseh do?

Well, we are told in 2 Kings 21 and 2 Chronicles 33 that Manasseh built the high places for worship of Baal, which his father Hezekiah had broken down. He reared up altars and groves for Baalim and worshiped the host of heaven (devils). He was a prochoice advocate in that he had his children pass through the fire in the valley of the sons of Hinnom. That is, he sacrificed his firstborn son to the god Molech in the belief that he would thus prosper financially. In addition, Manasseh was also into astrology as he observed times. He followed the occult and practiced wizardry and witchcraft. He even carved an idol and placed it into the house of God. Thus, we learn, "So Manasseh made Judah and the inhabitants of Jerusalem to err, and to do *worse* than the heathen, whom the Lord had destroyed before the children of Israel" (2 Chronicles 33:9).

Next we read, "And the Lord spake to Manasseh, and to his people: But they would not hearken" (2 Chronicles 33:10).

The Lord, through the prophet Jeremiah, warned the king and the people, but their ears were closed.

So let's see and understand what our God did in Manasseh's life. We will learn of a death, burial, and resurrection!

The death and burial of Manasseh's reign occurred in the next verse.

> Wherefore the Lord brought upon them the captains of the host of Assyria, which took Manasseh among the thorns, and bound him with fetters, and carried him to Babylon.
>
> 2 Chronicles 33:11

This verse illustrates Manasseh's demise and his burial, for he was taken away to Babylon—he died and was buried, so to speak. The resurrection of Manasseh is found in verses 12 through 16. We learn that in his affliction he besought the Lord and humbled himself. Manasseh prayed earnestly, and God heard his prayer and by his incredible grace brought Manasseh back to Jerusalem to once again rule over his kingdom.

Did you catch that?

God by his incomprehensible grace re-enthroned the *worst* king in Judah's history!

Why?

Because Manasseh humbled himself before God. Apparently God said, "Okay, now I can use you. Back to your position of leadership you go!"

What happened next is just brilliant! A great verse jumps out of the page.

Then Manasseh *knew* that the Lord he was God!

2 Chronicles 33:13b

Manasseh made an about-face, he had repented, and I dare say we will even see him in heaven!

So, to summarize Manasseh's story, we see that his evil reign as king of Judah lead to the death of his leadership. He was buried in Babylon and was resurrected back as king after he truly repented to the Lord.

The Story of Isaac

The New Testament is written to us as believers in Jesus Christ. We have personal letters from God the Father and Jesus his Son as noted in the opening remarks in many of the books of the New Testament.

Conversely, the Old Testament was written for our learning. These were books written to the people of Israel. Paul told us in Romans, 1 Corinthians, and other letters that Israel's experiences need to be seen as examples. They are admonishments to help us see God and his ways, to help us draw closer to him (1 Corinthians 10:6, 11).

Yes, the Old Testament is one gigantic picture book! It is chock full of illustrations and allegories that picture spiritual truths. Battles against physical enemies in the Old Testament symbolize battles against spiritual ones for us in the New. Certain key characters also can be seen as allegories of God's plan. And of course, as Jesus explained to the two disciples on the road to Emmaus, the Old Testament speaks of him (Luke 24:27).

Such is the case in the story of Isaac. Isaac is a powerful picture of Jesus Christ. As we examine his story, it is good to cross-reference Jesus' story with Isaac's. Wonderful truths are there waiting for one to see!

The other main characters in his story are Abraham, Sarah, Hagar, Ishmael, and Rebekah. They also allegorically represent spiritual truths, as we shall note.

The story we will examine is found in Genesis 21 through 25. It is a story that in biblical typology speaks of God's dealings with Israel and the church of Jesus Christ.

In chapter 21, we begin Isaac's story.

The Lord visited Sarah, and she conceived in her old age. This conception was foretold and was miraculous in that it was decades past the age of a woman's fertility. They named the promised son Isaac, which means *laughter*. What a great name! Sarah said, "God hath made me to laugh, so that all that hear will laugh with me" (Genesis 21:6).

Indeed, all who call upon the name of the greater One than Isaac will have reason to laugh also!

Later, when Isaac was weaned, Abraham made a feast for Isaac. At the party, the son of Hagar, Ishmael, mocked Sarah's son. This infuriated Sarah, and she demanded Abraham to "cast out this bondwoman and her son: For the son of this bondwoman shall not be heir with my son, even with Isaac" (Genesis 21:10).

Abraham was upset, as would be expected, and was reluctant at first to heed his wife's request. But God said, "Let it not be grievous in thy sight because of the lad, and because of thy bondwoman; in all that Sarah hath said unto thee, hearken unto her voice; for in Isaac shall thy seed be called" (Genesis 21:12).

Abraham indeed did rise up early the next morning and sent Hagar away into the desert with the measly provisions of some bread and water.

Abraham, as Isaac's father, is a picture of God the Father. Sarah, as his mother, is a type of spiritual Israel. Jesus came from the Father and was born into the spiritual Jewish world. The Bible says that he came unto his own, but his own did not receive him. He was of Israel.

Hagar is a picture of the Law. She births the first child, if you will, which cannot save. Ishmael is a type of the flesh. He is the product of Abraham and Sarah's fleshly attempt to help God out. Instead of believing in God's grace, they worked for their son. This obviously contrasts the false doctrine of salvation by works versus salvation by faith.

But you may say, "I'm not so sure about these associations you are making!"

If you doubt me, then look in Galatians.

> For it is written, that Abraham had two sons, the one by a bondmaid, the other by a freewoman. But he who was of the bondwoman was born after the flesh; but he of the freewoman was by promise. Which things are an allegory: For these are the two covenants; the one from mount Sinai in Arabia *(the Law)*, and answereth to Jerusalem which is now, and is in bondage with her children; *(those still living under the Law)*. But the Jerusalem which is above is free, which is the mother of us all; *(Sarah)*. For it is written, Rejoice, thou barren that bearest not; break forth and cry, thou that travailest not: For the desolate hath many more children than she which hath a husband. Now we, brethren, as Isaac was, are the children of promise. *(We are heirs with Jesus!)* But as then he that was born after the flesh persecuted *(mocked)* him that was born after the Spirit, even so it is now. *(The flesh continues to war against the spirit.)* Nevertheless what saith the scripture? Cast out the bondwoman and her son:

(Clearly we are not under the Law and we are to cast off the flesh.) For the son of the bondwoman shall not be heir with the son of the freewoman. So then, we are not children of the bondwoman, but of the free.

Galatians 4:22–31

Also speaking of the same allegory, Paul preached in Romans, "But put ye on the Lord Jesus Christ, and make not provision for the flesh, to fulfill the lusts thereof" (Romans 13:14).

Now we can begin to see in our story of Isaac why God had Abraham send Hagar and Ishmael away with only bread and water. He represents the truth that we are not to live under the Law and, importantly, we are to send the flesh away without making provision for it. It's important not to compromise with our fleshly desires.

Chapters 22 through 24 show us a type of death, burial, and resurrection, a type seen in Isaac, which mirrors what we see in our Lord.

And it came to pass after these things.

Genesis 22:1a

After what things?

After all the lessons God had worked in Abraham thus far in his life in order to bring him to this important time in his life. Chapter 22 is the moment in time we shall see that made Abraham great!

This was about to be Abraham's greatest moment. It was to be his Moriah moment!

That God did tempt Abraham …

Genesis 22:1b

What? I thought the Bible says in James that no man is tempted of God. That God does not tempt any man (James 1:13). It does. But what we must understand is that in Hebrew, the same word for *tempt* is also used for the word *proved.* God was about to prove Abraham. He was about to refine him as a silversmith would prove or perfect silver.

> And he said, Take now thy son, thine only son Isaac, whom thou lovest.
>
> Genesis 22:2a

What a minute! I thought Abraham had two sons! Ishmael and Isaac.

He does. But in God's eyes, Ishmael is forgotten. Ishmael, as a mighty picture of the flesh, is forgotten. Just as God forgets our sins and fleshly works (Psalm 103:12), he has forgotten Ishmael in relation to this story.

> And get thee into the land of *Moriah* ... upon one of the *mountains* I will tell thee of. And Abraham ... went unto *the place* of which God had told him.
>
> Genesis 22:2b, 3b

Moriah means foreseen of the Lord. God told Abraham to go to the mount of Moriah. "Go Abraham, to the place."

Now just where is this place? Can we know?

Second Chronicles speaks of Mount Moriah in a spine-tingling way as we consider these things.

> Then Solomon began to build the house of the Lord at Jerusalem in mount Moriah, where the Lord appeared unto David his father, in the place that David had prepared in the threshing floor of Ornan the Jebusite.
>
> 2 Chronicles 3:1

Wow! Mount Moriah is the temple mount, the site that God told Abraham to travel to became the future site of the temple. The place where sacrifice to God would be made! This is the same site where David offered sacrifice to God and the destroying angel was stayed (1 Chronicles 21).

I hope the picture of Jesus' sacrifice in this story is starting to develop.

Now the words *the place* are also significant.

> And when they were come to *the place,* which is called Cal-
> vary, there they crucified him.
>
> Luke 23:33

You see, Mount Moriah is actually a ridge in Jerusalem.
On the south end is the temple mount and the ridge rises
slightly to the north, to the site north of the city later called
Calvary. This is the place Jesus died for our sins, and this is the
place God will take Abraham and Isaac in order to show us
this picture, this powerful allegory of Jesus' sacrifice!

> And offer him there for a burnt offering...
>
> Genesis 22:2b

We should look in Leviticus chapter 1 to understand just
what a burnt offering was to be. It also wonderfully illustrates
our Savior! Reading, you will see that the burnt offering was a
voluntary sacrifice for the atonement of sin. An unblemished
animal was to be sacrificed before the priests and burnt over
wood with fire. It was to be totally consumed. It was to be
sacrificed on the north side of the altar.

This sacrifice speaks of Jesus, doesn't it? He voluntarily
offered his sinless body for the sin of mankind. He took the
wood of the cross and was consumed by the fire of God's wrath.
The priests witnessed his sacrifice on the north of the city!

Continuing with Isaac's story, Abraham and Isaac traveled
the next day to Moriah. Along with them traveled two young
men. (These men are representative of the two thieves in Jesus'
story.) When they arrived, Abraham told the young men to
abide with the donkeys, "and I and the lad will go yonder and
worship, and come again to you" (Genesis 22:5b).

This is great! Abraham understood that he was to sacrifice
Isaac, yet he believed God would resurrect his son.

> By faith Abraham, when he was tried, offered up Isaac: And
> he that had received the promises offered up his *only begot-*

ten son. Of whom it is said, That in Isaac shall thy seed be called: Accounting that God was able to raise him up, even from the dead; from whence also he received him in a *figure.*

Hebrews 11:17–19

Could it be any clearer? This story is a figure, a picture, a type. Abraham as the father offers up his only begotten son—his promised son—believing he would be resurrected. By this time in Abraham's life, his faith has become huge!

And Abraham took the wood of the burnt offering, and laid it upon Isaac his son: And he took the fire in his hand, and a knife; and they went both of them together.

Genesis 22:6

The types abound in this verse. The wood Isaac was given illustrates Jesus' cross, which he carried up this same mountain. This was the cross his father gave him to carry. The fire in this story pictures God's wrath. In the Bible, fire can be a picture of the Holy Spirit, but often it is a figure of God's wrath, as it is here in this allegory. Abraham also took a knife. Whenever we read of a knife or a sword in the Bible, we need to remember that they almost always typify God's Word.

"Take…the sword of the Spirit, which is the word of God" (Ephesians 6:17).

And, "The word of God is quick, and powerful, and sharper than any two-edged sword" (Hebrews 4:12a).

This knife speaks of God's Word, which would tell of the upcoming day of his Son's sacrifice.

Lastly, this verse states that they both traveled together. Indeed, Jesus always did the Father's will. He prayed in Matthew, "O my Father, if it be possible, let this cup pass from me: Nevertheless not as I will, but as thou wilt" (Matthew 26:39b). They were one; they traveled together!

Isaac then asked his father where the lamb was for the burnt offering.

Abraham answered by inspiration, "My son, God will provide *himself* a lamb for a burnt offering" (Genesis 22:8a).

Abraham unwittingly was prophesying what God would later do. That God indeed would provide *himself* to be the sacrifice.

Abraham's greatest moment then came. He took Isaac and went through with the sacrifice, not knowing ahead of time of the outcome. Not knowing that the angel of the Lord would prevent the completion of the sacrifice. Not knowing that he was about to pass the test!

Abraham heard God praise his faith and obedience.

> For now I know that thou fearest God, seeing thou hast not withheld thy son, thine only son from me.
>
> Genesis 22:12b

Abraham illustrates the Father greatly in this analogy, as the Father later would do the same for us in sacrificing his only begotten Son!

We next learn of a new name of God. It's a name that speaks of an aspect of God's nature. We find out a side of God that is on display for all to see in this story and in Jesus' story. For Abraham beheld a ram caught in a thicket and offered it instead of Isaac. He called the name of that place, the place we know as Calvary, "Jehovah-jireh," meaning "the Lord will provide." Indeed, if the Lord has provided the sacrifice for all time, and he has, he will also provide for our needs today!

The story continues with God blessing Abraham and his progeny, saying that his seed will be multiplied as the stars in the heavens and that in his seed shall all nations be blessed. Verse 19 then states, "So Abraham returned unto his young men, and they rose up and went together to Beersheba" (Genesis 22:19).

Implicitly, Isaac is present, but he is not mentioned any more in the story until much later. We see Abraham leave Moriah, but Isaac, who you remember typifies Jesus Christ, isn't seen again until he meets his future bride, Rebekah, at the end of chapter 24. During this time of Isaac's absence, we learn of the death of Sarah in chapter 23. Now, recall the allegory found in Galatians that was cited (Galatians 4:22–31). Sarah illustrates spiritual Israel. At this point in the story, she dies. Likewise, in Jesus' story, what happened to Israel after his sacrifice? Israel died. When they rejected the Messiah, when they said they would not have this man rule over them, they died both spiritually and physically. The church became God's ambassador in the world, and Israel was buried in the Gentile nations as we have noted previously.

Chapter 24 then tells of Rebekah. It explains to us how Abraham, the father of Isaac, finds his son a bride. The allegory is wonderful, for in it we see God the Father finding a bride for his Son Jesus. Rebekah as the bride of Isaac represents the church, for the Bible teaches that the church is the bride of Christ.

Looking at this calling of the bride in detail will reveal some important truths.

> And Abraham was old, and well stricken in age: And the Lord had blessed Abraham in all things. And Abraham said unto his eldest servant of his house, that ruled over all that he had, Put, I pray thee, thy hand under my thigh: And I will make thee swear by the Lord, the God of heaven, and the God of the earth, that thou shalt not take a wife unto my son of the daughters of the Canaanites, among whom I dwell: But thou shalt go unto my country, and to my kindred, and take a wife unto my son Isaac.
>
> Genesis 24:1–4

A period of time has occurred after the Mount Moriah moment in chapter 22 and after Sarah's death in chapter 23, for Abraham was old and well stricken in age. He called his eldest and most trusted servant to the task of finding a suitable bride for his son. It is important to note that this servant, who plays a very important role in this story, is not named. The reason is simple. This servant is a picture of the Holy Spirit.

You will recall Jesus' description of the Holy Spirit.

> Howbeit, when he, the Spirit of truth, is come, he will guide you into all truth: For he shall not speak of himself; but whatsoever he shall hear, that shall he speak: And he will show you things to come: He shall glorify me; for he shall receive of mine, and shall show it unto you.
>
> John 16:13–14

The Holy Spirit does not speak of himself. He does not glorify himself. But he speaks of Jesus. He glorifies Jesus. Likewise, the analogy in our story of Isaac is perfect. This important yet unnamed servant was sent to find a bride for Isaac, just as the Holy Spirit finds people to become Jesus' bride. We understand that it is the Spirit that quickens. That is, the natural man cannot comprehend the things of the Spirit (1 Corinthians 2:14). Without God's Spirit, no one will come to a saving knowledge of his Son!

Yet the Holy Spirit does not force himself upon a person. If a person doesn't want to believe, then he or she is free to make that poor decision. Likewise in our story, Abraham, representing the Father, told the servant to woo, not force himself on, the chosen woman (Genesis 24:8).

> And the servant took ten camels of the camels of his master, and departed; for all the goods of his master were in his hand.
>
> Genesis 24:10a

The servant traveled to the land of Abraham's kindred with ten camels where he met Rebekah. The Bible speaks of her in these wonderful terms, "And the damsel was very fair to look upon, a virgin, neither had any man known her" (Genesis 24:16).

The servant had asked God for a sign, which was fulfilled in Rebekah. Thus, he gifted her with a golden earring and two golden bracelets. He also proposed the offer of marriage to Abraham's son, Isaac.

The story goes on to tell that she accepted the proposal and traveled with the unnamed servant upon the ten camels where she met Isaac, who was meditating at the well of Lahairoi. True to type, Lahairoi means "Living One!"

> And Rebekah lifted up her eyes, and when she saw Isaac, she lighted off the camel.
>
> Genesis 24:64

She no longer needed to ride the camels. We learn a few verses later, "And Isaac brought her into his mother Sarah's tent, and took Rebekah, and she became his wife; and he loved her: And Isaac was comforted after his mother's death" (Genesis 24:67).

This story is loaded with figures that apply to the Lord and his church. The unnamed servant, picturing the Holy Spirit, took the ten camels with gifts to find the Father's son a bride from his people. The people he loves. These ten camels illustrate the Law, that is, they typify the Ten Commandments. The Bible teaches that a man cannot appreciate that he needs a savior until he understands that he is a sinner. The people on the *Titanic* didn't recognize their need for the lifeboats until they understood that the ship was going down! The Bible says, "If we say we have no sin, we deceive ourselves, and the truth is not in us" (I John 1:8).

It teaches,

> Wherefore the law was our schoolmaster until Christ, that we might be justified by faith. But after faith *(faith in Jesus)* is come, we are no longer under a schoolmaster.
>
> Galatians 3:24–25

We need the Law to show us our need for salvation, to show us our doomed and damnable condition. But when we understand our pitiful state and come to Jesus, as Rebekah came to Isaac, we no longer need to ride the camels. We can light off them as she did and be with our husband!

The golden earring and bracelets given by the servant to Rebekah obviously picture the gifts of the Holy Spirit given to us. During our time of engagement to Jesus, before we actually meet him face to face, we have the gifts his Father has given us.

> Wherefore he saith, when he ascended up on high, he lead captivity captive, and gave gifts unto men.
>
> Ephesians 4:8

We saw that Rebekah accepted the servant's proposal, just as we accept the Spirit's work bringing us to faith in the greater than Isaac. And we meet our Isaac at the well of Lahairoi, at the well of the Living One.

Lastly, Rebekah saw her future husband, and they were married. They went to Sarah's tent and became man and wife. This speaks of the rapture of the church and our seven-year honeymoon with Christ in heaven. We finally meet Isaac again in the story after a significant period of time, just as a long period of time has passed from the time of Jesus' sacrifice to his future return.

It's also interesting that Rebekah was brought into Sarah's tent and that Isaac was comforted after the death of Sarah, his mother. Remember, Sarah is a type of Israel. After the death of Sarah, or in type after the death of spiritual Israel, the woman in Isaac's life becomes Rebekah. Likewise, after Israel rejected Jesus, the church took the place of Israel. It moved into the tent previously occupied by Sarah.

Now I am *not* saying, as some have falsely said, that the church becomes Israel. No. The Bible teaches, "And so all Israel shall be saved: As it is written, There shall come out of Zion the Deliverer, and shall turn away ungodliness from Jacob" (Romans 11:26).

But in this dispensation of God's grace, in this time period we are living in now after the cross, we have taken her place.

For further independent study, chapter 25 of Genesis illustrates the revival of Israel during the millennium dispensation. It speaks of Abraham (God) remarrying a woman named Keturah, a woman who once again typifies God's marriage to the nation of Israel!

In closing this wonderful story of Isaac, we not only see the premise we have been speaking of in this book about death, burial, and resurrection, but we also see a different twist. We see a picture of the second coming of the Lord.

Yes, Isaac sacrificially died on Mount Moriah. He was buried upon the altar. And he was resurrected in type, as the angel of the Lord called out to Abraham. But then he left the story for a time while his mother died and his father's servant found him a bride. We do not see him again until the marriage feast with his bride.

It's interesting that in a Jewish marriage feast, the groom presents his bride to the people after a seven-day time of seclusion in their tent. Likewise, Jesus will present us as his bride to the world after a seven-year honeymoon in heaven (Revelation 4 and 5). That being when our Savior will come back as King of kings and Lord of lords at the second coming. When he returns, the Bible says that we will return with him.

> And the armies which were in heaven followed upon white horses, clothed in fine linen, white and clean.
>
> Revelation 19:14

We will be in our wedding dress! We will be clean and white. We will be wearing the clothes of salvation! Oh, what a happy day that will be!

Moses and the Ark

Earlier, we spoke of the story of Noah and his famous ark. But the great Moses also had an ark, which is another picture of God's plan of death, burial, and resurrection. In fact, without Moses's ark, the rest of his story could not even be told. He would have died as an infant. To use an obstetrical analogy, he would have been a miscarriage instead of a birth.

This story is found in the book of Exodus, chapters 1 and 2.

The seventy souls that came from Jacob, which traveled to Egypt under Joseph's guidance, grew and multiplied in the generations following Joseph's death. The Bible states, "And the children of Israel were fruitful, and increased abundantly, and multiplied, and waxed exceeding mighty; and the land was filled with them" (Exodus 1:7).

> Now there arose up a new king over Egypt, which knew not Joseph. And he said unto his people, Behold the people of the children of Israel are more and mightier than we: Come on, let us deal wisely with them; lest they multiply, and it come to pass, that, when there falleth out any war, they join also unto our enemies, and fight against us, and so get them up out of the land.
>
> Exodus 1:8–10

This is a typical response the people of the world will display when they see a group of God's children who are blessed by him. They will become suspicious and will often endeavor to bring us down. Don't be surprised or shocked when this occurs. It happened in the seventeenth century BC, and it will happen today also!

> And the king of Egypt spake unto the Hebrew midwives, of which the name of one was Shiphrah, and the name of the

other Puah: And he said, When ye do the office of a mid-wife to the Hebrew women, and see them upon the stools; if it be a son, then ye shall kill him: But if it be a daughter, then she shall live.

Exodus 1:15–16

Apparently Pharaoh thought he could enlist the two Hebrew midwives to do his dirty work. It was not enough that he enslaved God's people, but now he wanted to destroy them also.

This thought rings of the one Pharaoh pictures, the greater than Pharaoh, Satan! Jesus declared, "The thief *(speaking of Satan)* cometh not, but for to steal, and to kill, and to destroy" (John 10:10a).

But the midwives feared God, and did not as the king of Egypt commanded them, but saved the men children alive.

Exodus 1:17

And Pharaoh charged all his people, saying, Every son that is born ye shall cast into the river, and every daughter ye shall save alive.

Exodus 1:22

As the Hebrew midwives were not advancing Pharaoh's designs for Israel, Pharaoh called upon his own people to bring down God's children. We see this type in the tricks of Satan also. He uses both internal and external means to break down the church—division in the body of believers as well as attacks from the outside. These are well documented through-out church history, and I suspect the reader will agree, these happen in each of our own individual churches as well.

With this background we come to the story of Moses and the ark, the story of a death, burial, and resurrection experienced by the baby Moses.

Chapter 2 explains that Moses's parents were from the priestly tribe of Levi. His mother hid him for three months after his birth. But as every mother knows, as babies grow, they become nosier. They can cry loudly! Moses's mother was no longer able to keep his birth from the Egyptians. Thus, she devised a way of escape, which mirrors the way God delivered Noah. She made a basket, which acted as an ark or a boat and put the child therein along the shore of the river where the water was still.

This little ark was daubed with pitch. This sticky substance from trees would keep the craft from taking in water and sinking. Pitch is the same substance that God told Noah to use for his massive ark.

A beautiful truth also is found in the word *pitch*. *Pitch* and *atonement* are the same word in Hebrew. The pitch would keep the ark from sinking, just as Jesus' atonement, his sacrifice for you and me, keep us from sinking!

But not only is the pitch significant, but the entire ark is an Old Testament illustration God was using to show mankind what he was planning to do through his Son, Jesus. The two arks, Noah's and Moses's, are types of Jesus. Just as Jesus said that Scriptures speak of him, indeed these arks picture his deliverance of us from the waters of destruction. They show our deliverance from the tide of judgment we deserve!

In deciding that Moses must go into the ark, his mother chose a type of death so that he might live. Moses died in the analogy and was buried in the little ark. His resurrection in figure came next. Incredibly, it was from the same river where Pharaoh told his people to kill the Hebrew boys, and, almost comically, it was by his own daughter! Truly God has a sense of humor!

Pharaoh's daughter came down to the river with her maidens to wash herself, and she saw the ark. She had a choice to make at that point: to turn the baby over to men who would have killed Moses or to have compassion on the child. We know she took the latter approach.

Thus, against seemingly terrible odds, God shows us his

pattern once again of deliverance through death, burial, and resurrection.

Next, at the end of his life, Moses again also illustrates this truth. Let's look at Moses and Mount Nebo.

Moses and Mount Nebo

This story actually starts nearly forty years earlier in the wilderness of the modern day Sinai Peninsula.

Shortly after leaving Egypt, the children of Israel were camping in the desert while being tutored by God. He was preparing them for the promised land. When they arrived at their seventh camp—their seventh lesson, if you will—there was no water. The name of this camp was Rephidim, which means rest. That's funny. They were in the desert with no water at a place called rest! But that's exactly what God wanted them to learn. Even in hot and dry times, if we rest in him, we will be refreshed. Let see how this develops!

In Exodus 17, we learn that the people did chide with Moses. They thirsted for water and murmured against Moses. They even longed for their old life of bondage in Egypt at this point.

So Moses did a wise thing and cried unto the Lord.

> And the Lord said unto Moses, Go on before the people, and take with thee of the elders of Israel; and thy rod, wherewith thou smotest the river, take in thine hand, and go. Behold, I will stand before thee there upon the rock in Horeb; and thou shalt smite the rock, and there shall come water out of it, that the people may drink. And Moses did so in the sight of the elders of Israel.
>
> Exodus 17:5–6

God told Moses to smite the rock and out would come waters of refreshment for the people. This verse is loaded with significance. It is a powerful representation of Jesus, his passion, and of the Holy Spirit.

Paul teaches in his letter to the Corinthians that Jesus was that very rock in type. "And did all drink the same spiritual drink: For they drank of that spiritual Rock that followed them: And that Rock was Christ" (1 Corinthians 10:4).

Jesus is the rock that quenches our thirst.

Continuing, we see that Moses obediently does as God directs, and the story proceeds.

Shortly thereafter, the children of Israel were given the Law. They then built the tabernacle and were ready to move into the promised land after their one-year sabbatical in the desert with God. Unfortunately, though, ten of the twelve men they had sent to spy out the land brought back an evil report, and the people lost their faith. The Israelites rebelled against God and were banished to the desert to live out the duration of the lives of the faithless men who were over twenty years of age at that time.

It was sometime during this thirty-eight-year time period that they came to the desert of Zin and abided in Kadesh. This is where we pick up our story in Numbers chapter 20.

The Bible tells us that once again they found themselves in a dry place, a place without water. God was giving his children yet another chance to trust him. But as often happens with me, and I suspect with you also, they began to chide and murmur instead of walking in faith. They criticized Moses and Aaron for their apparent poor leadership. They even said their present fate seemed worse than what happened to Korah, Dathan, Abiram, and their followers when they rebelled against Moses and Aaron and were subsequently swallowed up by the earth! They were having such a pity party over their situation that they actually preferred God's judgment over the dry place!

To Moses's credit, he and Aaron took this to the Lord instead of responding to the unreasonableness of the people.

> And the Lord spake unto Moses, saying, Take the rod, and gather thou the assembly together, thou, and Aaron thy brother, and *speak unto the rock* before their eyes; and it shall give forth his water, and thou shalt bring forth to them water out of the rock:
>
> Numbers 20:7–8

As before when they found themselves in a dry place, God answered his man, Moses. But notice the instructions are similar but not identical. Earlier, God told Moses to smite the rock and water would gush forth; this time he was to speak to the rock. This seemingly small point is vitally important, as we shall see.

> And Moses took the rod from before the Lord, as he commanded him.
>
> And Moses and Aaron gathered the congregation together before the rock, and he said unto them, Hear now, ye rebels; must *we* fetch you water out of this rock?
>
> Numbers 20:9–10

Uh-oh, this is not good! What are you doing, Moses? This is not God's heart for the people. God did not say that the people were rebels. He was not angry, and he didn't intend for Moses to be either.

Unfortunately, Moses had had enough of the unbelieving nation, and he misrepresented the Lord seriously due to his anger. He actually forgot to acknowledge that it is by God's grace that water would flow. Incredibly, he asked, "Must we fetch you water?" As if it were in his power to provide.

> And Moses lifted up his hand, and with his rod he smote the rock twice: And the water came out abundantly, and the congregation drank, and their beasts also. And the Lord spake unto Moses and Aaron, Because ye believed me not,

to sanctify me in the eyes of the children of Israel, therefore ye shall not bring this congregation into the land which I have given them.

Numbers 20:11–12

Moses was demoted! His anger kept him from sanctifying the Lord in front of the people. Understand, dear reader, hostility diminishes authority. As James declared, "For the wrath of man worketh not the righteousness of God" (James 1:20).

Moses grabbed the glory instead of giving the glory to the one who deserves all glory and praise. God does not share his glory with any man. When a leader loses sight of this fact, the inevitable loss of his ministry will follow. The first example of this is seen in Lucifer's fall, and here also we see Moses succumbing.

Moses misrepresented God's heart and smote the rock twice. Now you will remember that this rock typifies Jesus Christ. We know that Jesus died once and for all time for the sins of the world. He was smitten once! His perfect sacrifice did not need to be repeated as did the covenant sacrifices of the priests for the covering of the nation's sins. His sacrifice not only covers but cleanses our sin away!

Thus, Moses did not follow the type God was giving by smiting the rock again. Jesus is not to be sacrificed again, as the book of Hebrews declares, "If they shall fall away, to renew them again unto repentance; seeing they crucify to themselves the Son of God afresh, and put him to an open shame" (Hebrews 6:6).

As an application to this, when I strike out and smite God's children angrily, when my pride keeps me from representing God to my tribe correctly, I'm really smiting Jesus personally!

Nevertheless, even though Moses was prideful and disobedient, God still showed his true heart. He graced the people with water pouring forth abundantly. Moses rebounded wonderfully from the chastisement he received and continued to lead the people through their journey in the wilderness.

They traveled from Sinai to modern-day Jordan, where they defeated the kings of the Amorites, Sihon, and Og. When they came to the edge of the promised land, Moses reminded the people of his upcoming fate as their leader. He reminded them of his upcoming death.

> And Moses went and spake these words unto all Israel. And he said unto them, I am an hundred and twenty years old this day; I can no more go out and come in: Also the Lord hath said unto me, Thou shalt not go over this Jordan. The Lord thy God, he will go over before thee, and he will destroy these nations from before thee, and thou shalt possess them.
>
> Deuteronomy 31:1–3a

Moses pointed out correctly that it would be God who would deliver them in the land they were going to possess.

> And Joshua, he shall go over before thee, as the Lord hath said.
>
> Deuteronomy 31:3b

Moses understood, as did John the Baptist, that he must decrease and another will increase.

Now, Joshua, wonderful Joshua! We must speak of him.

His name means "Jehovah saves." Throughout the Bible, he is a wonderful and powerful picture of the greater than Joshua, Jesus Christ. In fact, we know Jesus by his Greek name of Jesus, but this is not a name people actually called him during his earthly life. His name in Aramaic is Yeshua. That's how people knew him. The Hebrew translation is Joshua!

Yes, Joshua led the people into the promised land, just as Jesus leads us into the promised land of the Spirit-filled life, into the land of the new covenant walk. Into the land, as Jeremiah 31:33 points out, where God writes his will on our hearts.

Understanding Joshua's role in this story gives us a beautiful picture of God's plan of salvation. You see, Moses represents the Law, the Ten Commandments, the Old Testament. Joshua represents Jesus, the new covenant, the age of grace. The Law, as we have discussed earlier, is our schoolmaster to bring us to Christ. It is the ten camels that Rebekah rode to find Isaac that we ride to find our greater than Isaac, Jesus Christ. It brings us to the promised land, but Jesus brings us in. When we get to the promised land, we are no longer under the Law but under grace. We go from the Old Covenant of rules and regulations to the New Covenant of grace, the place where we have God's will written upon our hearts! Yes, God wonderfully paints a picture in passing the leadership of his people from Moses to Joshua.

Thus, after commissioning Joshua, Moses died and was buried.

> And Moses went up from the plains of Moab unto the mountain of Nebo, to the top of Pisgah, that is over against Jericho. And the Lord showed him all the land of Gilead, unto Dan. And all Naphtali , and the land of Ephraim, and Manasseh, and all the land of Judah, unto the utmost sea. And the south, and the plain of the valley of Jericho, the city of palm trees, unto Zoar. And the Lord said unto him, This is the land which I sware unto Abraham, unto Isaac, and unto Jacob, saying, I will give it unto thy seed: I have caused thee to see it with thine own eyes,
>
> Deuteronomy 34:1–4a

This is marvelous! God, in his grace, allowed Moses to look upon the promised land before his death. He miraculously showed Moses the entire land from the north in Dan to the west against the sea and unto the south.

> But thou shalt not go over thither.
>
> Deuteronomy 34:4b

To be true to the type, you will not go in, Moses. It is for Joshua to take the people into the land.

> So Moses the servant of the Lord died there in the land of Moab, according to the word of the Lord. And he buried him in a valley in the land of Moab, over against Bethpeor: But no man knoweth of his sepulcher unto this day.
>
> Deuteronomy 34:5–6

Moses died and was buried. And so ends his story.

Or does it?

Wonderfully not! For we find Moses alive again in the New Testament. He was resurrected! But not only do we find him alive again, we find him *in* the promised land. God in his infinite grace brought Moses into the land anyway. He snuck him in through the back door, if you will. Let's see how he does this!

> And after six days Jesus taketh Peter, James, and John his brother, and bringeth them up into an high mountain apart. (Scholars teach this mountain was Mount Hermon in the north of Israel.) And was transfigured before them: And his face did shine as the sun, and his raiment was white as the light. And, behold, there appeared unto them Moses and Elias talking with him. Then answered Peter, and said unto Jesus, Lord, it is good for us to be here: If thou wilt, let us make here three tabernacles; one for thee, and one for Moses, and one for Elias.
>
> Matthew 17:1–4

God fulfills the type we are picturing in this section. Moses died, was buried, and later resurrected. And he found himself in the promised land in the presence of the greater than Joshua: the Messiah, Jesus the Christ. Also, he was with Peter, James, and John, who represent the children of Israel, the nation over which he was given charge!

Praise God! For truly, his ways are unsearchable!

As a postscript to this story, we need to ask the question: how did Moses and Elijah end up alongside Jesus in their resurrected bodies in the first place?

Paul did teach that to be absent from the body is to be present with the Lord (2 Corinthians 5:8). But he also taught that Jesus was the firstfruits of the resurrection and we, as the latter harvest, will be resurrected later. He has explained that our bodies will be resurrected upon the return of the Lord, that day when the Lord will descend from heaven with a shout with the trump of God (1 Thessalonians 4:16). So again I ask how did Moses and Elijah get to have their resurrected bodies before this future event?

Well, it's not hard to place Elijah on the mount of transfiguration. The Old Testament clearly teaches that Elijah was taken up into heaven in a whirlwind, along with a fiery chariot and horses (2 Kings 2:11). Elijah did not die but as God's man who symbolized the Old Testament prophets; he prophesies for all time of the resurrection with his rapture to heaven. Yes, we can see how Elijah was invited to the transfiguration.

But what about Moses? He died and was buried, as we saw in Deuteronomy 34. But in rereading verse 6 of chapter 34, we see it says, "He buried Moses in the land of Moab at a place unknown to any man." It sounds like God did the burying upon this reading. But wait! The short book of Jude sheds some light on this event.

> Yet Michael the archangel, when contending with the devil he disputed about the body of Moses, durst not bring against him a railing accusation, but said, The Lord rebuke thee.
>
> Jude 9

This difficult verse helps us to understand Moses's presence at the transfiguration. Apparently after Moses's death and burial, he was resurrected, and Michael and Satan battled over him. Michael rebuked Satan in the name of the Lord and received Moses's body unto him and unto God. Thus, Moses's spirit and resurrected body were reunited. Therefore, Moses also could have been invited to the sneak preview of Jesus' glory without contradicting Scripture.

Now that we understand that they are alive in bodily form, let me examine with you another time many scholars feel they pop up again in the New Testament.

Revelation 11:3–13 speaks of two witnesses who will speak of Jesus to Israel and the world during the last days. Just as Jesus sent out his disciples to the cities of Israel in groups of two, he will again send two disciples to Israel to proclaim the gospel during the tribulation period. They will prophesy for nearly three years in Jerusalem, and those who are determined against them will be tormented by their words. The witnesses will be indestructible during the time of their testimony and will have power over their enemies. They will shut up heaven so that rain will not fall and will have power over water to turn it to blood. As in the days of God's judgment of Egypt (which is a powerful picture of the tribulation judgment), they will be able to smite the earth with plagues.

Only after their message is complete will the satanically possessed antichrist be able to subdue them. The world will rejoice and celebrate an anti-Christmas! People will exchange gifts upon the deaths of their enemies, in contrast to Christmas where people exchange gifts to celebrate the birth of a friend.

They will lie rotting for all to see for three and a half days. Then the Spirit will cause them to stand up alive, and all who witness this event will fear greatly. The witnesses will hear those words, *Come up,* and will be resurrected into heaven as a final witness to the world. At that same hour, a massive earthquake will kill seven thousand in Jerusalem and the remnant of Israel will out of fright give glory to God.

Are these witnesses Elijah and Moses?

I think it is very likely!

As we have discussed, Elijah did not die but was taken to heaven. We see him with Jesus on Mount Hermon, and he represents all of the prophets to Israel. Elijah had a powerful anointing. He prayed to God, and the rain from heaven was shut for three years. That day on Mount Carmel when he called down fire from heaven has forever been imprinted in the world's collective memory. Lastly, Malachi prophesied to Israel in 430 BC, "Behold, I send you Elijah the prophet before the coming of the great and dreadful day of the Lord" (Malachi 4:5).

Yes, the identity of one of the two as Elijah is most likely.

The second of the witnesses as Moses is less certain but still a very likely possibility. As we have noted, the archangel Michael obtained Moses' body. Moses also was with Jesus and Elijah on the mount. Moses represents the Law in the eyes of his people, just as Elijah represents the prophets. Thus, in Moses and Elijah we see God's two witnesses of the Old Testament, that of the Law and the prophets. Lastly, Moses's anointing was also with potent power. God used Moses in directing the plagues of Egypt that set his children free. These plagues, interestingly, are eerily similar to the plagues of the tribulation period. In fact, the only thing we need to identify Moses as the second witness with the same certainty as Elijah is a verse from Malachi stating so!

So Moses and Elijah will very likely once again witness to Israel about Jesus. Just as God told those men of Israel— Peter, James and John—that Jesus was his beloved Son. So too, Moses and Elijah will tell the men of Israel that Jesus is the beloved Son!

Notice also that the two witnesses could not be harmed until they finished their testimony. In like manner, I firmly believe that Satan, whom the Bible says in Hebrews 2:14 has the power of death, cannot take our lives prematurely. That is, we will not die before we too have finished the testimony God has given each of us! That may be a long life or a relatively short one, but it won't end until we have finished the testimony God has given.

Lastly, we see the witnesses soaring as they ascend to heaven. Likewise you and I will soar as we witness with our lives and words God's wonderful message of salvation.

A Leper's Two Birds

Did you know the Bible pictures you as a leper? Me too!

You see, whenever the feared disease of leprosy is spoken of in the Old Testament, it can be spiritualized as sin in the New Testament. That is, leprosy in the Old Testament is a picture of sin for us living in New Testament times. A leper in the Old Testament typifies a sinner in the New. You and I are sinners. Thus, spiritually we are lepers!

You may wonder, *Just how is leprosy like sin?*

The answer lies in the nature of the disease itself.

Leprosy is a contagious disease that starts out small. It is below the surface initially. Often a small, white patch will appear on the skin or an area of scalp will lose its hair as the initial manifestation.

So too is sin. It's contagious and starts out small. We received our sin nature through contact with our ancestor, Adam. When we sin, it's usually the little things first—a little white lie or a little kickback at the job, a peek at that magazine, or just a little too much attention to that co-worker.

After a period of time, though, leprosy becomes very disfiguring and brutal. Sufferers will become hideous to look upon. Skin, toes, ears, and fingers slough away, and sores ooze throughout the skin. At this point, everyone can see that the leper is cursed! Nothing is under the surface any more. Nothing is hidden!

Likewise, after a period of time, a person caught in sin will become hideous and disfigured. Everyone can see that the sinner has become a leper. He is cursed.

The leper is cast out of the city. He leaves the fellowship of his family and is an outcast. He loses everything. He lives a hell on earth as he cries, "Unclean! Unclean!" for all to hear. He is without hope!

In like figure, the sinner also loses everything. The Bible states that "the wages of sin is death" (Romans 6:23a). The sinner is without hope. He is destined for hell. He has the stench of death upon him. He is destined for outer darkness.

With these introductory remarks, a story in Matthew's gospel will hopefully come alive!

> When he *(Jesus)* was come down from the mountain, great multitudes followed him.
>
> Matthew 8:1

Jesus had just finished his Sermon on the Mount discourse.

"The people were astonished at his doctrine: For he taught them as one having authority, and not as the scribes" (Matthew 7:28b-29).

It was an electric scene, and the multitudes followed gladly.

It is in this setting, after hearing the Word of God, that we see healing take place, literally of leprosy and figuratively of sin (Romans 10:17).

> And, behold, there came a leper and worshipped him, saying, Lord, if thou wilt, thou canst make me clean.
>
> Matthew 8:2

This pathetic man knew he was unclean, as did everyone else who witnessed this interchange.

But he worshipped the Lord. He recognized Jesus for who he was. He called him Lord! In type, he was born again!

No doubt those standing by were repulsed by the leper as he called out to Jesus. They may have also feared that they too could contract the terrible disease and thus wanted the leper to return to his isolation.

But not our Lord!

> And Jesus put forth his hand, and touched him saying, I will; be thou I clean. And immediately his leprosy was cleansed
>
> Matthew 8:3

Jesus was not afraid to touch the leper. Other translations say it more forcefully. It can read, "He reached forth and grasped him." Jesus bear-hugged the leper!

Certainly we see that Jesus was not too concerned about catching leprosy. Spiritually we understand this, as Jesus was sinless. He is the Living Water. He is a fountain. He is a spring. He cannot be contaminated by sin, just as a fountain or spring cannot be contaminated by pollutants.

This is not the case with you and me though. The Bible says we are earthen vessels (2 Corinthians 4:7a). We are as cisterns, which hold water. But our water is not limitless like our Lord's. If we hug a leper, we are not likely to heal the leper but to contract leprosy. Likewise, when we walk with a person caught in sin, instead of cleaning the sinner up, we end up getting dirty!

Solomon states it this way: "Go from the presence of a foolish man, when thou perceivest not in him the lips of knowledge" (Proverbs 14:17).

Or, if I may paraphrase, when a fool hangs out with Jesus, he will become wise, but when you or I hang out with a fool, *we* become stupid!

The Bible says, "If we confess our sins, he is faithful and

just to forgive us our sins, and to cleanse us from all unrighteousness" (1 John 1:9).

The man was cleaned immediately, just as I am when I confess my sins, when I bring my leprosy to the Great Physician!

> And Jesus saith unto him, See thou tell no man; but go thy way, show thyself to the priest, and offer the gift that Moses commanded, for a testimony unto them.
>
> Matthew 8:4

If I may paraphrase what Jesus said to the man, "Now that you've been healed, go witness your healing to the priest. Show him what God has done for you. And as a child of Jacob, offer the sacrifice of the leper written in the Law."

Similarly, we are to witness the healing from sin we have received from the Lord!

But wait a minute! The gift Moses commanded. What's that?

It's found in Leviticus 14, and it's not a sacrifice with which the priests were very familiar. That's because since the beginning of the nation, no man or woman had ever been healed of leprosy except Moses's sister, Miriam; Moses's hand when he witnessed his commission to the elders of Israel; and Naaman, the captain of the Syrian host. The latter was not a portion of Scripture that was reviewed very often by the priests!

I have to smile when I think of how Jesus, tongue in cheek, must have told the man to go to the priest and have that cleric do something that had never been done before in Israel: that of offering a gift for a cleansed leper. Never, that is, until Jesus!

Let's look at this gift. It beautifully pictures the death, resurrection, and ascension of Jesus in the first seven verses and pictures the death, burial, and resurrection of the sinner in verses 8 and 9.

> And the Lord spake unto Moses, saying, This shall be the law of the leper in the day of his cleansing: He shall be brought unto the priest: And the priest shall go forth out of

the camp; and the priest shall look, and, behold, if the plague of leprosy be healed in the leper; Then shall the priest command to take for him that is to be cleansed two birds alive and clean, and cedar wood, and scarlet, and hyssop:

Leviticus 14:1–4

In this story, the priest is a type of Jesus. Jesus is our Great High Priest (Hebrews 4:14), and often in Scripture when a priestly ministry is being preformed, it can reflect an aspect of Jesus' ministry also. So it is in this story, as you will see.

The priest was then to take two alive and clean birds along with cedar, scarlet, and hyssop. These two birds, along with the three items, picture our Lord's death and resurrection.

And the priest shall command that one of the birds be killed in an earthen vessel over running water.

Leviticus 14:5

Jesus, in his human body, is represented by that earthen vessel. Our bodies are dust. We are just clay pots, as was Jesus' body. He became a man. Think of that. God became a man!

The running water represents the Spirit. We know that the spirit is like a river of running water! Oh, how the Spirit had ordained that sacrifice!

The first bird was killed as a sacrifice for the leper, as a sacrifice for sin!

As for the living bird, he shall take it, and the cedar wood, and the scarlet, and the hyssop, and shall dip them and the living bird in the blood of the bird that was killed over the running water:

Leviticus 14:6

Christ is the living bird who died and now is alive. He took the cedar wood and hyssop of the cross and shed the blood of scarlet. He is *both* birds.

Look what next happens to the living bird!

> And he shall sprinkle upon him that is to be cleansed from the leprosy seven times, and shall pronounce him clean, and shall let the living bird loose into the open field.
>
> Leviticus 14:7

The blood of the killed bird is dipped onto the living bird and then upon the leper seven times. Seven is the number of perfection. The living sacrifice is perfect! The blood continues to cleanse as Jesus is alive. He has risen from the dead!

After that, the living bird flies away. So too after Jesus' sacrifice, he also flew away. He ascended back to heaven where he sits at the right hand of the Father interceding for us (Romans 8:34).

How exactly the gift Moses commanded for the leper pictures Jesus' death, resurrection, and ascension!

> And he that is to be cleansed shall wash his clothes, and shave off all his hair, and wash himself in water, that he may be clean:
>
> Leviticus 14:8a

The leper would wash his clothes of death. Next, he would shave off all of his hair. Then he would wash himself.

The Bible teaches that we are all unclean, that our righteousness is as filthy rags (Isaiah 64:6). But, thankfully, it also declares that God clothes us with the garments of salvation, with the robe of righteousness (Isaiah 61:10b).

In Bible days, hair represented maturity and glory, thus shaving off all hair would be a sign of consecration and humility. When we come to Christ, it must be in humility (Matthew 8:3–4).

Lastly, this verse points out the importance of washing in the Word after salvation. "Wherewithal shall a young man cleanse his way? By taking heed thereto according to thy word" (Psalm 119:9).

And after that he shall come into the camp, and shall tarry abroad out of his tent seven days.

Leviticus 14:8b

The leper has died. He has left his filthy rags behind and has cleaned himself in water. Now he must tarry abroad for seven days. He is buried away. The next verse completes the picture with the leper's resurrection.

> But it shall be on the seventh day, he shall shave all his hair off his head and his beard and his eyebrows, even all his hair he shall shave off: And he shall wash his clothes, also he shall wash his flesh in water, and he shall be clean.

Leviticus 14:9

After seven days of burial, the former leper was clean. He was resurrected.

In like analogy, after we, as former lepers, die and are buried, we will be resurrected on the seventh day. At the perfect time, we will be in God's presence. In his presence, we will be shaved of hair. There will be no place for pride! Our clothes and flesh will be washed. *We shall be clean* (Psalm 119:9)!

Paul's Shipwreck

Jesus said to Thomas shortly before his death, "I am the way, the truth, and the life: No man cometh unto the Father, but by me" (John 14:6).

Truly, it is *impossible* to reach the Father apart from Jesus. As an analogy to this truth, as we have discussed earlier, Jesus is illustrated as the ark that carried Noah and Moses safely over the waters of destruction.

Let's look at those waters.

Previously, we have noted that flowing water, living water, a spring or fountain of water typify the Holy Spirit. This is not the case with bodies of water. Oceans, lakes, and seas spiritually represent something very different.

In the Bible and to the Jewish psyche, bodies of water are an expanse, a gulf, or a chasm that cannot be easily crossed. The Jews were not a sea-going people, and God thus used bodies of water in the Bible to demonstrate spiritual truth.

To spiritualize this idea, a body of water represents the barrier between a Holy God and sinful man! Thus, in the Bible, whenever we see an ark, a fishing boat, or in Paul's case, a passenger boat, these all point to Jesus. It is Jesus who carries that person or group of people to a place they cannot reach on their own. He takes them over dangerous and sometimes stormy waters in order to reach their destination.

So in these terms, let me contrast salvation by works, that is, salvation by being a good and moral person versus salvation by faith in Jesus Christ.

Imagine you are standing on the pier in New York harbor and you want to go to Kingstown, Jamaica. It's very cold in New York, there is crime everywhere, and you've heard that a benevolent king rules over Kingstown. You can almost feel the warm tropical breezes, and you know that life will be good there. You want to go!

So you set out. You eat a good breakfast after a great night of sleep. You put on your nice new swimsuit, and you jump into the water and begin to swim to Kingstown!

Well, even if you are the world's greatest swimmer, you won't get very close to your destination. It's thousands of miles away! You will tire and ultimately drown. You won't make it! That's salvation by works! By my own efforts, trying to impress God by my goodness, generosity, and morality, I won't even come close. God is holy. I am not!

Alternatively, if I want to go to Kingstown, I can take a boat. At the pier I can board a boat and ride safely over the ocean. I can sail over those same waters that I could have never navigated myself. In our analogy, Jesus *is* that boat! Oh, there may be some storms and seasickness along the way, but he's going to get me there. I'm going to make it. And he's greater than the *Titanic;* he's unsinkable!

So whenever you read of a boat in the Bible, whether it's Jonah on the sea sleeping, the disciples on the lake in a tempest, Noah over the waters rained down from heaven, Moses on the river of Egypt, or here in our story of Paul on the stormy Mediterranean, realize that the boat typifies Jesus' ministry of salvation.

With these comments, let's look at Paul's trip to Rome. Of course, in it we will see pictured the figurative death, burial, and resurrection of *all* of the 276 travelers.

This story typifies God's deliverance to all who stay on the ship of salvation, all who stay connected to Jesus!

The book of Acts tells the story.

Jesus told Paul, as recorded in Acts 23, that he would travel to Rome to stand before Cesar. In Acts 27, we read of the journey.

Paul and other prisoners were delivered to the charge of a centurion named Julius. Julius had the honor of belonging to a group of military men whose unit was named after a previous emperor, Augustus Caesar. They set off from Caesarea and traveled north to Sidon. But only about half way to Rome they realized the trip had taken much more time than usual. It was autumn and the winds were a threat for sea travel at this time

Unfortunately, Julius felt that a short trip down the coast to the port of Phenice would be best, as that harbor faced a more favorable direction against the winter wind and waves.

Initially the winds were light out of the south, but not long after setting sail, the Bible tells us that a *tempestuous wind,* called a euroclydon, hit the area. This is better known to us as a Nor'easter and is a vicious winter storm that strikes the coastal areas of the Northern Hemisphere. The wind became uncontrollable out of the northeast, and the men had to ride out the storm in the open waters of the Mediterranean Sea so as to avoid crashing upon the rocks on one of the beaches of Crete. We learn that they were tossed and turned for two weeks in this powerful storm system.

On the fourteenth day of their ordeal, the sailors noted that they were coming up against land, as the depth of the sea was markedly diminishing. They sounded the bottom and found that it rose from twenty to fifteen fathoms over a short distance. This led the shipmen to fear that the ship would fall upon the rocks. The men let down a lifeboat and were ready to jump ship when Paul told Julius and the other soldiers, "Except these abide in the ship, ye cannot be *saved*" (Acts 27:31b).

Wonderfully, the soldiers believed Paul and did not abandon ship. Later that day they discovered the island of Melita, known today as Malta. They rode the ship into the rocks off the beach, and the Bible tells us that the forefront of the ship stuck fast in the sandy offshore bank while the hinder part was exposed to the waves and was broken. Julius came to Paul's rescue and kept the soldiers from killing the prisoners. All 276 men swam and floated to the beach safely without loss of life or limb.

What a story! The travelers survived because they believed God's anointed man, Paul, instead of going with their instincts and jumping ship.

Let's examine the death, burial, and resurrection in this story. We see the agonizingly slow, figurative death of the sailors during their fourteen-day ordeal on the Mediterranean Sea. The men went from being in control—or so they thought—of their own destiny to a point where they lost all hope and put their trust in a rabbi from Israel. They indeed died to self; they died to their agendas and their purposes and put their lives in Paul's hands.

As we have seen before in several other stories, these men were buried in the water. They were baptized, if you will, by Paul, to their figurative resurrection on the beautiful beach of Malta. They left the dangers of the sea and came to the safety of the land. Spiritually, they left their old life of terror and trouble, were buried in the sea, and rose to a new life in a place that pictures our new life in heaven.

Lastly, you will recall that the ship pictures Jesus. He is the one that carries us over stormy waters. Notice in our story that the forepart of the ship stuck fast in the sand and was unmovable (Acts 27:41a). This pictures our Savior as he, like a flint, moved forward to Calvary without wavering for you and me. But the hinder part was broken with the violence of the waves (Acts 27:41b). This, of course, is seen in the beating and death Jesus took to purchase our freedom.

Lastly, God told Paul that all the men traveling with him would be saved. All of the men on ship would be delivered safely. This is the way with our Lord. Jesus said to the Father, "While I was with them in the world, I kept them in thy name: Those that thou gavest me I have kept, and none of them is lost" (John 17:12a).

We are secure in Jesus. We are secure in our salvation. But also notice a few verses later, Paul had to tell the centurion, when the men were preparing to jump ship, that unless they stayed on the ship, they could not be saved. This is an important principle, which must be addressed from its spiritual perspective. Yes, we are secure in our salvation in Jesus. We cannot lose our salvation. But apparently we can jump ship. We can *walk away* from it.

So does that mean we can lose our salvation? No! It means we can walk away from it!

The picture is true. If Noah or Moses or the disciples had jumped off their boats, they would have died. Their covering would have left. That was exactly the fate that Jonah experienced when he jumped overboard. But as long as they stayed on the ship of salvation, as Paul told those sailing with him to do, they were safe. They were saved!

So it is for you and me too. Stay on the ship, dear believer!

Crucified with Christ

Did you know that sin has *no* power over you! That's right! It has no power over me either!

In the Christian manifesto called the book of Romans, we learn of our predicament as sinners and our wonderful deliverance from not only the *penalty* of sin, but also from the *power* of sin. Specifically, the first five chapters of Romans teach of our *justification*. This holy word can be broken down into the phrase, "Just as if I've never sinned." When God says I am justified, it means to him that I never sinned at all. It's as if it didn't happen!

These chapters describe how men are set free from the penalty of sin. We learn in chapter 1 of the perversity of sin and of how mankind's pathetic state is indicted by creation itself. We look around and can see that a glorious God must be present, as evidenced by creation, and yet we see that we fall woefully short of his glory. Chapter 2 picks up the indictment by revealing that we all have a conscience that speaks to us of our fallen state, and finally chapter 3 teaches that the Law of God also indicts us. Yes, we are shown guilty by creation, conscience, and the commandments.

After meticulously building the case for mankind's fallen state, we come to chapters 4 and 5. Here we see the wonderful truth that by *faith* in Jesus Christ the deserved penalty of sin is waived. We are set free indeed from the penalty of sin. The religious word for this concept is *sanctification.* We are set apart.

But it gets better. For if God had stopped there, we all would get to be in heaven later but would still be defeated now. The power that sin holds over me would continue to bring me down and take me out! That's why chapter 6 was written. This wonderful chapter sets the believer in Jesus Christ free from the power of sin.

Let's look at it in some detail. We will, of course, see a death, burial, and resurrection involved in obtaining our freedom.

> Know ye not, that so many of us as were baptized into Jesus Christ were baptized into his *death?* Therefore we are *buried* with him by baptism into death: That like as Christ was *raised* up from the dead by the glory of the Father, even so we also should walk in newness of life.
>
> Romans 6:3–4

There we see it again. The death, burial, and resurrection of Jesus are transferred to you and me so we can walk in newness of life! Instead of being defeated and destroyed by sin, we can be a new creation, one that can start our resurrected life the moment we call Jesus as Lord, not when we die and go to heaven. Jesus prayed to the Father about this very thing.

> And this is life eternal, that they might know thee the only true God, and Jesus Christ, whom thou hast sent.
>
> John 17:3

You see, in God's eyes, our new life started when we were baptized into Christ's death, when we believed. We have eternal life now! We don't have to wait. It's already started!

So the obvious response is to live life like eternity has already begun. Store up treasures in heaven, and don't worry so much about your 401(k)!

> For if we have been planted together in the likeness of
> his death, we shall also in the likeness of his resurrection:
> Knowing this, that, that henceforth we should not serve sin.
>
> Romans 6:5–6

Well, praise God! I can stop serving sin. I can stop being defeated by my "pet" sin, for I have been crucified with Christ.

But not so fast! A crucifixion is a long, slow, and agonizing death. It's death by degree. It's not a cardiac arrest where one minute a person is well and the next he's gone. The old man doesn't die the minute I come to Christ. But he is nailed to the cross at that time. I then have the choice of whether, like Jesus, I will lay my life down and die after six hours on the cross, or, like most sufferers who were crucified, will I fight the inevitable death and hang on torturously for days. It's my choice—start walking in newness of life or hang on to the old man!

The verse we are studying tells us that the body of sin and death is destroyed when we were crucified with Christ. A better translation for destroyed would be paralyzed. It is evident to even the most mature believer, the one who has walked with the Lord for decades, that the old man can still rise up.

Remember when you were young there was always a bully at school who would boss you around and generally torment you. If you didn't fall into line, he would slug you. Well, that's the old man. But now that bully is paralyzed. He was in an accident and had a neck injury. He's in a wheelchair and really can't do anything. He can't back up what he tells you to do any longer.

Likewise, the old man can't boss me around any longer either. He's in traction; he's paralyzed. Oh, he will still shout at me to look at this or indulge in that, but he has no power to make me go there or do that any longer. He was crucified!

> For he that is dead is free from sin. Now if we be dead with
> Christ, we believe that we shall also live with him: Know-
> ing that Christ being raised from the dead dieth no more;
> death hath no more dominion over him: For in that he died,

he died unto sin once: But in that he liveth, he liveth unto God. Likewise *reckon* ye also yourselves to be dead indeed unto sin, but alive unto God through Jesus Christ our Lord.

Romans 6:7–11

Reckon is not something Jed Clampett might say to Granny; it's an accounting term. You look at your bank statement and see that there's money in your account. Likewise, Christ died unto sin and lives unto God, so I can reckon, or account, that to be true for me also!

Let not sin therefore reign in your mortal body, that ye should obey it in the lusts thereof. Neither yield ye your members as instruments of unrighteousness unto sin: But *yield* yourselves unto God, as those that are alive from the dead, and your members as instruments of righteousness unto God.

Romans 6:12–13

Do you want to feel alive? Do you really want to live? Then yield yourself to God and stop serving sin.

In these ten verses, we see a key to crucifying the old man, to paralyzing him so that he can only bark but no longer bite, to being free from the power of sin.

First, we *recognize the truth* that the power of sin is broken, that the old man is destroyed, or better translated, paralyzed. Secondly, we *appropriate that truth.* We reckon or account it to indeed be true. We believe that we were really crucified with Christ! Lastly, we make the application. We *yield to the truth.* We yield our bodies unto the Lord. We don't have to cower anymore to the old man's bullying.

Now, in the Old Testament in the book of Judges, we find a story that illustrates these truths beautifully. It's found in Judges 4.

The setting is approximately 1270 BC, a little over one hundred years after the armies of Israel under Joshua's command had taken the promised land. Unfortunately, after General Joshua's death, the children of Israel entered a 335-year cycle of sin known as the time period of the book of Judges. It was a time interval that was characterized by the people falling into sin only to become slaves to a foreign leader. They then would call out to God, who was always faithful to deliver them. Subsequently, they would serve God for a time only to fall back into the cycle of sin after the particular judge died.

Of course, this book typifies our lives to a tee, doesn't it? We too, as believers in Jehovah, have been delivered. But unfortunately, we often fall into sin. We become slaves to that sin. Later, we come to our senses and call out to God for deliverance. He does deliver, and we serve him wholeheartedly for a time. Unfortunately, we often fall into the same or some other sin again, and the whole cycle starts over. Read the book of Judges in this light, and you will be blessed!

Let's look at the days of Deborah.

The Bible tells us that Deborah was a prophetess and a mother in Israel. Her name means *bee,* and indeed she was busy as women can become with their many job descriptions. She sat under a palm tree between Ramah and Bethel. Translating the meaning of her location, she was under the authority of Jesus (as sitting under a tree always pictures submitting to the work of the cross), and she presided between an elevated place, Ramah, and the house of God, Bethel.

As a prophetess, she apparently received revelation from God that he was about to deliver the children of Israel from Jabin, the king of Canaan. It was Jabin whom God allowed to enslave the people after they fell away from him. Deborah told her general, whose name was Barak, to take ten thousand men of the children of Naphtali and Zebulon and draw Jabin's general, Sisera, and his army to the Kishon River in northern Israel for a face-off.

Now, Sisera's army had nine hundred chariots of iron and thus was very powerful. Israel hadn't even entered the Iron Age by this time, and thus the Bible tells us that they were mightily oppressed for twenty years before they cried out unto the Lord (Judges 4:3).

Barak took the men and met Sisera at the river. He was reluctant, as he feared Sisera, not seeing the big picture as did Deborah. The Bible tells us, "And the Lord discomfited Sisera, and all his chariots, and all his host, with the edge of the sword before Barak; so that Sisera lighted down off his chariot, and fled away on his feet" (Judges 4:15).

The Lord caused a heavy rainstorm to trap the Canaanite army in the mud, rendering the chariots useless and a liability, as Judges 5 sings of the narrative. They were then easily taken out by the men of Israel.

Well, our story continues as General Sisera fled away to the tent of Jael, the wife of Heber the Kenite. Heber, whose name means *crossover*, was a Gentile from the people of Moses's father-in-law, the Midianites. He supported Jabin, and thus Sisera believed he would find refuge in the tent of a woman. Apparently he did not take the meaning of Heber's name literally!

Jael called Sisera into her tent and covered him in what he perceived was to hide him from the men of Israel. He knew that Barak would never look in a woman's tent for a man, and thus he felt safe. He then politely asked Jael for a little drink of water, but she gave him milk. Next, he demanded for her to stand in the door of the tent and to say to any men who would enquire about him that he was not there.

In this safe place, he slept, but Jael went to work.

> Then Jael Heber's wife took a nail of the tent, and took a hammer in her hand, and went softly unto him, and smote the nail into his temples, and fastened it into the ground: For he was fast asleep and weary. So he died.
>
> Judges 4:21

Jael killed Sisera with a tent stake and a hammer. This is the biblical type I would like for us to see.

Sisera represents the old man, the person before one comes to Christ, the powerful general who commands an awesome army against the "new man" we desire to become after believing in the Lord. We see that he can be polite as he asks Jael for a drink but also demanding, as noted, when he commanded her to guard the door to the tent.

But look how Jael destroys him. It's a perfect picture of how we can take out our "old man." When he wanted water, she gave him milk. As 2 Peter teaches, "As newborn babes, desire the sincere milk of the word, that ye may grow thereby" (2 Peter 2:2).

She then took a nail, a huge tent stake! Of course, this brings to mind the cross of Christ. The place where the stakes fastened his hands and feet and a sword pierced his side. Jael went to the cross to kill the old man. She also took a hammer. Jeremiah states, "Is not my word like a fire? Saith the Lord, and like a *hammer* that breaketh the rock in pieces" (Jeremiah 23:29).

She took the hammer of the Word of God and a nail, representing the cross of Christ, and killed the old man.

That's how we can defeat our enemy within also. Remember the cross. Give the communion table worth. Recall daily what Jesus did for you. And take the Word of God, which is called the Sword of the Spirit (Ephesians 6:17), and immerse your brain with it; drive it through your temples. Give the old man the milk of the Word instead of water when he asks for a drink, and when he demands you to obey him, take a stake and a hammer and kill him.

So the next time that bully yells at you to obey him, remind him he has been paralyzed. He has no control over you any longer. Remember the truth that his power over you is broken, reckon that truth to be true, and yield yourself to God. Then you will walk in the newness of life!

Traditions of Spring

I remember as a child that one of my favorite yearly traditions was hunting for Easter eggs, those little presents that the famous bunny had hidden. Little did I know then, despite being steeped in the Babylonian mystery religion, that this tradition to the believer in Jesus Christ points to his death, burial, and resurrection.

In like amusement, each year at the Passover meal called the Sadir, Hebrew children similarly partake in a little game where a piece of bread is hidden by the parents to be hunted and found by the children. This tradition also portrays in a biblical and clear way the death, burial, and resurrection of Jesus. In this case, it is to his earthly relatives, the Jews. Amazingly, they do not see it!

First, let's examine Easter.

Before God revealed himself to Abraham, Isaac, and Jacob and then more fully to their descendants through Moses and the Law, mankind sought incorrectly after God. We inherently wanted the relationship we lost with God after Adam's fall. The heart of this "religious" effort to reach God on man's terms was centered in Babylon, or present-day Iraq. Man's first organized attempt to "find God" was called the Tower of Babel. The Bible tells us that God was not pleased with this religion, and the language of man was scrambled at that point.

The Babylonian religion persisted, though, after the tower debacle. This religion, which was inspired by Satan, had many similarities to the gospel. This should not be surprising, as Satan is the father of lies. One of the best ways to tell a good lie is to tell a half-truth! And we know that one of Satan's strategies is to counterfeit God's plan. As the angel of light, with an IQ off the charts, Lucifer could deduce some of God's plan through prophecies he had available to him as given to Adam, Eve, and the early fathers. Thus, Satan started a religious system, which in varying forms still persists today. It's a group of traditions that counterfeit the gospel message of a child born to a woman who would die and later come back to life.

One of these early counterfeits was called the Feast of Ishtar. We, of course, get the word *Easter* from this pagan celebration. A baby named Tamuz was birthed miraculously from a mother named Semeramas. Tamuz later died yet came back to life according to the story. His story was centered on the feast of Ishtar. Ishtar was the Babylonian goddess of fertility. As you can probably imagine, other objects of fertility were included in the celebration, including eggs, rabbits, and new clothes.

The religion persisted as other cultures came on the scene. The names of the principles were changed, and you may recognize some of them. The Canaanites changed Semeramas to Ashteroth, followed by the Greeks calling her Diana and by the Romans naming her Venus. The baby's name was changed to Baal by the Canaanites and later to Cupid by the Greeks and Aphrodite by the Romans. Needless to say, these legends have a similar ring to them when compared to the gospel account!

Thus, when the Roman Empire under Constantine's dictate made Christianity the state religion, the followers of the Babylonian religion had a problem on their hands. Did they have to discard their hallowed traditions to accommodate the Christian teaching of the death, burial, and resurrection of the Savior, Jesus Christ? The answer, of course, is no. It was a simple thing to assimilate their religious practices into Christianity since the similarities were already in place. The Feast of Ishtar, which was already in the spring, was changed to Easter and celebrated on the Sunday of Jesus' resurrection. The hiding of eggs by a rabbit was also easily transferred due to their associations with new life.

So you may ask, since this holiday is a counterfeit, should we discard these traditions that children enjoy throughout the world every year? I really don't think that's the best response. The Bible states that we are in the world but not of the world (John 17:11, 15). I don't believe we should stick our collective heads in the sand and pretend that the Easter traditions from Babylon don't exist. Instead, I suggest we redeem the traditions. Realize that the eggs of Easter represent Jesus in his earthly body, a body that was as fragile as ours, yet without sin. He lived among us and was broken like an egg for our sins. Then, as we paint the Easter eggs, we can picture our Lord's body turning black, blue, and red in dying for our sins. We can talk about this to our kids. Of course, the burial of Christ is presented well as the Easter bunny hides the eggs at night to be found in the morning. Lastly, the resurrection clearly is depicted as the children happily find the treasure they are seeking.

Now the Passover meal, since God gave it to man, is a pure figure of God's plan of death, burial, and resurrection. It is the uncorrupted version of the Easter tradition.

During the Passover meal, the Jews would eat only unleavened bread. No leaven was to be found in the house during this week of remembrance. The reason is that leaven represents sin in God's economy, and the sacrifice of Passover was to be perfect, unblemished, without sin in a spiritual context.

Also, this bread was stripped. It had holes in it. To this day, the Jewish matzoh is noted for its striping. During the meal, the head of the family would take three loaves of the unleavened bread and would break the middle loaf in front of all present. He would then hide it. On the following Sunday, which was called the Feast of First Fruits, the children would look for and find the hidden loaf of unleavened bread.

Of course, Jesus told us he is the Bread of Life. Just as the Father gave the children of Israel bread, called manna, in the wilderness, the Father also gave his Son as the true bread from heaven. Jesus was born in Bethlehem, which in Hebrew means the house of bread. He made it clear to the multitude in John 6, and later to the disciples at the last supper, that true believers were to eat his body and drink his blood in remembrance of the true meaning of Passover, that of our sins being passed over!

The bread, as mentioned, was striped. As we know, Jesus was beaten and bloodied and broken for our sins. As Peter puts it, "By whose stripes ye were healed" (1 Peter 2:24b).

The holes in their bread tell of our Lord's torture for you and me.

In the Passover meal, three loaves of bread were used, and the middle loaf was broken. This pictures the triune God, the threefold character of God, with the middle person, the Son, being broken. That piece was hidden away or buried and then found or resurrected on the Feast of First Fruits. So too our Lord was buried on Passover and resurrected the following Sunday, the Feast of First Fruits!

Most Jews today have heard the gospel message that Christians believe that Jesus died for man's sins, was buried, and rose from the grave three days later. And, of course, they continue to observe the Passover and partake in the Sadir. Certainly, one may say they are blind to this connection in their practice, that they just don't get it! But it's probably more than that. Unfortunately, many have hardened their hearts. They've heard the gospel but refuse to believe.

Oh, Lord we look forward to the day when, as Paul teaches,

And so all Israel shall be saved. For I would not, brethren that ye should be ignorant of this mystery, lest ye should be wise in your own conceits; that blindness in part is happened to Israel, until the fullness of the Gentiles be come in. And so all Israel shall be saved: As it is written, There shall come out of Sion the Deliverer, and shall turn away ungodliness from Jacob:

Romans 11:25–26

Application: The Death, Burial, and Resurrection of Self

We've come to the point of book two where the "rubber meets the road." The point when we say, "Okay, now what do I do?" We've seen the pattern over and over of how in dying comes new life by the power of God. This *is* the secret. When we as believers see this, we become more than conquerors in this life. And we gain life eternal in the next!

> Verily, verily, I say unto you, Except a corn of wheat fall into the ground and die, it abideth alone: But if it die, it bringeth forth much fruit. He that loveth his life shall lose it; and he that hateth his life in this world shall keep it unto life eternal.
>
> John 12:24–25

The secret of a grand life is to *die to self.* It's paradoxical! As we die to self, to our agendas, to our worldly desires, we actually find life. We find fulfillment. As we bury the hatchet against that boss or ex-spouse who wronged us, as we forgive that parent who wasn't always there, as we let it go, we experience a resurrection of soul, which is the freedom Jesus wants you to experience.

Jesus put it this way:

> Therefore if thou bring thy gift to the altar, and there rememberest that thy brother hath ought *(a charge or indictment)* against thee: Leave there thy gift before the altar, and go thy way; first be reconciled to thy brother, and then come and offer thy gift.
>
> Matthew 5:23–24

The Lord is saying before you can truly worship him, you must clear up issues you are holding on to. The truth is those issues are holding on to you! They are holding you down. He used a play on words to make the point. He said before you go to the altar, you must be altered!

In the Bible, to initiate true reconciliation, there will always be a death. Look with me in the book of Genesis.

> Then Abraham gave up the ghost, and died in a good old age, an old man, and full of years; and was gathered to his people. And his sons Isaac and Ishmael buried him in the cave of Machpelah.
>
> Genesis 25:8–9

You will remember that the sons of Abraham were separated physically years earlier when God told Abraham to cast out the bondwoman and her son—Ishmael as a figurative picture of the flesh sent away. We never again see Isaac and Ishmael together in the narrative until this point, the point of their father's death. This literal example of reconciliation through death is what Jesus meant figuratively in teaching that to find life, a man must be willing to lose his life. To get to the altar of God, a person must reconcile his issues with others. He must be altered. He must die to self!

Of course, Jesus models our reconciliation to God through his death.

> For if, when we were enemies, we were reconciled to God by the death of his Son, much more, being reconciled, we shall be saved by his life.
>
> Romans 5:10

The tiny book of Philemon illustrates this principle in a very practical way. In this book, Paul is writing to a younger man in the faith whom he had brought to the Lord and had mentored. It seemed that a slave of Philemon called Onesimus (a name that means profitable) stole some money from Philemon and ran away to Rome where that same slave crossed paths with the Apostle Paul. Onesimus's encounter with Paul apparently led him to a saving knowledge of Jesus Christ, and the slave subsequently became a profitable co-worker with Paul. Now in those days, a slave had no rights, and this act of thievery and running away essentially put a death sentence upon Onesimus's head should Philemon ever catch up to him.

With that setting, let me paint the picture. Paul, who is a type of Jesus in this analogy, understood that reconciliation needed to occur in order for Philemon and Onesimus to function effectively in ministry. Onesimus owed a debt to Philemon, and Philemon needed to forgive Onesimus. So Paul told Onesimus that he needed to return to Philemon. He needed to right a wrong. So he sent Onesimus back to Philemon with a letter instructing Philemon to forgive his former slave. Not only that, but Paul went on to suggest that Philemon accept Onesimus no longer as a slave but as a brother.

The beauty of this letter is that it typifies what our Lord has done for us. Paul writes to Philemon, "If thou count me therefore as a partner, receive him as myself. If he hath wronged thee, or oweth thee ought, put that on mine account" (Philemon 17–18).

That's what Jesus did for you, what he did for me! He took our sins, he took the wrong things we have done in the sight of the Father, and he put them on *his account!*

Thus, Jesus models how I am to live. I must die to my fleshly tendencies of selfishness, greed, and unforgiveness. Bury them in a place where I won't dig them back up. Then I will live life in the resurrected manner he intended. You will too!

BOOK THREE

Sorrow to Joy

The Labor

> These things have I spoken unto you, that ye should not be offended. They shall put you out of the synagogues: Yea, the time cometh, that whosoever killeth you will think that he doeth God service. And these things will they do unto you, because they have not known the Father, nor me. But these things have I told you, that when the time shall come, ye may remember that I told you of them. And these things I said not unto you at the beginning, because I was with you. But now I go my way to him that sent me; and none of you asketh me, Whither goest thou? But because I have said these things unto you, sorrow hath filled your heart.
>
> John 16:1–6

Shortly before his passion, Jesus told his disciples, as noted in John 16, to expect dangerous times in this world. Thankfully, he ended his discourse with words of comfort.

> These things I have spoken unto you, that in me ye might have peace. In the world ye shall have tribulation: But be of good cheer; I have overcome the world.
>
> John 16:33

Jesus knew that some would be offended by the gospel, and consequently his disciples would suffer persecution (1 Timothy 3:12). He told his followers not to be surprised if religious people kicked them out of the synagogues (*churches*) and then blindly believed they had done God a service. As if it were possible to help God out! He explained that religious people would fight against the gospel because they didn't really know the Father or him.

Our Lord then revealed that he must leave so that the Comforter would come, which is the Spirit of Truth (John

16:7). Now picture this! Jesus had been with these men for nearly three years. They had left everything of earthly substance to follow him. They were excited about this Passover time, as just a few days earlier they saw their Master enter Jerusalem triumphantly in what was clearly a messianic prophecy fulfilled. They were expectant that this was the time that Jesus was going to usher in the reign of the king. And as his disciples, they surely believed that they to were going to be in positions of authority and power. So when Jesus stated that his time had come to leave, there must have been a collective jaw drop heard all the way down to Jericho! How could this be Jesus? David's son is to reign on his throne, and you are he, are you not Jesus?

It is with this backdrop that Jesus uttered the beautiful analogy that I would like to consider here.

> Verily, verily, I say unto you, That ye shall weep and lament, but the world shall rejoice: And ye shall be sorrowful, but your sorrow shall be turned to joy. A woman when she is in travail hath sorrow, because her hour is come: But as soon as she is delivered of the child, she remembereth no more the anguish, for joy that a man is born into the world. And ye now therefore have sorrow: But I will see you again, and your heart shall rejoice, and your joy no man taketh from you.
>
> John 16: 20–22

Wow! Yet I know this picture is indeed true, as I have witnessed it thousands of times. When a woman delivers her baby, all of the hours of agony and pain are eclipsed by the joy in the arrival of the baby. This is what our Lord was telling those men getting ready to start their own "labor and delivery." I doubt if any of those men sitting in that upper room had even seen a laboring woman. Nonetheless, they were about to experience labor firsthand.

Consider a short time later when Jesus told Peter and the others that they were all going to be scattered that night. Confidently, Peter believed that even if all would leave the Master, he would not. The prophet, of course, retorted that before the cock crew, he, Peter, would deny him three times! Ouch! The pangs began!

As they left the meal, they headed across the brook Kidron to the garden of Gethsemane. First, Jesus asked them to stay up and pray with him. He even singled out Peter, James, and John to come into his inner circle and support him. Unfortunately, they were too tired, as it was late and the hour of darkness was upon them.

And that's the way it is so often in our own hour of darkness. We can be spiritually sleepy, wanting to catch a few Zs instead of praying. As we know, Jesus reprimanded them three times for their complete failure at persevering in prayer with him (three being the number of completeness in the Bible). Three more pangs! To their amazement, one of their own, Judas of Iscariot, accompanied by a band of men arrived with "lanterns, torches, and weapons" (John 18:3b). They thought Judas went off earlier to make arrangements for the upcoming feast, as he had charge of the money. How could this be that the one that sat in the honored position next to Jesus at the dinner earlier that night would be leading a group to take away the Rabbi with such a show of force? My, that pang must have hurt!

This enraged Peter greatly, and, to his credit, he did what he had earlier told Jesus he would. That was to fight for him. You have to admire Peter for this even though it was completely misguided. Peter drew the sword, probably a fishing knife, and cut off the ear of Malchus, the servant of the high priest.

Jesus, always in control of the situation, stopped the uprising before it got out of hand. He knew that if it continued, not only would Peter and the others lose, but they would also likely die for the cause. This is not what Jesus had in mind when he said he was leaving. He firmly told Peter to put up his sword into the sheath and said, "The cup which my Father has given me, shall I not drink it" (John 18:11b).

Jesus touched Malchus's ear and restored it whole, just as the Spirit will do when you or I flail away with the sword. Then they led the Savior away while Peter and his brothers were feeling another birth pang.

Next, the Gospel of John tells us that Jesus was whisked away to an encounter with Annas, the father-in-law to the high priest, Caiaphas. After the disciples initially fled away from the scene of the Gethsemane arrest, Peter and "another disciple known to the high priest" followed. The other disciple went in, but Peter stood at the door without. It was then that the damsel that kept the door said unto Peter, "Art not thou also one of this man's disciples?" In a classic biblical understatement, Peter said, "I am not" (John 18:17). The pains were getting closer!

A bit later on that dark night, Annas sent our Lord bound to the house of Caiaphas the high priest. Again, Simon Peter followed as Matthew narrates, "Peter followed him afar off unto the high priest's palace, and went in, and sat with the servants to see the end" (Matthew 26:58).

Luke adds, "They had kindled a fire in the midst of the hall, and were set down together, Peter sat down among them" (Luke 22:55).

It was there that a certain maid beheld him as he sat warming himself by the fire. She excitedly spoke out so that the many around the fire could hear, "This man was also with him."

Peter's second denial (another birth pang) was directed to the woman but in range undoubtedly to all around. "Woman, I know him not" (Luke 22:56b–57).

Look at the succession here. Peter went from, "I am not" to "I *know* him not." Fear is beginning to grip the usually strong and brave man!

Lastly, Mark reveals, "A little after, they that stood by said again to Peter, surely thou art one of them: For thou art a Galilaean, and thy speech agreeth thereto. But Peter began to curse and to swear, saying, I know not this man of whom ye speak" (Mark 14:70–71).

Too bad they didn't have anesthesia for labor in those days, as Peter surely was in need of something now as the pains were getting very close and intense! Also, it's interesting that the Bible says his speech gave him away. Lord, I pray that *my* speech would also give me away. That my speech will indict me as your follower!

The Scriptures teach us that grace and forgiveness abound with the Lord. Earlier that night, Jesus had told Peter that Satan had desired to sift him like wheat but that he had prayed for him and after he was recovered, he was to strengthen the brothers.

When we spiritualize what happened to Peter, we can glean some truths for our own lives so as to not deny our Lord. Peter's downfall started at the supper when he boldly and confidently stated that he would never fall away after Jesus revealed the course of the night's events to the group. This speaks into the face of the proverb, "Pride goeth before destruction, and an haughty spirit before a fall" (Proverbs 16:18).

Next, we find Peter sleeping in the garden when he should have been praying. The devil would like nothing better than to have Christians sleep spiritually instead of praying. He knows prayer will bind him greatly (Matthew 18: 18–20).

Thirdly, as we have mentioned earlier, Peter was using a fleshly weapon to battle instead of a spiritual one. His fleshly sword injured while the sword of the Spirit, the Word of God, is effective against our real enemy. "And take … the sword of the Spirit, which is the word of God" (Ephesians 6:17).

Fourthly, Peter was following from afar. Whenever we fall to the back of the pack, we risk being picked off by the enemy. Lastly, we are told in multiple accounts that Peter *warmed* himself at the fire of the enemy. Folks, whenever we get comfortable in the system of the world's warmth and fire, we risk getting burnt! It is the wise man, woman, teenager, or child who can recognize that the warmth of the world's flame is not a safe place to stay.

So to summarize Peter's situation, he was fighting the wrong battle (fleshly instead or spiritual) with the wrong weapon (sword instead of Word) for the wrong reason (Jesus didn't need his help) with the wrong motive (he had just been sleeping instead of praying). Lord, help us to learn from Peter's failure lest we fall into the same pit!

As they were leading Jesus from Caiaphas's court, Jesus was apparently in view of Peter when the fisherman choked out his last denial as Luke records,

> And immediately the Lord turned and looked upon Peter. And Peter remembered the word of the Lord, how he had said unto him, Before the cock crow, thou shalt deny me thrice. And Peter went out and wept bitterly.
>
> Luke 22:61–62

Yet another labor pain!

From here on out, the agony of labor must have been unbearable. The disciples witnessed Jesus being escorted to Pilate then over to Herod and then back to Pilate. During the second visit to Pilate, they witnessed the people under the priests urging call for the release of Barabbas (which means son of the father) instead of the true Son of the Father. They also saw the result of the brutal scourging that Jesus underwent. They were on the street when Jesus carried his cross, and they heard him tell the daughters of Jerusalem to, "Weep not for me, but weep for yourselves, and for your children. For if they do these things in a green tree, what shall be done in the dry?" (Luke 23:28b).

How bad they must have felt when they witnessed Simon of Cyrene carry the cross for the dying Jesus because none of their number was near enough to offer this aide.

They saw their Lord stripped naked and then nailed to the tree while the soldiers were mocking him with vinegar and the priests were taunting him to come down if he were the Son of God, saying, "He saved others; himself he cannot save." They didn't realize that if he saved himself, then no one else would be saved.

They looked upon the superscription written over their Master, "In letters of Greek, and Latin, and Hebrew, *This Is The King Of The Jews*" (Luke 23:38).

They witnessed the incredible forgiveness their bruised Lord displayed in praying to the Father, "Forgive them; for they know not what they do" (Luke 23:34).

They felt the palpable darkness that enveloped the entire world from the sixth hour to the ninth hour.

They heard Jesus cry out in a loud voice, "*Eli, Eli, lama sabachthani*" (Matthew 27:46), as well as fulfill Scripture in saying, "I thirst" (John 19:28b).

They wondered at those wonderful words, "It is finished" (John 19:30), followed immediately by, "Father, into thy hands I commend my spirit" (Luke 23:46).

Incredibly, their leader was dead! Simultaneously, they felt the earth quake under the weight of that dark day's events. They saw his limp and bloodied body taken off the cross and laid in the tomb.

Oh, the tragedy of all these things! For the next three days, they hid for fear of the Jews, lest they suffer the same fate as the one they believed to be the Messiah.

Then to complete the picture perfectly, the baby was born, the morning came, Jesus their friend, rose from the grave! Their hearts rejoiced as John 16:22 prophesied they would. Let's look at the birth of their joy.

The Delivery

Matthew describes that as it began to dawn toward the first day of the week that a great earthquake occurred.

> For the angel of the Lord descended from heaven and came and rolled back the stone from the door, and sat upon it. His countenance was like lightning and his raiment white as snow.
>
> Matthew 28:2–3

The angel told the two Marys that Jesus had risen, and they departed with a mixture of fear and joy. The women then told Peter and John, who excitedly ran to the sepulcher where Peter saw "the linen clothes lie. And the napkin, that was about his head, not lying with the linen clothes, but wrapped together in a place by itself" (John 20:6b–7).

I wonder if Peter understood that Jesus, as a carpenter, had signed the resurrection with the carpenter's cloth signifying his finished work. You see, in the east, to this day, I am told that a master carpenter will note the completion of his work by placing a little cloth he had used for the job on top of the finished work. This, the Great Carpenter did also!

John then went into the sepulcher and witnessed the empty tomb. The Bible says he saw and *believed.*

This reminds me of that wonderful promise in Romans.

> That if thou shalt confess with thy mouth the Lord Jesus, and shalt believe in thine heart that God hath raised him from the dead, thou shalt be saved.
>
> Romans 10:9

Incredible joy probably doesn't reveal how John felt at that moment. Jesus' many references to his passion and mission were now starting to make sense. What wonder and amazement he must have felt!

After Peter and John left the empty tomb, Mary, not yet understanding what had happened, was weeping when Jesus himself came up to her and asked, "Woman, why weepest thou?" (John 20:15).

Jesus then revealed himself to her in what undoubtedly

was the happiest moment of her life! Her sorrow indeed was turned to joy!

Next, Luke tells us that Jesus intercepted two believers on the road to Emmaus, which was seven miles from Jerusalem. Jesus' reprimand to them applies to all when he said,

> O fools, and slow of heart to believe all that the proph-
> ets have spoken: Ought not Christ to have suffered these
> things, and to enter into his glory? And beginning at Moses
> and all the prophets, he expounded unto them in all the
> scriptures the things concerning himself.
>
> Luke 24:25–27

Wow! What a Bible study that must have been!

Luke goes on to tell us that they didn't recognize Jesus until they broke bread with him. Isaiah states, "He has no form or comeliness ... no beauty that we should desire him" (Isaiah 53:2).

Apparently, in his resurrected body, Jesus looked different.

Also, it's interesting that, like in our time now after the cross, that the believers did not recognize Jesus as Lord until they broke bread with him. The application of giving worth to communion is obvious!

The Bible says, "Their eyes were opened, and they *knew* him" (Luke 24:31a).

Lord, I want to know you like this!

> And they said one to another, did not our hearts burn within
> us by the way, and while he opened to us the scriptures?
>
> Luke 24:32

Later that evening, John placed the disciples, less Thomas, together behind closed doors. Jesus entered through solid matter "and stood in the midst and saith unto them, Peace be unto you" (John 20:19).

He showed them his hands and his side, and in the Greek it says the disciples were hilariously glad (John 20: 20). Next he "breathed on them and saith unto them, receive ye the Holy Ghost" (John 20:22).

When this scene was repeated eight days later for Thomas, his doubting was replaced by saving faith when he uttered those most famous words of his, "My Lord and my God" (John 20:28b).

Jesus then spoke that awesomely wonderful statement for you and me when he said, "Thomas, because thou hast seen me, thou hast believed: Blessed are they that have not seen, and yet have believed" (John 20:29b).

Praise God for that remark as it warms my heart. We are those who have not seen yet believe!

God Is Faithful

God specializes in turning sorrow into joy. Not only did he do it for the disciples, but the Bible is full of similar examples of this principle. Jacob, when he learned that his son Joseph was apparently dead, he rent his clothes, put sackcloth on, and mourned many days (Genesis 37:34). The Bible says he refused to be comforted but said he would go down to the grave in mourning. Seventeen years later, in chapter 42, when Jacob feared he would now lose his beloved son Benjamin, in addition to Joseph, he said, "all these things are against me" (Genesis 42:36b).

Obviously to us armchair quarterbacks nearly four thousand years later, Jacob didn't get the big picture. He did not know this most famous verse from the book of Romans, "And we know that all things work together for good to them that love God, to them who are the called according to his purpose" (Romans 8:28).

The baby was finally born for Jacob after his seventeen-year labor. Chapter 45 reveals that when Jacob's sons came back from Egypt, they said, "Joseph is yet alive, and he is governor over all the land of Egypt" (Genesis 45:26).

The account states that Jacob's spirit was revived. What joy he must have felt!

I'll give you one more example of this pattern of God turning sorrow to joy, of turning labor to delivery. There are numerous ones to pick from. We could look at the accounts of Ruth or Esther. Or we could study the praying saints at John Mark's mother's house when Peter was rescued out of Herod's jail by the angel of the Lord, but let's look at Hannah. Her story is found in the first book of Samuel, chapters 1 and 2.

Hannah, whose name means favored, was married to a man of Ephraim named Elkanah. The Bible reports that Elkanah had two wives, Hannah and Peninnah. (Peninnah's name means rich hair.) Peninnah indeed did have it all, or so it would seem, as verse 2 states, "Peninnah had children, but Hannah had no children" (1 Samuel 1:2).

Every person of Israel knew that in the Law, barrenness was considered a curse from God. Thus, Hannah lived with a weight upon her heart. To make things worse, we read in verse 6, "Her adversary also provoked her sore, for to make her fret, because the Lord had shut up her womb" (1 Samuel 1:6).

Don't miss the analogy here of *our adversary* provoking us when we don't quite understand God's plan!

Every year, the three would travel to Shiloh "to worship and to sacrifice unto the Lord" (1 Samuel 1:3).

Even though Hannah received the greater portion from Elkanah to offer to the Lord in that year, for verse 5 says that he loved her, the Bible says she wept and would not eat.

In speaking of her sorrow, in speaking of her labor we learn,

She was in bitterness of soul, and prayed unto the Lord, and wept sore. And she vowed a vow, and said, O Lord of hosts, if thou wilt indeed look on the affliction of thine handmaid, and remember me, and not forget thine handmaid, but wilt give unto thine handmaid a man child, then I will give him unto the Lord all the days of his life.

1 Samuel 1:10–11

Indeed this prayer summarized the sorrow she had been experiencing these many years. As she labored in prayer, the Bible tells us that Eli the high priest marked her mouth and thought she was drunk, not understanding her grief. When Hannah answered with her story, Eli (who illustrates our Great High Priest, Jesus Christ, in this section) "answered and said, Go in peace: and the God of Israel grant thee thy petition that thou hast asked of him" (1 Samuel 1:17).

Hannah's sorrow now turned to joy. The labor was over, and the baby was delivered. The book of Samuel tells us she went her way, did eat, and her countenance was no longer sad. Later that year, she conceived and bore her first son, Samuel (in God's grace she had a total of five children), and she indeed kept her promise and "lent him to the Lord" (1 Samuel 1:28).

Now let's apply what we've seen.

Every day across the world, women have their sorrow turned to joy as they labor and then deliver their babies. Let this profound illustration remind us that when it looks terrible—for the pain of labor must be terrible—that's when the Lord will resurrect you. That's when you will deliver the baby! In over twenty-five years of delivering babies, I've never had a patient not deliver the baby, even when she must have thought it would never arrive!

So too, dear reader, take heart. God is not finished with you. The old saying, "It ain't over till it's over," is indeed true in this regard. For God demonstrates his love to us in that we all deserve labor, "for all have sinned, and come short of the glory of God" (Romans 3:23), yet we get the delivery. We get the joy! Yes, it might not even be in this life, but know this, dear saint: those of you who are indeed his will come into a joy unspeakable on that day when you hear him say, "Well done, thou good and faithful servant: enter thou into the joy of thy Lord (Matthew 25:21).

BOOK FOUR

*The Prices of Idolatry: The
Babylonian Conquest of the Judeans*

Judah's Adulterous Affair

For I have heard a voice as of a woman in travail, and the anguish as of her that bringeth forth her first child, the voice of the daughter of Zion, that bewaileth herself, that spreadeth her hands saying, Woe is me now! For my soul is wearied because of murders.

Jeremiah 4:31

Indeed, the anguish a woman experiences during labor and delivery is magnified in the birth of her *first* child, for the birth canal has not yet been passed. When a woman is asked years later, it is her first birth that is often the one that stands out. Often, I will ask my second-time mothers if they know the old doctor's joke about a second birth. We say the second birth makes the doctor look good! Thus, when Jeremiah tells about Judah's upcoming labor pains, he rightly compares it to the first labor a woman experiences.

We have heard the fame thereof: Our hands waxed feeble: Anguish has taken hold on us, and pain, as a woman in travail.

Jeremiah 6:24

What wilt thou say when he shall punish thee? For thou hast taught them to be captains, and as chief over thee: Shall not sorrows take thee, as a woman in travail?

Jeremiah 13:21

How gracious shalt thou be when pangs come upon thee, the pain as a woman in travail!

Jeremiah 22:23b

And I will punish Bel in Babylon, and I will bring forth out of his mouth that which he has swallowed up: And the nations shall not flow any more unto him: Yea, the wall of Babylon shall fall. My people, go ye out of the midst of her, and deliver ye every man his soul from the fierce anger of the Lord.

Jeremiah 51:44–45

When Jeremiah tells of Judah's deliverance from Babylon, he also reveals that Babylon will have a birth process of her own when he speaks of Babylon bringing forth (birthing) that which he (she) has swallowed up.

Now why dost thou cry out aloud? Is there no king in thee? Is thy counselor perished? For pangs have taken thee as a woman in travail. Be in pain, and labor to bring forth, O daughter of Zion, like a woman in travail: For now shalt thou go forth out of the city, and thou shalt dwell in the field, and thou shalt go even to Babylon; there shalt thou be delivered; there the Lord shall redeem thee from the hand of thine enemies.

Micah 4:9–10

"Is there no king in thee?" We know that Jesus is her king and ours!

"Is thy counselor perished?" We know that our wonderful counselor *did* perish, and now he ever lives to make intersession for the saints!

These passages in Jeremiah and Micah tell of the eminent judgment of which Judah and Jerusalem could expect. Scholars believe that these two prophets were speaking to their contemporaries, much like we might hear Billy Graham or other spiritual leaders give a warning to our nation due to our own despicable behavior. Both Jeremiah and Micah tell the nation that the eastern power of Babylon was soon going to come and the result was going to be metaphorically like a horrific labor. And as we have seen, with labor comes delivery. Micah gives that hope in the passage quoted.

God in his graciousness had given Judah and Jerusalem

notice after notice of their upcoming judgment. He spoke audibly to the children of Israel the Ten Commandments, of which the first one is, "Thou shalt have no other gods before me" (Exodus 20:3).

Solomon, even with all of his wisdom, fell away from this command and division of the nation was the result.

The second, "Thou shalt not make unto thee any graven image" (Exodus 20:4a), was discarded also as Ahaz, the twelfth king of Judah and the eighth king after David, led Judah away.

> Ahaz was twenty years old when he began to reign, and he reigned sixteen years in Jerusalem: But he did not right in the sight of the Lord, like David his father: For he walked in the ways of the kings of Israel, and made also molten images for Baalim.
>
> 2 Chronicles 28:1–2

Now, the reader will recall that the northern kingdom of Israel fell away from Jehovah many years prior to Judah's downfall. They began to break the first two commandments of worshiping false gods and of worshiping God falsely, approximately two hundred years before Ahaz led Judah astray. It was Israel's first king, named Jeroboam, who introduced idolatry to Israel as a way of keeping his subjects from traveling to Judah and Jerusalem for the annual feasts.

Because of their earlier downfall, God gave Israel over to the Assyrians during the reign of Judah's King Hezekiah in 722 BC. Judah had greater than one hundred years to witness and consider the example of how God will deliver his people. They saw the judgment of the Assyrians against Hezekiah when the angel of the Lord smote 185,000 soldiers in one night (2 Kings 19:35). Conversely, they should have considered what comes as the result of God withdrawing his grace. Indeed, they were witnesses to the Assyrian conquest of their sister nation of Israel, which came about as the result of her idolatry (2 Kings 17:5–18).

Nevertheless, when Manasseh, who was the son of Hezekiah, ruled, Judah crossed the line of no return! In chapter 21 of 2 Kings, we are told that Manasseh "did evil in the sight of the Lord, after the abominations of the heathen, whom the Lord cast out before the children of Israel" (2 Kings 21:2).

We are informed that Manasseh built altars for Baal like Ahab, the king of Israel, had previously done.

Now, you may remember Ahab most notably as being the husband of the infamous Jezebel. For Manasseh to be compared to Ahab was certainly not a good thing! We learn also that Manasseh worshiped devils, used enchantments, dealt with familiar spirits and wizards, and "he wrought much wickedness in the sight of the Lord, to provoke him to anger" (2 Kings 21:6b).

The Lord went on to say,

> Because Manasseh king of Judah hath done these abominations, and hath done wickedly above all that the Amorites did, which were before him, and hath made Judah also to sin with his idols: Therefore thus saith the Lord God of Israel, Behold, I am bringing such evil upon Jerusalem and Judah, that whosoever heareth of it, both his ears shall tingle. And I will stretch over Jerusalem the line of Samaria, and the plummet of the house of Ahab: And I will wipe Jerusalem as a man wipeth a dish, wiping it, and turning it upside down. And I will forsake the remnant of mine inheritance, and deliver them into the hand of their enemies; and they shall become a prey and a spoil to all their enemies.
>
> 2 Kings 21:11–14

Jeremiah confirms the role Manasseh played in the downfall of Judea. "And I will cause them to be removed into all the kingdoms of the earth, because of Manasseh the son of Hezekiah, king of Judah, for that which he did in Jerusalem" (Jeremiah 15:4).

One may ask why the entire nation fell because of the sins of one man. Well, the principle is clear whether it be a king, a president, or a father. If a leader gets sucked into sin, often those who are under him, the people or the family, will also be taken down and wiped out! This is a sobering word to fathers. We can take our entire family out when we sin willfully and persistently. We may count the cost of sin and feel a particular sin is worth taking the risk, for the Bible states that sin is pleasant for a season. But what is often not factored in is the injury to the family, the impact to those caught in the crossfire, the collateral damage!

A moment ago, I mentioned that due to Manasseh's idolatry, Judah crossed the line. Considering that our God is so gracious, how can this be?

Indeed, in the book of Exodus, God told Moses in chapter thirty-four that he is "merciful and gracious, longsuffering, and abundant in goodness and truth" (Exodus 34:6b).

Yes, this is true, yet we see in the New Testament that the one who practices sin habitually is on very thin ice. After listing idolatry and sixteen other works of the flesh in Galatians 5, Paul exclaims that they who practice such things shall not inherit the kingdom of God. Also, in Colossians 3, after noting a similar list of evil practices, Paul stated, "For which things sake the wrath of God cometh on the children of disobedience" (Colossians 3:6).

Yes, the Lord is gracious and longsuffering, but he is also just. Judah started her own "labor" due to Manasseh's disregard of God and his Word when he should have known better as godly Hezekiah's son.

Her Pregnancy

Sometimes before labor begins there is a time of increased energy and activity that a woman will experience. And so it was for Judah. Two years after Manasseh's evil fifty-five-year reign, his grandson, Josiah, became king at the tender age of eight. Apparently he did not have time to learn from his grandfather, as the Bible says Josiah did that which was right in the sight of the Lord. In fact, near the end of his account in 2 Kings 23, the Lord revealed,

> And like unto him was there no king before him, that turned to the Lord with all his heart, and with all his soul, and with all his might, according to all the law of Moses; (see Deuteronomy 6:4–5) neither after him arose there any like him.
>
> 2 Kings 23:35

So what is it about Josiah's story that won him this appraisal from God?

When Josiah was twenty-four years of age, he ordered a renovation of the house of the Lord. While Hilkiah, the high priest, was working, he found the book of the law. He found the Torah! Now, understand this is 622 BC, nearly eight hundred years after God, through Moses, had given it to the children of Israel. In that time, it had been lost and only the oral tradition through memorization of the Psalms and other Scripture was being carried forward from generation to generation. This was ample time for God's revelation given to Moses, David, and others to be diluted.

When the law was read to Josiah, the Bible tells us, "And it came to pass, when the king had heard the words of the book of the law, that he rent his clothes" (2 Kings 22:11).

Josiah was distressed, for he realized that his people had

not and were not following the Law. He saw in Deuteronomy 28 the curses that God had promised his people if they did not follow the Law. And he likely understood that these curses had *already* happened to the northern tribes of Israel. He feared that the same fate was in store for his nation.

Thus, he had Hilkiah inquire of the Lord through Huldah, the prophetess. This is the word she faithfully delivered:

> Thus saith the Lord God of Israel, Tell the man that sent you to me, Thus saith the Lord, Behold, I will bring evil upon this place, and upon all the inhabitants thereof, even all the words of the book, which the king of Judah hath read: Because they have forsaken me, and have burned incense unto other gods, that they might provoke me to anger with all the works of their hands; therefore my wrath shall be kindled against this place, and shall not be quenched. But to the king of Judah which sent you to enquire of the Lord, thus shall ye say to him, Thus saith the Lord God of Israel, As touching the words which thou hast heard; Because thine heart was tender, and thou hast humbled thyself before the Lord, when thou heardest what I spake against this place, and against the inhabitants thereof, that they should become a desolation and a curse, and hast rent thy clothes, and wept sore before me; I also have heard thee, saith the Lord. Behold therefore, I will gather thee unto thy fathers, and thou shalt be gathered into thy grave in peace; and thine eyes shall not see all the evil which I will bring upon this place.
>
> 2 Kings 22:15–20

After receiving this message from God, Josiah demonstrated his invigorated faith by cleaning out the hot spots of sin that were so grossly being flaunted in his nation. In chapter 23, we learn that all vessels of idolatry to Baal were burnt. All the priests of Baal, of the sun, the moon, the planets, and of the host of heaven were put down, and the groves were stamped into powder. In other words, Josiah was serious about his nation serving the one true God!

Here is another key for leaders, whether it be the leader of a family or of a nation. Humility and brokenness in the face of recognized sin saved the nation while Josiah was in command, and it will make a difference in our lives and nation also.

Her Labor

Now let's study the waves of labor pains that Judah experienced after Josiah, which are found in 2 Kings 23–25 and 2 Chronicles 36.

Josiah died in 609 BC in the historic town of Megiddo at the hands of Pharaoh Nechoh, the king of Egypt. The Bible tells that the people took Jehoahaz, the son of Josiah, and made him king at the age of twenty-three. We are told by the Lord that Jehoahaz "did that which was evil in the sight of the Lord, according to all that his fathers had done" (2 Kings 23:32).

After a short three-month reign, Pharaoh put Jehoahaz in bands and installed his older half-brother as his puppet king. Pharaoh taxed the land a hundred talents of silver and a talent of gold (a lot of money), and the new king, Jehoiakim, passed Pharaoh's demands along to the people in the form of a tax. The Bible states that Jehoiakim also did evil in the sight of the Lord.

The next pang quickly came upon Judah in 605 BC as the first wave of the Babylonians arrived. Nebuchadnezzar, the Babylonian king, made Jehoiakim his servant, but after three years, Jehoiakim unwisely rebelled against the Babylonian. The result was that Jehoiakim was put down after Jerusalem was besieged. The Bible tells that he was bound in fetters and carried away to Babylon.

Also, the temple was plundered, "and he carried away all Jerusalem, and all the princes, and all the mighty men of valor, even ten thousand captives, and all the craftsmen and smiths: None remained, save the poorest sort of the people of the land" (2 Kings 24:14). Ezekiel, Daniel, Shadrach, Meshach, and Abednego likely went to Babylon at this time.

Nebuchadnezzar then installed Zedekiah as king. We learn in 2 Chronicles "he did that which was evil in the sight of the Lord his God, and humbled not himself before Jeremiah the prophet speaking from the mouth of the Lord" (2 Chronicles 36:12).

Zedekiah rebelled against the prophet of God, which really was not a good idea. The result of that rebellion was predictable. We learn that the Chaldees "had no compassion upon young man or maiden, old man, or him that stooped for age" (2 Chronicles 36:17b).

They burnt the house of God and broke down the wall of Jerusalem. And those that were not killed were deported to Babylon. In 586 BC, this final defeat occurred. Zedekiah was the last of David's sons to reign in Judah. That is, of course, until Jesus Christ will reign in the future as promised in the books of Zechariah, Revelation, and elsewhere.

From Jeremiah, we learn in 25:11 that Judah would serve the king of Babylon for seventy years. This prophecy was fulfilled in the years 605 to 536 BC.

In that latter year, we are told that Cyrus, the king of Persia, proclaimed,

All the kingdoms of the earth hath the Lord God of heaven given me; and he hath charged me to build him an house in Jerusalem, which is in Judah. Who is there among you of all his people? The Lord his God be with him, and let him go up.

2 Chronicles 36:23

No doubt Daniel, who was a prince during Cyrus's reign and had intimate access to the king, witnessed to the king of the true God of Israel. He must have shown the king the scripture from Isaiah's prophecy, proclaimed 170 years earlier, which spoke of Cyrus by name!

> That saith of Cyrus, He is my Shepard, and shall perform all my pleasure: Even saying to Jerusalem, Thou shalt be built; and to the temple, Thy foundation shalt be laid.
>
> Isaiah 48:28

With that wonderful proclamation, Judah's labor had come to its end.

Her Delivery

To fit the type, the birth has come! Judah and Jerusalem had labored and now were delivered. The call to return to the promised land had been made, and the Jews rejoiced!

Ezra says it best:

> And when the builders laid the foundation of the temple of the Lord, they set the priests in their apparel with trumpets, and the Levites the sons of Asaph with cymbals, to praise the Lord, after the ordinance of David king of Israel. And they sang together by course in praising and giving thanks unto the Lord; because he is good, for his mercy endureth forever toward Israel. And all the people shouted with a great shout, when they praised the Lord, because the foundation of the house of the Lord was laid. But many ... ancient men, that had seen the first house, when the foundation of this house was laid before their eyes, wept with a loud voice; and many shouted aloud for joy: So that the people could not discern

the noise of the shout of joy from the noise of the weeping
of the people: For the people shouted with a loud shout.

Ezra 3:10–13

Truly, once again, and as a witness for all times, God had
shown his faithfulness to deliver his people. By crossing the
line, so to speak, Manasseh's idolatry put Judah on an irrevers-
ible course. But God all along had a better plan for his children. The student of the Bible and of history understands that
since their return from Babylon, the Jews, to this day, have not
fallen back into idolatry. They are unique from other cultures
and groups on the earth in that they elevate Jehovah as the one
true God. And one will not find any graven images of God in
their ranks. Yes, they have their issues; foremost was not rec-
ognizing the Messiah when he came as the suffering servant,
but they now understand the importance to God of his first
and second commandments. Throughout their history, they
have subsequently worshipped God, and God alone, and they
have not been sucked back into idolatry as is so common in
other cultures of our world.

This story, of course, has an application for us also. We too
should be reminded that like Judah, if we continue to ignore
his call to repentance when we sin, he will chastise us.

We read in Hebrews,

For whom the Lord loveth he chasteneth, and scourgeth
every son whom he receiveth ... Now no chastening for the
present seemeth to be joyous, but grievous: Nevertheless
afterward it yieldeth the peaceable fruit of righteousness
unto them which are exercised thereby.

Hebrews 12:6, 11

The Jews have appreciated their relationship with God to
a much greater degree after their time in Babylon. Likewise,
we too can grow close to our Father as a by-product of his
discipline toward us. As we are dependent and in touch with

the Vine, as John 15 teaches, we come to that place of bearing much fruit. That is what I crave!

Lastly, a beautiful picture is hidden in this story for us to pull out and apply. Moses declares in Psalm 90 that the days of man are three score and ten years. That is, the typical life span of a man or woman is seventy years. Then, after our time here on this planet, we will go home to be with the Lord.

So it is in this story. The children of Israel were away from their home for seventy years, the length of a man's life. Indeed, the captivity of Israel in Babylon is a picture of our life here on earth!

Jeremiah told the people in chapter 29 that they were to build houses, till the ground, take wives, beget sons and daughters, and seek the peace of the land that they were carried away to as captives. Then we see the wonderful promise of their return home.

> For thus saith the Lord, That after seventy years be accomplished at Babylon I will visit you, and perform my good word toward you, in causing you to return to this place. For I know the thoughts that I have toward you, saith the Lord, thoughts of peace, and not of evil, to give you an expected end.
>
> Jeremiah 29:10–11

This promise is for you and me also. After seventy years, figuratively, after a full lifetime literally, the Lord will visit us and take us to our true home with him in heaven. He indeed has peaceful thoughts for us, and our hope for our expected end is wonderful!

In the meantime, while we are here in this life, we are called to stay engaged. Paul exhorts Timothy to pray for all men, especially for those in authority, so that we as believers may lead quiet and peaceable lives in godliness and honesty (1 Timothy 2:1–2).

Realize that God is ultimately on the throne. He will raise up kings, and he will put them down. He's in control. When I realize this, I can take a whole lot more things a whole lot less seriously! As Jeremiah told Israel to make lives in Babylon, so too we need to make lives here. But understand this is not your home. Realize that some day soon the Lord will take you to a place that is infinitely more permanent. So don't take this life too seriously!

God's blessings as you consider these things.

BOOK FIVE
Paul's Travail

Paul's Calling

The Apostle Paul was given a unique calling, as he was a Jewish scholar and rabbi with an anointing from God to preach the gospel of Jesus Christ to the Gentiles! In fact, the Bible states that Paul was given charge of birthing the administration of grace.

> For though I preach the gospel, I have nothing to glory of: For necessity is laid upon me; yea, woe is unto me, if I preach not the gospel! For if I do this willingly, I have a reward: But if against my will, a dispensation of the gospel is committed unto me.
>
> 1 Corinthians 9:17

Also,

> For this cause I Paul, the prisoner of Jesus Christ for you Gentiles, if ye have heard of the dispensation of the grace of God which is given me to you-ward.
>
> Ephesians 3:1–2

Paul was truly one of a kind. He was trained at the feet of the great rabbi Gamaliel, he had command of the Hebrew and Greek languages, and he had zealously persecuted the believers in Jesus Christ. With the Roman roads in place throughout the known world, Paul was the perfect man at the perfect time for Jesus to use in spreading the gospel to the world. He was a brilliant, motivated scholar who understood our Lord's grace in his life!

But this calling was not without a price. Everywhere Paul traveled, trials and persecutions followed. It got so bad that Paul compared his course in ministry to the pain of a woman in labor, to the seemingly unending, grinding, relentless travail of a woman about to deliver a baby! But he also knew that the baby would be born; he knew that Christ *would* be formed in his spiritual children.

> My little children, of whom I travail in birth again until Christ be formed in you.
>
> Galatians 4:19

Paul suffered greatly in order to see his children grounded and established in the faith of Jesus Christ. He labored to see the good news of the grace of God revealed through our Lord.

But he kept his eyes on the goal. He looked toward the "delivery." He told the Colossian believers,

> If ye continue in the faith grounded and settled, and be not moved away from the hope of the gospel, which ye heard, and was preached to every creature which is under heaven; whereof I Paul am made a minister: Who now rejoice in my sufferings for you, and fill up that which is behind of the afflictions of Christ in my flesh for his body's sake, which is the church: Whereof I am made a minister, according to the dispensation of God which is given to me for you, to fulfill the word of God.
>
> Colossians 1:23–25

Paul understood that he was suffering for the sake of the body of Christ. He knew his sufferings were for the church, just as a mother willingly suffers the intense pain of labor in order to receive the baby!

Later, near the end of his life, Paul still understood what his travail was accomplishing. He wrote shortly before his execution to Timothy, his son in the faith:

> Whereunto I am appointed a preacher, and an apostle, and a teacher of the Gentiles. For the which cause I also suffer these things: Nevertheless I am not ashamed: For I know whom I have believed, and am persuaded that he is able to keep that which I have committed unto him against that day.
>
> 2 Timothy 1:11–12

Paul sensed that the fruit of his ministry would continue because he understood that "God is able." But I doubt if he understood just how important his contribution to our faith would be.

Herein lies a key to effective ministry. Do what God calls you to do, and don't worry about what the fruit appears to be. Many times the fruit of a person's labor isn't apparent until later; much like the fruit of a woman's labor, the baby, does not mature into a grown man or woman at the time of the delivery. It takes time!

On a similar note, as a woman expects to have pain during the labor and delivery process, we also should not be surprised by problems, difficulties, and pain during our "labor." Paul stated it well as he preached to Timothy and by extension to you and me: "Yea, and all that will live godly in Christ Jesus shall suffer persecution" (2 Timothy 3:12).

Paul didn't say you might have problems because of Christ. He said you *shall* have difficulties, issues, pain, and problems. In short, you will feel persecuted because you belong to Jesus Christ. Expect it so as to not be stunned when it happens.

In the delivery arena, I see this principle on a frequent basis. The woman who is prepared for the labor and delivery invariably does well and is often proud of her effort after the process is completed. But the woman who is unprepared, well, she is in for the shock of her life as waves of labor pangs make her lose focus and hope and reduce her to an out-of-control train wreck!

So again, don't be surprised when you have travail in this life!

Paul understood that although he was bound, the Word of God was not. He shared with Timothy about the baby, about what will come from the pains of his labor.

Remember that Jesus Christ of the seed of David was raised from the dead according to my gospel: Wherein I suffer trouble, as an evil doer, even unto bonds; but the word of

God is not bound. Therefore I endure all things for the elect's sake, that they may also obtain the salvation which is in Christ Jesus with eternal glory.

2 Timothy 2:8–10

Paul taught that suffering as an evildoer, that persecutions for Christ actually bring people to a saving knowledge of Jesus as Lord. As people see a man or a woman of God standing in the face of adversity, they will be drawn to the Lord. Obviously, you may want to keep this in mind as you go though your next trial. People are watching to see how you will react. Will you or I handle the labor with focus and resolve, or will we check out, not trusting in the Lord for his strength?

Look at where Paul put his trust.

At my first answer no man stood with me, but all men forsook me: I pray God that it may not be laid to their charge. Notwithstanding the Lord stood with me: that by me the preaching might be fully known, and that all the Gentiles might hear: And I was delivered out of the mouth of the lion. And the Lord shall deliver me from every evil work, and will preserve me unto his heavenly kingdom: To whom be glory for ever and ever. Amen

2 Timothy 4:16–18

Paul related to Timothy how at his first trial in the judgment hall of Nero, none of the believers in Rome stood by at his defense. Apparently fear was a factor, much like the fear that led the disciples to forsake our Lord after he was taken by the cohort of men in the garden of Gethsemane. Paul reminded Timothy that he indeed was delivered out of the mouth of the lion. The lion is often a type of the devil in Scripture, as it certainly is here. Nero, as the devil's man, is called the lion. Paul recalled how he was set free after what church history tells us was his first incarceration in Rome. So now that he is once again a prisoner in Nero's jail, he understands that the Lord will again deliver and preserve him. No, he doesn't say the Lord will break him out of jail again, and we know by history that this indeed did not happen, but he boldly preaches that the Lord will deliver and preserve him right into heaven, right to the place where all suffering will cease, to the ultimate delivery of the baby, to the place where his joy will be full!

Let's look more closely at Paul's labor pains of persecution, and then at the end we will see the baby he births! The Acts of the Apostles tells the story.

Paul's Conversion

Paul first appeared in the narrative as we read of the martyr Stephen's death. We learn in chapters 7 and 8 that young Paul was present and consenting of the stoning of Stephen. He believed it was a proper Jewish execution and took it personally upon himself to help crush this aberrant sect of Judaism that was being propagated. This carpenter from Nazareth did not fit his picture of the Messiah.

Thus, we see in chapter 9:

> And Saul, (Saul is Hebrew, Paul is Greek) yet breathing out threatenings and slaughter against the disciples of the Lord, went unto the high priest, and desired of him letters to Damascus to the synagogues, that if he found any of this way, whether they were men or women, he might bring them bound unto Jerusalem.
>
> Acts 9:1–2

Paul was a "hit man!" He was nothing more than a thug at this point in his life! Worse, his mission in life was to squash the followers of Jesus. This was as natural to him as breathing.

You see, at this time, the "way" was still part of Judaism. Jews were getting saved and were still meeting with their brothers in the synagogues. Thus, Paul used the authority of the high priest to legalize his murderous behavior.

As we know, Jesus had other plans for Paul on that fateful trip to Damascus. The Messiah knocked Paul off his horse, made the reality of his lordship known to him, and then blinded him for three days. During those three days, Paul learned of his labor pains.

> But the Lord said unto him (Ananias), Go thy way: For he is a chosen vessel unto me, to bear my name before the Gentiles, and kings, and the children of Israel: For I will show him how great things he must suffer for my name's sake.
>
> Acts 9:15–16

The threefold ministry God had planned for Paul is stated plainly here (three being the number of completeness). He was to witness to the Gentiles, to kings, and to Israel. We know after the fact, after Paul's life was completed, that he did exactly that!

At the very beginning of his ministry, Paul was given a revelation of what was in store. This, of course, as we have mentioned, was a good thing. Paul was not surprised when persecutions later arose, as he was shown by the Lord that it would be so.

Well, it didn't take very long for trouble to develop in his life. Ananias went to the repentant Paul. He was filled with the Holy Spirit, received his sight, and was baptized. Then amazingly, until one considers Paul's personality, the Bible reveals that "straightway he preached Christ in the synagogues, that he is the Son of God" (Acts 9:20).

He went to the very places where he was authorized to capture Christians—the synagogues—and witnessed that he had seen Jesus and that he indeed is the Messiah!

We learn that Paul, as a learned Jewish scholar, had a successful ministry by earthly standards initially in Damascus. He amazed the people by the circumstances of his conversion, and he confounded the people with his ability to prove that Jesus was the very Messiah.

The Bible states that after many days, though, the Jews took council to kill Paul. They couldn't win a debate with Paul, so they wanted to shut him up. What better way than to kill him? Fortunately, the murderous plot became known to Paul. So the disciples took him by night and let him down over the city walls in a basket so as to not be apprehended and killed by the Jews. Thus, Paul felt his first labor pain of persecution in seeing Christ formed in his children!

Paul's Quiet Time with the Lord

The first chapter of Galatians reveals the next stop on Paul's journey. Paul told the Galatian church that after his conversion, he left Damascus and went to Arabia for three years. He went to the desert where Jesus revealed his Word more fully to him.

> But I certify you, brethren, that the gospel which was preached of me is not after man. For I neither received if of man, neither was I taught it, but by the revelation of Jesus Christ.
>
> Galatians 1:11–12

Paul said he didn't learn this knowledge of the grace of God, of salvation through belief in the atoning work of the cross of Christ, by his sitting at the feet of Gamaliel or by his extensive grasp of the Scriptures. He proclaimed that this gospel he was entrusted with came by no other source but by direct revelation from Jesus himself! It was during this time in the desert of Arabia that this revelation apparently occurred.

Now, it's interesting that Paul heard from Jesus in the desert. He was in that dry place without water when the water of the Word of God was given to him. This is often the pattern seen in Scripture.

I think of Moses on the backside of the desert for forty years, tending the sheep of his father-in-law, Jethro when he saw the I AM in the burning bush that was not consumed. From there he was sent out.

We think of Jesus in the desert for forty days taking on the devil and also from there being sent out on his public ministry. So it may be with you. You may be called to a dry place, to a place of trial (forty being the number of trial in the Bible). It is there in that place that God will reveal himself to you before sending you out on your calling, on what he has planned for you. So *pay attention* when you are in that desert place. God will talk to you!

After his time in Arabia, Paul returned to Damascus and then went up to Jerusalem for the first time since his conversion. This was three years later. We are told that he spent fifteen days with Peter and James before going back to his hometown of Tarsus.

Actually, he was whisked away from Jerusalem, as you might have guessed, because of more trouble! During those fifteen days, we are informed in Acts 9 that Paul "spake boldly in the name of the Lord Jesus, and disputed against the Grecians: (Grecians were Greek speaking Jewish men who were living the Greek culture of the day.) But they went about to slay him" (Acts 9:29).

There we have it again! Paul wins the debate, if you will, but nearly loses his life. We're going to see that Paul will soon learn that he would better spend his time preaching to the sheep instead of wasting his breath on the goats, so to speak, that is, those men who think they are wise in God's ways are often the fools who won't listen. Instead, they are the ones who lash out against the messenger bringing the good news. This still occurs today. As the proverb states, "Reprove not a scorner, lest he hate thee: Rebuke a wise man, and he will love thee" (Proverbs 9:8).

After his close call in Jerusalem, Paul spent several years out of the limelight, if you will, back home in Tarsus. We are not told anything in the narrative about this time. But I can't help wondering if Paul thought he had failed his calling. He had seen the risen Lord, but nothing much was happening. Had the Lord decided to use someone else because he was ineffective in Damascus and Jerusalem?

These thoughts certainly must have crossed his mind! Of course, we know this was not the case. Often there is a time gap between planting and harvesting. So it was for Paul and so it can be expected for you and me too!

While Paul was waiting in obscurity, the Lord was using Peter to begin his call to the Gentiles. The house of the Roman centurion, Cornelius, came to the Lord and the gospel was spreading outside of Israel due to persecution from the unbelieving Jews. Antioch in Syria became the major center for the Way.

We learn in chapter 11 that Barnabas, who earlier had a positive encounter with the newly saved Paul back in Jerusalem, went to Tarsus to bring Paul back for the work going on in Antioch. Paul was back in a place of ministry, and we are told, "And it came to pass, that a whole year they assembled themselves with the church, and taught much people. And the disciples were called Christians first in Antioch" (Acts 11:26b).

Paul was now getting to release the things that the Lord had taught him to people who wanted to hear. What a great feeling this must have been for him! It will also be for you as you release to open ears the things the Lord has shown you!

Paul's First Missionary Journey

The time now was AD 44, and the prophet Agabus informed the disciples in Antioch that there would be a great dearth throughout all the world in the days of Claudius Caesar (Acts 11:28). History tells us that this indeed occurred in that time. As a result, Paul and Barnabas were commissioned to bring a financial gift from the believers in Antioch to the brethren in Judea who were especially hard hit. They did this with joy and afterward returned to Antioch, fulfilling their ministry. No persecutions occurred during this visit as Paul apparently avoided the unbelieving Jews.

The next phase of Paul's life was about to begin. In chapter 13, the Holy Spirit told the church to separate Barnabas and Paul for a special work. They were to be sent out. The model of a church sending out missionaries is first seen here. It is the model that the Lord continues to use today. God will reveal a need to a body of Spirit-filled believers, and he will then raise up men and women who want to go out and answer that call. So it was for Barnabas and Paul. They left on what is known as Paul's first missionary journey, taking a young man named John Mark along with them. This is the same man who later became a disciple of the Apostle Peter and penned the Gospel of Mark from Peter's narrative.

After a successful work in Cyprus, where the deputy of the country became a believer in Jesus, Paul and his company sailed to nearby south-central Turkey. The nation we know as Turkey was called Asia in Paul's day. John Mark left, but Paul and Barnabas witnessed powerfully in Pisidia to both the Jews and the Gentiles as described in chapter 13. The chapter ends with these words:

And when the Gentiles heard this, they were glad, and glorified the word of the Lord: And as many as were ordained
to eternal life believed. And the word of the Lord was published throughout all the region. But the Jews stirred up
the devout and honorable women, and the chief men of the
city, and raised persecution against Paul and Barnabus, and
expelled them out of their coasts. But they shook off the
dust of their feet against them, and came to Iconium. And
the disciples were filled with joy, and with the Holy Ghost.

Acts 13:48–52

After preaching to the Jews, Paul and Barnabas took the
gospel to the Gentiles, and they rejoiced. All of the region
buzzed because of the wonderful message of salvation. Then,
as can sometimes be the case, women were stirred up and
started talking and men started persecuting. Paul and Barnabas, realizing that it was time to move on, traveled eastward
for Iconium. They left in their wake a group of joyous, Spirit-
filled new believers.

Again at Iconium, the people had a choice to make. Many
Jews and Gentiles believed, but once again the unbelieving Jews stirred up other unbelieving Gentiles, and the city
became divided. This really is the way of the Lord in this age
we live. Jesus said he would bring division. The gospel is not
something people can be ambivalent about. They instead will
choose up sides and battle to defend their choice! Chapter 14
tells that an assault was planned to stone Paul and Barnabas—
another labor pain for Paul. They thankfully became aware of
it and fled south to nearby Lystra.

In Lystra, though, Paul was not so fortunate. A congeni-
tally lame man was healed as they were preaching, and the
people, influenced by Greek mythology, believed the two must
be the gods Jupiter and Mercury come down to men. They
were ready to worship Paul and Barnabas. But the two evangelists made known the truth of the miracle, and the sacrifice
was stayed. Almost immediately, though, the people of Lystra

turned on their two ministers from God. Jews from nearby Iconium and faraway Antioch took it upon themselves to follow and resist Paul and Barnabas.

As an aside, Paul shouldn't have been surprised. That was exactly what he was doing before he was converted. He too was traveling on a mission to hold back the spread of the gospel. It's true that a man will reap what he sows!

Paul was apprehended in Lystra and was stoned! He, like Stephen before him, was killed for his faith in Jesus Christ. But in this case, Paul's testimony was not complete (Revelation 11:7). The Bible states that the disciples believed he was dead, yet Paul rose up, and the next day, he and Barnabas departed to the east to the town of Derbe. That had to have been a labor pain that Paul would remember for a long time though!

Things went well in Derbe, and after preaching and teaching the gospel in that city, Paul and Barnabas backtracked their entire Asian route, building up the believers in the cities they had previously evangelized. They returned to Antioch, fulfilling the work to which the Holy Spirit had called them.

Thus ended Paul's first missionary journey. The gospel had now leapt out of Palestine and was running wild!

Paul's Second Missionary Journey

Several years likely passed for Paul, as the Bible states, after they returned to Antioch and they abided a long time with the disciples (Acts 14:28).

Then after that time interval, Paul and Barnabas traveled to Jerusalem in chapter 15 of Acts to answer the question that certain Judeans were propagating, that question being did the

Gentiles need to be circumcised in order to be saved? Although no persecution occurred in Paul's life during this chapter of his story, the importance of what happened cannot be underestimated. If Paul and Barnabas, along with James, had not won the debate over circumcision that day, the doctrine we enjoy of salvation by faith in Jesus Christ would look totally different. I'm afraid it would look like a works doctrine!

Upon returning to Antioch, Paul and Barnabas again spent time in their role as teachers in the church at Antioch (Acts 15:35).

> And some days after Paul said unto Barnabas, Let us go again and visit our brethren in every city where we have preached the word of the Lord, and see how they do.
>
> Acts 15:36

Barnabas was determined to bring the now older and more mature John Mark along. This did not sit well with Paul. You will remember that John Mark flaked out on the two in Asia, and Paul didn't want to be left holding the bag again. This rift split the team of Paul and Barnabas, but when seen from God's perspective, it was ordained. Barnabas took John Mark and sailed to Cyprus while Paul chose Silas and began his second missionary journey. Thus, from God's point of view, he now had two teams of evangelists instead of one!

For his second journey, Paul traveled overland from Antioch. He stopped in Derbe then on to Lystra. I wonder if he was a bit apprehensive there when he recalled his stoning, which took place a few years earlier! In Lystra, he met a young disciple named Timotheus, who began traveling with the outreach team. We know him as Timothy. The Bible states that they were forbidden to preach in Asia, so they hiked the entire length of Turkey from the southeast to the northwest were the Spirit led them into Macedonia. This region is present-day northeastern Greece. As I think upon the difficulty of traveling on foot for those distances, I am humbled at the tenacity of Paul and his co-workers!

The chief city of that region was Philippi, and Paul was given the green light from God to preach and evangelize. A woman named Lydia, who was not even from Macedonia but hailed from the western Turkish city of Thyatira, became the first convert to Christianity in Macedonia. Her entire household was baptized, and she gave lodging to the group for their continued work.

Trouble soon developed for Paul though. It seemed a woman who was possessed with an evil spirit had been harassing Paul. The spirit's name was Python. He was a powerful spirit that was the keeper of the temple of Zeus. The Bible states that after many days Paul became grieved, and he turned and commanded Python in the name of Jesus Christ to come out of the woman. Thus, the woman in whom the spirit dwelt no longer possessed the powers of divination that she used to gain money for her masters. With their financial cash cow lost, the men caught Paul and Silas and brought them to the local magistrates. The slave owners got the crowd involved as well by trumping up the charges, and the puppet leaders had no choice but to have Paul and Silas brutally beaten to appease the mob. The two were then cast into the inner prison with their feet chained to the stocks.

The Bible reveals that that very night at midnight while Paul and Silas were singing praises to God, with the other prisoners and the jailor no doubt listening, that a mighty earthquake occurred. The captives were freed, and we learn that the jailor and his house were saved in the course of the events.

After leaving Philippi, Paul, and Silas traveled westward to Thessalonica. As was Paul's manner, he reasoned with the Jews in the synagogue before going to the Gentiles. He taught out of the Scriptures how the Messiah had to suffer and rise from the dead. He skillfully made the connection that Jesus was that very prophetic fulfillment. Some of the listeners believed and were saved, as were many Gentiles, during the course of this work. But as we have seen so many times before, the unbelieving Jews were moved with envy and gathered a company of rabble-rousers to cause an uproar in the city. Jason, who had been hosting the evangelists, was taken, but Paul and Silas escaped the mob and were immediately sent away by the believers during the night for their own safety.

They came to the nearby town of Berea where again many received the Word of God—both the Jews and the Greeks. As you have already guessed, when the unbelieving Jews from Thessalonica learned that Paul and Silas were preaching in Berea, they came over and stirred up the people. Thus again, a labor pang of persecution forced Paul out of town while Silas and Timothy felt they could stay and finish their work.

Paul traveled to the city of Athens where he boldly preached to the wise men of the day in the midst of Mars Hill. He spoke of the unknown God who was now revealed. Again fruit was seen as certain men clave unto him and believed.

Next, Paul came down to Corinth and lived with Aquila and Priscilla. They were a wonderful husband and wife team from Rome who were expelled when Emperor Claudius commanded that all Jews leave Rome during his evil reign. The two were tentmakers like Paul and came to be an important couple in the early church. Silas and Timothy joined Paul in Corinth, and the group was given eighteen months of freedom from persecution during which time they taught the Word of God boldly.

As their season of freedom from persecution ended, the Jews rose up and took their case against Paul to Gallio, the deputy of the province of Achaia. Gallio would not have any of their nonsense and expelled them from the judgment seat. The Bible then tells us that the Greeks took the chief ruler of the synagogue, named Sosthenes, and beat him before the judgment seat.

Now this would only be an interesting footnote in history, that of the Jewish leader who wanted to persecute Paul actually being the one who was beaten, if it were not for the opening verse in the book of 1Corinthians: "Paul, called to be an apostle of Jesus Christ through the will of God, and Sosthenes our brother" (1 Corinthians 1:1).

Sosthenes apparently became a believer and a co-worker! Did the beating that he took make a difference? We don't know. But later Paul calls him a brother, and he is to this day involved in the ongoing ministry of Paul via that wonderful correctional epistle to which he is attached!

Paul continued in Corinth for a season and then concluded his second missionary journey in chapter 18. He sailed to Ephesus, where he left Aquila and Priscilla, and then sailed to the Israeli port of Caesarea. He went up to Jerusalem for one of the feasts and then traveled back home to Antioch.

Thus we have come to the end of Paul's second missionary journey. The gospel now had blazed its trail from Turkey to Greece!

The Word of God Prevails

After spending some time in Antioch, Paul began his third missionary journey. He first retraced his steps of previous ministry in eastern and central Turkey, known as Galatia. Then he traveled through a new section of Turkey known as Phrygia. In Phrygia are located the important biblical cities of Colossae and Laodicea.

Next, Paul returned to Ephesus, on Turkey's western coast, where a wonderful door for ministry was opened. The Bible states that Paul spoke boldly in the synagogue of Ephesus for three months. But after the Jews became hardened, he departed their company, and we are told that he disputed daily in the school of one Tyrannus. Paul continued teaching there for two full years, and we learn that all those who dwelt in Asia heard the Word of God through this ministry. Can you believe that! There was such a move of the Holy Spirit that everyone, that means *everyone,* heard the message of salvation. All people living in Turkey, that country the size of California and Texas put together, heard the Word. Truly the gospel was now out to the public. The mustard seed of the kingdom of God was now growing into a great tree as Jesus told his disciples it would.

This section of Paul's ministry concluded with the great summary statement,

So mightily grew the word of God and prevailed.

Acts 19:20

Paul indeed was used mightily during this period of his ministry, and the wonderful doctrinal epistle to the Ephesians is a testimony to that fact!

Sincerity Is No Guarantee for Truth

Continuing with our story of Paul's travail and joy, of his labor and delivery to see Christ formed in his children. We pick it up at the end of his third missionary journey.

After these things were ended, Paul purposed in the spirit, when he had passed through Macedonia and Achaia, to go to Jerusalem, saying, After I have been there, I must also see Rome.

Acts 19:21

Paul's plan was to visit Greece again to build up and perfect his flock in that country before visiting those two contrasting spiritual centers of the world, Jerusalem and Rome. We know from reading later in the Book of Acts that Paul did indeed visit Jerusalem and Rome, but not in the way he likely intended, for he was imprisoned during both!

But first, just as Paul was preparing to leave and after he had sent Timothy and Erastus on ahead to Macedonia, Demetrius the silversmith led an uprising against the Way. It seemed that since people were turning to the Lord by the countless thousands in Turkey that the demand for his craft in forming silver idols was waning. Specifically, the Greek goddess of Diana, who was worshiped in Ephesus, was being denigrated as people could see the folly of believing in gods made with the hands of men. Since Demetrius and his cohorts made their livelihood in this work, it is not hard to see why they had a problem with this new religion.

A huge uprising boiled over, and Paul saw this as his message to move on with his plan to travel across the Aegean Sea over to Macedonia and Achaia. This he did as the first half of chapter 20 documents. On his return trip through Ephesus, with his course now set toward Jerusalem, Paul revealed to the brethren what the Lord had shown to him about his upcoming travails and the joy to follow.

> And now, behold, I go bound in the spirit unto Jerusalem, not knowing the things that shall befall me there: Save that the Holy Ghost witnesseth in every city, saying that bonds and afflictions abide me. But none of these things move me, neither count I my life dear unto myself, so that I might finish my course with joy, and the ministry, which I have received of the Lord Jesus, to testify the gospel of the grace of God.
>
> Acts 19:21

Wow! What a man! Paul is focused on one thing and one thing only: to finish strong! To complete the ministry to which the Lord had called him. That's my prayer for me and for you too!

Unfortunately for Paul, sincerity is *no* guarantee for truth! Paul was sincere in his plan to go back to Jerusalem, but it was apparently not the Lord's primary will for him. Look in chapter 21 with me. There are no less than four times the Holy Spirit tells him not to go up to Jerusalem.

> And finding disciples, we tarried there seven days: Who said to Paul through the Spirit, that he should not go to Jerusalem.
>
> Acts 21:4

> And the same man (Philip the evangelist) had four daughters, virgins, which did prophesy. (Context suggests they also told Paul not to go to Jerusalem.)
>
> Acts 21:9

> And as we tarried there many days, there came down from Judea a certain prophet, named Agabus. (The same man who years earlier in 44 a.d. prophesied of the world-wide famine.) And when he was come unto us, he took Paul's girdle, and bound his own hands and feet, and said, Thus saith the Holy Ghost, So shall the Jews at Jerusalem bind the man that owneth this girdle, and shall deliver him into the hands of the Gentiles.
>
> Acts 21:10–11

> And when we heard these things, both we, and they of that place, besought him not to go up to Jerusalem.
>
> Acts 21:12

Verse 13 states that despite this clear warning from the respected Agabus, as well as the others in the Spirit, Paul was not to be dissuaded from his goal of returning to Jerusalem.

Next we come to a difficult verse, which does not fit with the flow of the story. Verse 14, as reported in the King James Version of the Bible, reads as follows: "And when he would not be persuaded, we ceased, saying, The will of the Lord be done" (Acts 21:14).

The only problem was it *wasn't* the Lord's will that Paul should go Jerusalem at that time. That is made crystal clear in the proceeding verses. So why would the disciples just give up and say to Paul to go ahead; it's the will of the Lord?

Actually, they didn't!

You see, the meaning of this verse hangs on the placement of the commas in verse 14. Apparently an early scribe thought it sacrilege that the Apostle Paul might go outside of the will of God by this time in his ministry, so he tried to help Paul out by adding a comma. Verse 14 should read, "And when he would not be persuaded, we ceased saying the will of the Lord be done." In other words, they realized that Paul was going to do his own thing, so they just stopped telling him to listen to the Lord.

Remember, the Bible tells us that in our flesh dwells no good thing (Romans 7:18). We might think we are pleasing God when we are in fact outside of his will. The key is, are we walking in fleshly religiousness as Paul was in this section, or are we walking in the Spirit?

Paul's Jerusalem Trial and Travail

Well, indeed Paul traveled to Jerusalem where he met with the church leader James and the other elders. They discussed Paul's ministry to the Gentiles, and the men saluted Paul for his efforts.

Unfortunately, the Jewish believers in Jerusalem had become zealous for the Law and sucked Paul into their religious ways. They suggested to Paul that to purify himself in the eyes of the multitude he should shave his head and act like an observant Jew while he was visiting town. This backfired on Paul as Asian Jews, who had seen Paul in Turkey, noted the hypocrisy of Paul's actions and stirred up all the people in the crowded temple. They cried out to the men of Israel that Paul was the man who had taught far and wide against the Jews, the Law, and the temple. They also said that Paul had brought Gentiles into the Temple. As you can imagine, this set off a firestorm against Paul, and he was nearly killed. Just in the nick of time, the chief captain of the Roman band learned of the uproar and took soldiers to rescue Paul. He was beaten badly but survived the ordeal.

Now the captain, not knowing the nature of the uprising, had Paul bound with two chains and demanded to know who he was. The multitude, in their confusion, could not give the captain a clear answer, but Paul, who had command of the Greek language, did. He was allowed to give a beautiful summation of his personal testimony and of the grace of God toward him, but when he spoke of his commission to the Gentiles, the Jewish intolerance toward non-Jews came back to the surface.

They cried out again with such intensity that the chief captain commanded that Paul must be worthy of scourging in light of the multitude's feelings against him. Luckily for Paul, he played the Roman citizen card, which was able to keep the whip off his back! But the prophecy of Agabus, the labor pain of Jerusalem, was certainly coming to pass.

The next day, the captain commanded the chief priests and all their council to appear, and he brought Paul down and set him in their midst. Chapter 23 tells of this meeting.

Paul initially addressed the council as brethren and proclaimed that he had lived with a clear conscience. The high priest had him smitten in the mouth for this statement, which led Paul to change his tactics toward the assembly. He perceived that the group was divided between the Pharisees and the Sadducees. Thus, he played on the contention the two groups had concerning the resurrection of the dead. This indeed did move the focus off of him, but the two groups become so agitated that the captain of the guard feared that Paul would be seriously hurt in the fray. Thus, once again Paul needed to be rescued from injury.

The next day, more than forty Jews bound themselves with oath that they would neither eat nor drink until they had killed Paul. They asked the council to call for Paul again under the pretense of more discussion. The plan was to assassinate Paul by overcoming the small contingent of Roman guards that would be present during Paul's trip from the Roman castle to the Jewish court.

Once again, certain death was averted as the chief captain became aware of the plot and had Paul whisked away by night under heavy Roman guard. Paul spent the next several years of his life under arrest in the Roman military city of Caesarea. These were likely lonely days where he may have questioned the wisdom of his decision to return to Jerusalem.

But as we know, the Lord had further plans for Paul!

Paul's Reality

Paul spoke of his many "labor pains" most directly in the books of 1 and 2 Corinthians.

> Even unto this present hour we both hunger, and thirst, and are naked, and are buffeted, and have no certain dwelling place: And labor, working with our own hands: Being reviled, we bless; being persecuted, we suffer it: Being defamed, we intreat: We are made as filth of the world, and are the offscouring of all things unto this day. I write not these things to shame you, but as my beloved sons I warn you. For though ye have ten thousand instructors in Christ, yet have ye not many

fathers: For in Christ Jesus I have begotten you through the gospel. Wherefore I beseech you, be ye followers of me.

1 Corinthians 4:11–16

For we would not, brethren, have you ignorant of our trouble which came to us in Asia, that we were pressed out of measure, above strength, insomuch that we despaired even of life.

2 Corinthians 1:8

We are troubled on every side, yet not distressed; we are perplexed, but not in despair: Persecuted, but not forsaken; cast down, but not destroyed: Always bearing about in the body of dying of the Lord Jesus, that the life also of Jesus might be made manifest in our body.

2 Corinthians 4:8–10

But in all things approving ourselves as the ministers of God, in much patience, in afflictions, in necessities, in distresses, in stripes, in imprisonments, in tumults, in labors, in watchings in fastings: By pureness, by knowledge, by longsuffering, by kindness, by the Holy Ghost, by love unfeigned: By the word of truth, by the power of God, by the armor of righteousness on the right hand and on the left: By honor and dishonor, by evil report and good report; as deceivers, and yet true: As unknown, and yet well known; as dying, and behold, we live; as chastened, and not killed: As sorrowful, yet always rejoicing; as poor, yet making many rich; as having nothing, and yet possessing all things.

2 Corinthians 6:4–10

In labors more abundant, in stripes above measure, in prisons more frequent, in deaths oft. Of the Jews five times received I forty stripes save one. Thrice was I beaten with rods, once I was stoned, thrice I suffered shipwreck, a night and a day I have been in the deep: In journeyings often, in perils of waters, in perils of robbers, in perils by mine own countrymen, in perils by the heathen, in perils in the city, in perils in the wilderness, in perils in the sea, in perils among false brethren: In weariness and painfulness, in watchings, often, in hunger and thirst, in fastings often, in cold and nakedness. Besides those things that are without, that which cometh upon me daily, the care of all the churches.

2 Corinthians 11:23b–28

Wow! After reading these verses, one must ask just what made Paul tick! How could a man stand in the face of such hardship and persecution?

The answer's threefold.

First, Paul knew of the *reality of eternity*. We learn in chapter 12 of 2 Corinthians that Paul was caught up to the third heaven. He was taken to paradise and heard unspeakable words.

Secondly, Paul understood the *potency of the gospel*. He knew that the Word of God is like a lion in a cage. All he had to do was let it out, and it would not be stopped!

Lastly, Paul remembered the *mystery of God's mercy*. He recalled how he previously had been a persecutor of the gospel and yet was spared by the grace of the Lord.

Along with these understandings, Paul stayed connected to the vine. He made it of utmost priority to stay close to Jesus. We would call this having daily devotions today. Paul found his compassion for the lost by contemplation with his Lord!

Paul's Thorn in the Flesh

Indeed, 2 Corinthians is Paul's most personal letter. In this letter, he revealed the intensity of his labor pains received in order to see Christ formed in his children. He spoke of a "thorn in the flesh" near the end of the epistle.

And lest I should be exalted above measure through the abundance of the revelations, there was given to me a thorn in the flesh, the messenger of Satan to buffet me, lest I should be exalted above measure. For this thing I besought the Lord thrice, that it might depart from me. And he said unto me, My grace is sufficient for thee: For my strength is made perfect in weakness. Most gladly therefore will I rather glory in my infirmities, that the power of Christ may rest upon me. Therefore I take pleasure in infirmities, in reproaches, in necessities, in persecutions, in distresses for Christ's sake: For when I am weak, then am I strong.

2 Corinthians 12:7–10

These verses discussing Paul's thorn in the flesh are pregnant with truths that should be brought out.

First of all, we are not told what the thorn is. It's anonymous, so we can all relate. Truly every person has his or her own personal thorn, if you will. Everyone has an issue to deal with in this life. Things never will be perfect this side of heaven. That's one of the very things that should make one look and long for heaven, that place where all *will* be perfect!

Secondly, the thorn in the flesh was benevolent. It was given to Paul so he could experience God. I think back to the book of Daniel as Shadrach, Meshach, and Abednego experienced a walk with the Angel of the Lord when they were *in* the fiery furnace. When they came out, the Lord remained in the fire (Daniel 3:1–30).

Thirdly, Paul was perceptive concerning this thorn. He knew Satan sent it but that God allowed it! He understood the words of Joseph to his brothers when he said to the effect, what (Satan) meant for evil, God meant for good (Genesis 50:20).

Fourthly, the thorn was for Paul's protection. He realized that God allowed the thorn to keep pride away. Paul had been given much, and his flesh would tend to become prideful with the abundance of revelations he had received. Paul understood that it was actually a gift!

Lastly, Paul walked in the power of God because of his thorn in the flesh. His power was not from within but totally from without. His power came from God! "For when I am weak, then I am strong" (2 Corinthians 12:10b).

Scholars over the years have written and speculated about what this anonymous thorn in the flesh was that Paul suffered. They most often note the idea that Paul had an eye problem, as he had others actually pen his epistles and had to write large letters at the end of some of his dictations as a way of signature (Galatians 6:11).

Also, it is noted that he told the believers in Galatia that he was thankful concerning their tolerance to his visual limitations. He was blessed that they would have gladly given their own eyes to him in order to minister to his needs (Galatians 4:15).

An eye disease is likely something Paul suffered through, but I don't think that was his thorn in the flesh. A better explanation comes from what we have been discussing in this section. The thorn is the persecution, distress, and trial that Paul received at the hands of men!

I say this because of a simple rule of biblical study that we should apply in understanding the thorn. That is, when a word is not clear in the Bible, look where it is used before to gain its meaning. God will define a word for us by applying the word as it is used previously in the Bible.

Let's look at some prior usages of the word *thorn* and see how it speaks of men, how it speaks of people, and how it speaks of the enemies of God.

> But if ye will not drive out the inhabitants of the land from before you; then it shall come to pass, that those which ye let remain of them shall be pricks in your eyes and thorns in your sides, and shall vex you in the land wherein ye dwell.
>
> Numbers 33:55

God spoke through Moses to tell the children of Israel that the *people* of the land would become pricks in their eyes and thorns in their sides if they did not drive them out when they went in to take the promised land. Thorns are people in this example.

> Know for a certainty that the Lord your God will no more drive out any of these nations from before you: But they shall be snares and traps unto you, and scourges in your sides, and thorns in your eyes, until ye perish from off the good land which the Lord your God hath given you.
>
> Joshua 23:13

Once again people are the thorns.

"But the sons of Belial shall be all of them as thorns thrust away" (2 Samuel 23:6a). Those who resisted God, the sons of Belial, are pictured as thorns.

Indeed, time after time, Paul needed to interrupt his ministry; he needed to move on. At the hands of the unbelieving Jews, Paul received blows and persecution at the hands of men. People were Paul's thorn in the flesh, people who Satan inspired and God allowed, thorny people who Paul asked the Lord three times to have depart from his life.

Yes, Paul's course is compared to a hard, long labor. But he does deliver the baby! As every mother has experienced, the pain of labor is eclipsed by the joy of delivering the baby.

Let's look at Paul's joy!

The Crown of Rejoicing

> For what is our hope, or joy, or crown of rejoicing? Are not even ye in the presence of our Lord Jesus Christ at his coming? For ye are our glory and joy.
>
> 1 Thessalonians 2:19–20

That's it! Just as Paul's thorn in the flesh was actually people, just as his labor and travail came at the hands of people, so was his baby. Those who rejected and resisted the gospel became thorns while those whom Paul brought to the saving knowledge of Christ became his baby. Those who received salvation through faith in the finished work of Jesus Christ on the cross and believed in the subsequent resurrection became his glory and crown!

Paul speaks of the delivery, the glory of the birth, powerfully in 2 Corinthians.

> For our light affliction, which is but for a moment, worketh for us a far more exceeding and eternal weight of glory.
>
> 2 Corinthians 4:17

The reality of eternity and the hope of heaven shared with those countless people who heard the Word of God through Paul would be an eternal crown of rejoicing. It would be glorious for Paul, and that's the only way he could say that his present circumstances were light affliction! We have seen previously that what happened to him was anything but light compared to earthly standards.

Now think about a crown of rejoicing with me for a moment.

A crown denotes royalty. It is worn by a man or woman

who has ascended to the top of the kingdom. It denotes someone very special.

Rejoicing is that wonderful inward mental state of pure peace, satisfaction, and happiness. Indeed, the person upon whom a crown of rejoicing is bestowed has ascended and is in a state of perpetual bliss!

Paul will be wearing the crown of rejoicing in the presence of the Lord Jesus, but so can you, so can I.

Remember the reality of heaven and meditate daily on the fact that Jesus is coming back for you. Live your life and speak words that glorify Christ. And above all, remember that "the fear of the Lord is the beginning of knowledge" (Proverbs 1:7). But "the fear of man bringeth a snare" (Proverbs 29:25).

Don't fear man, but fear God! That is, respect the Lord and give him worth.

Children Walking in Truth

In closing, I would like to look at the words of the Apostle John.

> I rejoiced greatly that I found of thy children walking in truth.
>
> 2 John 4a

> I have no greater joy than to hear that my children walk in truth.
>
> 3 John 4

John is noted as the apostle of *love*, yet he rejoiced and found joy in the fact that another's children and his children were walking in *truth*.

Like his brother Paul, John also travailed in labor for his spiritual family, and he received the joy that comes with the delivery. He rejoiced in finishing his course and seeing his children walk in truth. He understood that his children were moving forward.

You may be thinking, *That's great for Paul and John. They had a special evangelistic anointing. But I'm just one of the children.*

That's okay too. Listen to the encouragement John gives to the children.

> I write unto you, little children, because your sins are forgiven you for his name's sake. I write to you, fathers, because ye have known him that is from the beginning. I write to you, young men, because you have overcome the wicked one. I write unto you, little children, because ye have known the Father.
>
> 1 John 2:12–13

Your sins are forgiven; you know the Father! It doesn't really get any better than that.

Okay, we are the children that our spiritual parents are rejoicing in as we walk in truth. But the question must be asked, what does walking in truth look like?

Well, first of all, it's a process. It doesn't happen all at once. It's also a decision that you and I make. It's not an emotion!

Let me give you three keys that may help you to keep moving forward, keys to walking in truth.

First, it's important to *pace yourself*. We are body, soul, and spirit. All three areas need nurturing in order to be successful.

Secondly, *enjoy life's journey*. Stop and smell the roses, and don't wish away today. You'll never get it back. Live in the present and don't dwell on the mistakes of the past while learning from them.

Lastly, *hope for that future day*, specifically, that future day with the Lord in heaven. And absolutely, positively, don't set your hope on the temporal things of this life! You'll only be disappointed!

Look at the big picture. Life is not about getting that new job, moving to that better home, seeing your candidate win, or even marrying that perfect mate. Sure, those things are well and good, but when they come to pass, they will *never* fulfill completely. It's only the Lord Jesus Christ who can fill that place in your heart with a joy that never ends!

God bless you as you prepare your mind for the "labors" of life. In the end, you will rejoice in the birth of the baby!

BOOK SIX

Of Blood and Water

The Second Adam

After this, Jesus knowing that all things were now accomplished, that the scripture might be fulfilled saith, I thirst. Now there was set a vessel full of vinegar: And they filled a sponge with vinegar, and put it upon hyssop, and put it to his mouth. When Jesus therefore had received the vinegar, he said, It is finished: And he bowed his head, and gave up the ghost. The Jews therefore, because it was the preparation, that the bodies should not remain upon the cross on the Sabbath day, (for that Sabbath day was an high day,) besought Pilate that their legs might be broken, and that they might be taken away. Then came the soldiers, and brake the legs of the first, and of the other which was crucified with him. But when they came to Jesus, and saw that he was dead already, they brake not his legs: But one of the soldiers with a spear pierced his side, and forthwith came there out blood and water. And he that saw it bear record, and his record is true: And he knoweth that he saith true, that ye might believe. For these things were done, that the scripture should be fulfilled, A bone of him shall not be broken. And again another scripture saith, They shall look on him whom they pierced.

John 19:28–37

Jesus of Nazareth, the Christ, died for the sins of humanity. He was murdered in a dastardly plot by the leaders of the Jewish nation so they could maintain their position and power over the nation. But he was not taken against his will, for he laid down his life. The Scripture clearly states that all of his actions, including his death, were the fulfillment of Scripture. He truly was in command of the situation, even in his death!

But I find it intriguing in reading this account of the last moments of Jesus' life that we see a picture of an event of which every mother, every grown woman, is familiar. That is, we see a reference to the birth of a baby.

When the soldier pierced his side, out came blood and water. This is a powerful reference to the combination of fluids that are seen in no other place in medicine other than with the birth of a baby. Indeed, as Jesus died, a birth also occurred. That birth was *ours!* He died, and we were born!

But medically was this a miracle? How could water flow from a wound? The answer comes from an understanding of the physiology of the heart. As our Lord was dying, his heart began to fail. This process, known as congestive heart failure, is due to the heart becoming unable to pump blood adequately throughout the body. Thus, blood backed up in his venous system, causing tissue edema. His body likely swelled with water, similar to what is observed in late pregnancy. The covering of Jesus' heart, a sac called the pericardium, also received watery fluid as a result of this physiologic process. Therefore, when the soldier pierced the Savior's side, the spear apparently ruptured both the pericardium and the ventricle of his heart. When the soldier removed the spear, the combination of blood from the heart and water from the pericardium tracked out of the wound, much like air escaping a tire that has run over a nail.

Let's spiritualize these two fluids for a moment.

> For the life of the flesh is in the blood: And I have given it to you upon the altar to make atonement for your souls: For it is the blood that maketh an atonement for the soul.
>
> Leviticus 17:11

This is a key verse in the Old Testament, for it proclaims that without the shedding of blood there is no remission of sins. There is no atonement, or as has been said, there is no "at-one-ment."

Thus the blood that flowed speaks of our forgiveness.

In the last day, that great day of the feast, Jesus stood and cried, saying, If any man thirst, let him come unto me, and drink. He that believeth on me, as the scripture hath said, out of his belly shall flow rivers of living water. (But this spake he of the Spirit, which they that believe on him should receive: Because that Jesus was not yet glorified.)

John 7:37–39

It's easy to comprehend that the water that gushed forth from Jesus is a type of the Spirit that is given to those who believe on him. It will not be a trickle, a stream, or a pond. It will flow forth as a river of living water as the Scripture declares!

So we see in our study text that Jesus' death, his blood and water, led to our birth. This helps me understand his famous words to Nicodemus. He told that ruler of the Jews that a man could not see the kingdom of God unless he was born again, unless he was born from above. He told Nicodemus that a man is born the first time of a woman, of the flesh. The second birth, on the new birth, is of the Spirit.

Now Paul teaches in his epistle to the Corinthians that Jesus is the second Adam (1 Corinthians 15:45–48). We understand that Adam is a picture of Christ in many ways. One similarity concerns what we have been discussing here. Just as Jesus had his side opened and a birth occurred, so did Adam.

And the Lord God said, It is not good that man should be alone; I will make him an help meet for him … And the Lord God caused a deep sleep to fall upon Adam, and he slept: And he took one of his ribs, and closed up the flesh instead thereof: And the rib, which the Lord God had taken from man, made he a woman, and brought her unto the man.

Genesis 2:18, 21–22

Here we have, back in the second chapter of the Bible, the account of the first surgical procedure. God induced general anesthesia (he caused a deep sleep to fall upon Adam), he surgically opened up Adam's side, removed a rib, and closed him up. Then God fashioned the rib into woman!

Just as Jesus' side was opened and a birth occurred, so Adam's side was opened, and he birthed the woman. Eve was formed. The part Adam was now missing, God used to bless him beyond his wildest imagination! Eve completed Adam just as my wife completes me! For indeed God intends for a woman to complete a man. If you doubt this statement, look at the next two verses.

> And Adam said, this is now bone of my bones, and flesh of my flesh: She shall be called Woman, because she was taken out of Man. Therefore shall a man leave his father and his mother, and shall cleave unto his wife: And they shall be one flesh.
>
> Genesis 2:23–24

Without the woman, something was missing. That sensitivity, that compassion, that beauty that Adam lost when God took his rib was restored when he clave unto his wife and once again became one flesh. So it is with you and me also.

But there is a glaring dissimilarity in looking at the two surgeries of Adam and Jesus. Adam's surgery was bloodless! There is no mention of any pain or blood being shed. That's because sin was not a factor for Adam. But for Jesus, he who knew no sin became sin for us that we might be made the righteousness of God in him (2 Corinthians 5:21). Jesus' side was bloodied because his surgery was for sin!

So we see that our Lord birthed something wonderful that day as he died upon the cross of Calvary. But if a birth occurred, then we know that a labor also had to have happened.

We need look no further that the last hours of Jesus' life, which are documented from four perspectives, the four gospels, as well as from Old Testament prophecies, in order to understand the intensity of his labor pains.

Scripture Buildup

First of all, in order to comprehend Jesus' labor, we need to grasp what labor was like in times of old, for it was somewhat different than in our day today.

In our time, labor is tough. Don't get me wrong! I'm quite convinced that I would fare poorly if I had even an inkling of the pain a woman experiences with labor. But today's births are not like births before our modern times. That's because today a woman does not go into labor wondering whether or not she will survive the ordeal. It's a given that she will deliver a baby that should do well, and she also expects that she will suffer no permanent ill effects.

That was not the case in times past. A woman had no more assurance of surviving the labor and delivery experience than a man did of going to war. Both were potentially lethal. Thus the fear that a woman experienced during her pregnancy as she looked toward the labor and delivery is not comprehended in our day. The setting is entirely different. Dying is not in the equation!

As a man, the best example I can think of to picture how a woman likely felt before going into labor would be the feeling that a young soldier may have experienced prior to landing onto Omaha Beach on D-day. You didn't have a choice; you had to get out of the landing craft and hit the beach. But you realized that you might not make it. So it was for a woman. She had no choice. She had to deliver the baby. But she knew she might not make it!

Also, today, labor still is very painful. But pain medicines and anesthetics are available. If things get out of hand, there is a course that can bring needed relief. Obviously, the pain remedies of old did not match up to the choices we have today.

Lastly, in our day, if the labor isn't progressing, if the cervix isn't dilating, then medications are used to hasten the process. In fact, the average duration of active labor today is eight hours. And if a baby is too large to deliver, if it just won't come out, a C-section can be done. In contrast, in olden days, labor was much longer, with forty hours being common! And if the baby wasn't progressing forth, the mother and baby would die a slow and painful death after approximately seventy-two hours of agony.

So it is in this light that we should examine the labor of Jesus.

The four Gospels of Matthew, Mark, Luke, and John give a detailed account of the passion of our Lord. God chose to use four different writers, as the number four in the Bible is associated with the world. Truly, these four books speak to the entire earth of the message of salvation. They indeed are inspired works, which show varying views of the Jesus' life and of his death. In fact, by comparing scriptures from the gospels, when more than one narrative is given on a specific topic, we can get a better focus on the events, timing, and course of Jesus' last hours. The scholastic term for the process of putting the story together like a jigsaw puzzle is called *Scripture buildup.*

Also helpful in putting together the four accounts is an understanding of the perspective each gospel writer is revealing. The first gospel, the one penned by the apostle Matthew, reveals Jesus as the King from heaven. It was written to explain Jesus to the Jewish people, and Matthew consistently refers back to the Old Testament with nearly two hundred references. The term the *kingdom of heaven* is only used in Matthew. The genealogy of Jesus through King David is also emphasized in this wonderful gospel.

Mark's gospel, which is the shortest, pictures Jesus as the servant. Its primary audience is the Roman culture. No genealogy is given, as one would not expect a servant to have a special lineage.

Luke portrays the Messiah's humanness. He is writing primarily to the Greek world. In this gospel, the genealogy of Jesus is connected with the first man, Adam. Jesus emphasizes himself as the Son of Man in this book.

Lastly, the gospel according to John emphasizes Jesus' divinity. His unity with the Father as the Son of God is its central view. This account starts out proclaiming that Jesus is the "Word made flesh" and ends with the statement that the world itself cannot contain the books that should be written about him. John obviously is writing with the whole world in mind!

With these opening remarks, let's dive into the study of the gospel accounts of the Savior's last hours—the study of how he labored to deliver the baby in ways that we, two thousand years later, do not fully appreciate. We will see that time and tradition have dimmed the memory of much of our Lord's passion, like a woman's recall of the pain of labor is minimized after the joy of the baby's arrival!

The Garden Arrest

The scene is in the garden of Gethsemane. It is late at night after the Last Supper and after Jesus had prayed three times to the Father that the cup he was about to suffer would pass. He had agonized in prayer, realizing the enormity of what he was about to undergo. By no coincidence, Gethsemane means *olive press*, and we understand that our hero was pressed greatly from this point forward.

We have seen earlier in our study of the sign of Jonah that Jesus was in the heart of the earth for three days and three nights just as Jonah was in the belly of the great fish for three days and three nights (Matthew 12:40). We also know that Jesus was seen early on the first day of the week; that is, he was first seen on Sunday morning. Thus, counting backwards from there, we understand that our Lord actually died late on Wednesday afternoon, which was Passover that year, the fourteenth of Nisan, and rose from the grave exactly seventy-two hours later.

One of the points to be made in this study is that of an understanding of the timing of the events of Jesus' passion. We will see that far too many things occurred in the four gospel narratives of Jesus' passion to have been sandwiched in an eighteen-hour period, as tradition teaches.

Actually, the setting in the garden of Gethsemane was approximately forty hours prior to our Lord's death. It was late Monday night around midnight, slightly less than two days before the Lord's Passover, which occurred at sunset on Wednesday the fourteenth of Nissan (Leviticus 23:5). We should also note, though, that the Hebrew day started at sunset. Thus it was the day before Jesus' death by their reckoning. It was early on the thirteenth of Nisan with his death near the end of the fourteenth of Nisan. Not coincidentally, this was at the exact time the Passover lambs were being slaughtered for the Passover meal! Truly, as Paul stated in 1 Corinthians, "For even Christ our passover, is sacrificed for us" (5:7b). Jesus is the Passover!

As we have noted, in days gone by, the typical duration for a first time labor of a baby was forty hours. We also know that forty is the number associated with trial in the Bible. Yes, the Lamb of God labored in a picture-perfect way in order to bring forth the baby!

> And while he yet spake, lo, Judas, one of the twelve, came, and with him a great multitude with swords and staves, from the chief priests and elders of the people.
>
> Matthew 26:47

It was Judas, the apostle from Judea, the educated one, the one who had a position of authority being the one who handled the money, who betrayed the Master. Earlier that night, Judas was sitting next to Jesus in a seat of honor at the Last Supper. Significantly, in that culture, if a man shared a meal with another, a bond of trust was forged, and an act of betrayal would be unthinkable. David spoke of the significance of this prophetically as he sang of his own betrayal by the hand of his trusted advisor, Ahithophel. "Yea, mine own familiar friend, in whom I trusted, which did eat of my bread, hath lifted up his heal against me" (Psalm 41:9).

John points out that this act was a fulfillment of Scripture. "I speak not of you all: I know whom I have chosen: But that the scripture may be fulfilled, He that eateth bread with me hath lifted up his heal against me" (John 13:18).

We see that a great multitude came out against Jesus and his disciples, and they were well armed. John's account adds that the multitude was actually a *band* of men and officers (John 18:3). Scholars teach that this group totaled six hundred men. We also see in this account, as well as Mark's and John's, that the men were sent out by the chief priests, Pharisees, scribes, and elders (Mark 14:43, John 18:3). The leaders of the nation were clearly driving this murderous plot.

History tells us that Caiaphas, the high priest, was of the sect of the Sadducees. We understand that the Sadducees and the Pharisees often did not see eye to eye, but in this case—their plan to destroy Jesus of Nazareth—they were united in one purpose.

> Now he that betrayed him gave them a sign, saying, Whomsoever I shall kiss, that same is he: Hold him fast. And forthwith he came to Jesus, and said, Hail, master; and kissed him. And Jesus said unto him, Friend, wherefore art thou come?
>
> Matthew 26:48–50a

The night was lit by the nearly full moon of the Passover week, but Judas and the leaders were concerned that Jesus could escape into the darkness of the garden, and thus the sign of a kiss was prepared. Judas knew that he could likely use his position as one of the men in Jesus' inner circle to get the captors close to the one they so desperately wanted to arrest. The irony, of course, is that in the Eastern mind, a kiss is a sign of friendship. An Eastern man would never betray another with a kiss. In our culture, this would be the same as a man marrying a woman and then immediately sneaking away with one of the bridesmaids while the wedding party was still in progress!

We must note that Jesus, always the loving and merciful one, calls Judas friend. Even this late in the game, Jesus is opening the door for Judas to repent!

At this point in the story, John includes some new information, which is wonderfully pertinent.

> Jesus therefore, knowing all things that should come upon him, went forth, and said unto them, Whom seek ye? They answered him, Jesus of Nazareth. Jesus saith, unto them, *I am* he. And Judas also, which betrayed him, stood with them. As soon then as he had said unto them, *I am* he, they fell backward, and fell to the ground. Then asked he them again, Whom seek ye? And they said, Jesus of Nazareth. Jesus answered, I have told you that *I am* he: If therefore ye seek me, let these go their way: That the saying might be fulfilled, which he spake, Of them which thou gavest me have I lost none.
>
> John 18:4–8 (emphasis mine)

When you think about it, this scene is truly comical! Six hundred men armed to the teeth come out and one man steps forward and knocks down the entire band with the force of his words. Of course, those words were incredibly powerful as Jesus said three times I AM he! We remember when Moses asked God his name, he told him it is I AM THAT I AM (Exodus 3:14). God told Moses that he is I AM. He is whatever we need! In this case, man needs a Savior and Jesus connects himself as one with the Father in revealing his name to the captors as I AM.

But the doubter of this point may say that Jesus said I am he, not I AM. But look closer. In the King James Version of the Bible, the translators place a word in italics when it is not found in the original text. When they add a word for clarity, they correctly tell us. As you will note, in each of these three instances, the word *he* is in italics. The translators admit that they added this word to Jesus' answer as they thought it made more sense. My point is they are wrong! The italicized words are not inspired by God. Jesus could not topple over six hundred men by saying, "Here I am," but he could by saying, "I am God!"

> Then came they, and laid hands on Jesus, and took him. And, behold, one of them which were with Jesus stretched out his hand, and drew his sword, and struck a servant of the high priest's, and smote off his ear.
>
> Matthew 26:50b-51

Nevertheless, the men laid hands upon Jesus. I can imagine that after being embarrassed by him that this was not a gentle scene! This change, of course, for Jesus inspired one of his companions into action! He drew a sword, which was more correctly a large knife, and cut the servant of the high priest's ear off! John adds that it was Simon Peter who drew the sword and that the servant's name was Malchus (John 18:10).

It is likely that the other gospel writers did not include the information that Peter was the swordsman because their accounts were written before Peter's death. They did not want to implicate him should those in authority choose to prosecute him for this crime.

I find the naming of Peter and Malchus intriguing for two reasons. First, we know that Peter told the Lord earlier that night that he would not forsake him even if all others did. Of course, we know that Peter did deny the Lord later in the evening, but here, in the garden, Peter is being true to his words. He is fighting for his Lord!

The second point is that John gives us the name of the injured servant. Now remember, John penned this gospel many years after the events occurred. To include the servant's name implies that this person was well known to the contemporary readers of his gospel. Could it be that Malchus became a follower of Jesus Christ through his experience of this night?

Luke, in his gospel, includes the information that Jesus touched the ear of the wounded servant and healed him (Luke 22:51). I think it very likely indeed that Malchus became a committed believer in Jesus as the Messiah at that point!

> Then said Jesus unto him, Put up again thy sword into his place: For all they that take the sword shall perish with the sword.
>
> Matthew 26:52

This remark is only included in Matthew's gospel. Obviously, this verse is both literal and figurative. Sermons throughout our age of grace have been penned discussing the implications of this great statement.

I will briefly focus on the figurative analogies herein. The best way is to place it alongside other words of God!

> But if ye bite and devour one another, take heed that ye be not consumed one of another.
>
> Galatians 5:15

Also:

> Be not deceived: God is not mocked: for whatsoever a man soweth, that shall he also reap. For he that soweth to his flesh shall of the flesh reap corruption: But he that soweth to the Spirit shall of the Spirit reap life everlasting.
>
> Galatians 6:7–8

And:

Blessed are the merciful: For they shall obtain mercy.

Matthew 5:7

Lastly:

For he shall have judgment without mercy, that hath showed no mercy; and mercy rejoiceth against judgment.

James 2:13

It is clear from God's Word that our actions, whether good or bad, will come back on us!

John alone includes a statement which was made next.

Then said Jesus unto Peter, Put up thy sword into the sheath: The cup which my Father hath given me, shall I not drink it?

John 18:11

Jesus is somewhat sarcastically asking Peter if he would rather not have him do the Father's will. "Peter, would you rather I not take the cup of wrath for your sins as well as for the sins of the whole world?"

Earlier that evening, Jesus had prayed exactly that. He asked the Father three times to take away the cup he was about to suffer if there was any other way. The agony of the prayer caused our Lord to sweat blood! The answer was that there was no other way.

Thinkest thou that I cannot now pray to my Father, and he shall presently give me more than twelve legions of angels?

Matthew 26:53

The traitor was accompanied by a band of six hundred men. Yet our Lord had at his disposal more than twelve legions of angels. Now to appreciate the impact of this statement, it helps to understand that a legion is the largest unit of the Roman army. It includes infantry and cavalry and numbers twelve thousand. Thus Jesus told Peter that if he had so desired he could pray to the Father and more than 144,000 angels would immediately come to his rescue!

When I consider this, I am humbled by our Lord's restraint. His actions and ways are so different than mine! He truly practiced what he preached. He said to turn the other cheek, and that's what he did!

> But how then shall the scriptures be fulfilled, that thus it must be? In that same hour said Jesus to the multitudes, Are ye come out as against a thief with swords and staves for to take me? I sat daily with you teaching in the temple, and ye laid no hold on me. But all this was done, that the scriptures of the prophets might be fulfilled. Then all the disciples forsook him, and fled.
>
> Matthew 26:54–56

Luke adds in his account of this statement that this was their hour and the hour of the power of darkness (Luke 22:53b).

Matthew, Mark, and Luke include this question of Jesus. The irony of the mob's action is not missed by Jesus in their taking him under the cover of night when he was daily present in the temple.

Thus ends this early labor pang, that of the garden arrest, which occurred around midnight on the thirteenth of Nisan. Again, the timing was approximately forty hours before our Lord's death, and the account of the arrest is found in all four gospels in varying degree of detail (Matthew 26:47–56, Mark 14:43–52, Luke 22:47–53, John 18:2–12).

Appearance Before Annas

The Savior was taken next to Annas for the first of three illegal trials. John gives us the details.

> Then the band and the captain and the officers of the Jews took Jesus, and bound him, and led him away to Annas first; for he was father-in-law to Caiaphas, which was the high priest that same year. Now Caiaphas was he, which gave council to the Jews, that it was expedient that one man should die for the people.
>
> John 18:12–14

We learn from John that before Jesus was tried by Caiaphas and the entire Sanhedrin, Jesus had a relatively private audience with Annas, who was Caiaphas's father-in-law. The reason scholars believe this occurred was that Annas was the real powerbroker of the Jewish priesthood. Annas was the high priest from AD 7 through 14, and five of his sons were the high priests before his son-in-law, Caiaphas, was promoted to the position.

It is germane to the story to understand that the appointment to the position of high priest had been terribly corrupted by this time. Originally, God ordained Aaron and his sons to the position, but now the Romans were deciding who would be the high priest. Apparently Annas was connected to the Romans and was able to have a family business in his position as former high priest.

Under Annas, an extortion racket prospered. Worshipers traveling great distances to Jerusalem would fear bringing their own animals to sacrifice, as the priests would often deem them blemished and thus unfit to sacrifice to the Lord. Thus the priests under Annas's lead were able to sell multitudes of their unblemished animals for sacrifice—all of this at a nice profit, of course!

Also, the priests were in charge of the moneychangers. Since Rome was in control of the territory, Roman money was in circulation. But when pilgrims traveled to the temple, they would need to change their Roman money for Judean shekels, again, a profitable opportunity for Annas and his family!

This was not the first time that the Jewish priestly position was corrupted in regard to the sacrifices of the people. You may remember how the sons of Eli were also stealing the sacrifices that the worshipers were bringing to the tabernacle during the Prophet Samuel's early years at Shiloh (1 Samuel 2:12–17).

Now we understand that our hero had a problem with these godless activities. His righteous anger flared upon two separate occasions due to this type of extortion. He cleansed the Temple as he overturned the moneychangers' tables and drove out the animal dealers early in his public ministry when he visited Jerusalem during the Passover celebration (John 2:13–17). Then more recently—earlier in the week we are discussing—Jesus cast out the sellers and overthrew the moneychangers' tables after riding into the city in that famous Messianic procession (Matthew 21:12–13). Thus it's not difficult to believe that Annas held hatred in his heart toward Jesus. This prophet from Nazareth had to be silenced!

Annas's purpose during this late-night audience with our Lord was to listen to Jesus' story and then trump up a charge so an indictment could be brought before the entire Sanhedrin, which was being gathered at the adjacent house of Caiaphas.

> The high priest (John calls Annas the high priest, again indicating between the lines where the real power resided!) then asked Jesus of his disciples, and of his doctrine.
>
> John 18:19

Don't think for a minute that Annas wanted to hear words from the greatest rabbi of Israel. This was his attempt to twist a response into something that could be used against his enemy.

Of course, Jesus was not going to fall for that pathetic ploy, for the Bible says of Jesus, "In whom *(Jesus)* are hid all the treasures of wisdom and knowledge" (Colossians 2:3).

> Jesus answered him, I spake openly to the world: I ever taught in the synagogue, and in the temple, whither the Jews always resort; and in secret have I said nothing. Why askest thou me? Ask them which heard me, what I have said unto them: Behold, they know what I said.
>
> John 18:20–21

Jesus saw straight through this trap and mocked the outrageousness of this meeting, which was against all legal precedents of both the Jews and of the Romans. Specifically, our Lord pointed out that a legal indictment was to come from others and not from the accused. He was alluding to the proper way that a formal charge was to be brought forth and that was at the mouth of two or three witnesses (Deuteronomy 17:16).

The verbal beating Annas took resulted in a physical beating given to the Savior.

> And when he had thus spoken, one of the officers that stood by struck Jesus with the palm of his hand, saying, Answerest thou the high priest so? Jesus answered him, If I have spoken evil, bear witness of the evil: But if well, why smitest thou me? Now Annas had sent him bound unto Caiaphas the high priest.
>
> John 18:22–24

Jesus retorted that he had responded to Annas according to the Law, and he again clearly separated his righteous actions from their unrighteous ones.

Thus, with that defeat, Annas sent the accused across the common courtyard to the large home of Caiaphas where the entire Sanhedrin had gathered for their illegal nighttime inquisition.

The Night Trial

Fifty-one verses in the gospel accounts are dedicated to the first trial, the illegal nighttime trial (Matthew 26:57–75, Mark 14:53–72, Luke 22:54–65, John 18:24–27). Only seven verses cover the legal daytime trial (Matthew 27:1, Mark 15:1, Luke 22:66–71). Thus, most casual readers of the Bible have missed that two trials occurred. But with a close reading of all four narratives, it is clear that our Lord appeared before Caiaphas and the Sanhedrin twice. The short second trial was the one the group considered official as it occurred in the morning (during daytime), as was proper according to Hebrew jurisprudence.

During this nighttime trial, all four writers speak of Peter's denials, but Matthew and Mark give us much insight into Jesus' plight, whereas Luke includes only one new insight, and John does not speak of either trial proceeding other than to mention that it was occurring during Peter's last two denials.

John had the benefit of knowing that the other writers had included an inspired summary of the trials before Caiaphas and the Sanhedrin, but he saw that the appearance before Annas had not yet been revealed to the Christians. Thus he filled in the information we discussed of Jesus before Annas to complete the account for us.

For the nighttime trial, we will use Mark's account as our main text with reference to Matthew and Luke as needed for further clarity.

> And they led Jesus away to the high priest: And with him were assembled all the chief priests and the elders and the scribes. And the chief priests and all the council sought for witness against Jesus to put him to death; and found none.
>
> Mark 14:53, 55

This trial wasn't about finding innocence or guilt. They had already decided Jesus needed to die. This was about coming up with a charge that could stick with the Romans since Annas had been unsuccessful in his private endeavor.

As an aside, scholars believe that Annas had officially been deposed from his high priest's position earlier by the Romans for just this scenario: that of executing capital punishment without Roman consent. Thus, the need for a formal charge was becoming palpable!

> For many bare false witness against him, but their witness agreed not together.
>
> Mark 14:56

The Law clearly stated that two or three witnesses were required to establish that a crime had been committed. Also, it proclaimed that if a false witness arose, and it was determined that the witness was indeed false, then that witness would receive the same punishment that would have been dealt out to the accused (Deuteronomy 19:15–20).

> And there arose certain, and bare false witness against him, saying, We heard him say, I will destroy this temple that is made with hands, and within three days I will build another made without hands. But neither so did their witness agree together.
>
> Mark 14:57–59

Is that what Jesus said? Of course not. He didn't say he was going to destroy the temple. He said, "Destroy this temple, and in three days I will raise it up" (John 2:19).

He was saying that if you destroy me, the temple of my body, I will raise it up in three days. He said this to the Jews three years earlier. It was after he had overturned the moneychangers' tables and drove out the animal sellers that the Jews asked for a sign for his authority to do such a thing. He said my resurrection will be the sign of my authority!

Pathetically, the leaders were reaching back far in time in order to find anything that might stick. This sort of reminds me of some of the false witnesses that come forward from a man's past in our present-day political campaigns! Nothing's really changed!

> And the high priest stood up in the midst, and asked Jesus, saying, Answerest thou nothing? What is it which these witness against thee? But he held his peace and answered nothing.
>
> Mark 14:60–61a

Continuing in the similar vein that he took with Annas, Jesus did not respond to these bogus charges. He chose not to give them anything to use to incriminate him.

But this was about to change!

> Again the high priest asked him, and said unto him, Art thou the Christ, the Son of the Blessed?
>
> Mark 14:61b

Matthew put the question this way: "And the high priest answered and said unto him, I adjure thee by the living God, that thou tell us whether thou be the Christ, the Son of God" (Matthew 26:63).

This question from the high priest in this format put a legal demand upon Jesus to answer. It is similar to our present-day court subpoena. If we do not respond, we are held in contempt of court. This was now the dilemma our Lord was in. He was compelled to answer. And answer he did!

> And Jesus said, I am: And ye shall see the Son of man sitting on the right hand of power, and coming in the clouds of heaven.
>
> Mark 15:62

Earlier in the garden when the mob asked if he was Jesus of Nazareth, he responded I AM. Now responding to Caiaphas, we see Jesus use God's name in answer to his identity. Then, after this strong affirmative answer to the question, the Savior gave a stirring prophecy of his future power and glory—a prophecy that is yet to be fulfilled but one that all will see one day!

Jesus alluded to Daniel the prophet, who spoke also of the Son of Man.

> I saw in the night visions, and, behold, one like the Son of man came with the clouds of heaven, and came before the Ancient of days, and they brought him near before him. And there was given to him dominion, and glory, and a kingdom, that all people, nations, and languages, should serve him: His dominion is an everlasting dominion, which shall not pass away, and his kingdom that which shall not be destroyed.
>
> Daniel 7:13–14

> Then the high priest rent his clothes, and saith, What need we any further witnesses? Ye heard the blasphemy: What think ye? And they all condemned him to be guilty of death.
>
> Mark 14:63–64

Now, Caiaphas had what he so desperately wanted. Until this point, he was not sure the Sanhedrin would have the resolve to push for the death penalty. He may have feared they might settle for some lesser punishment. But the position of Jesus as the Messiah, the Son of God, the Jewish leadership was not ready to accept. The entire Sanhedrin voted that Jesus should die. They were in effect saying, "We shall not have this man rule over us."

They still had the problem that this charge may not be enough for the Romans though. But it was a start, and it was something we will see they built upon in their dealings with the Roman governor Pontius Pilate.

Two subtle points concerning these events need to be brought forward at this point. First, we see that the entire governing body voted against our Lord. I am told that according to Jewish tradition, a unanimous decision immediately disqualified the verdict as biased! It is probable that believers in Jesus as the Messiah, which were in the Sanhedrin (Nicodemus and Joseph of Arimathea), voted for the verdict for just this reason. They were hoping that the judgment would be ruled illegal. As we know, this did not happen!

Secondly, Caiaphas rent his clothes in a bogus attempt to show how shocking this statement was to him. The renting of a man's clothes was a sign of grief in the Eastern mind. Yet the Law specifically forbade those in priestly ministry from displaying their grief in this manner. In fact, God told Moses that renting of the clothes would disqualify a man from the priesthood (Leviticus 10:6 and 21:10). Thus this act symbolically marked the transfer of the Jewish high priesthood from Caiaphas, and those that would follow him, to Jesus, whom the Bible calls the Great High Priest (Hebrews 4:14).

> And some began to spit on him, and to cover his face, and to buffet him, and to say unto him, Prophesy: And the servants did strike him with the palms of their hands.
>
> Mark 14:65

Luke adds that the men mocked Jesus, and after blindfolding his eyes, they taunted him to reveal to the onlookers which of them had struck him on his face (Luke 22:63–64).

Obviously, Jesus could have answered those taunts to their amazement. Yet once again our Lord demonstrated superhuman restraint in allowing his Father's will to be done over the natural inclination that he and we all possess.

One comment concerning the spitting our Lord took. In our day, if a man spits into the face of another, it would be at least scandalous, and, at worst, it could escalate into a murderous rage. As bad as this would be to us, multiply the reaction for the Jewish mindset. This was the ultimate insult, which would be considered unforgivable in their culture. Thankfully for mankind, God's ways are higher than our ways (Isaiah

56:9). The Savior does forgive us even of this insult, which he received in atoning for our sins.

Almost simultaneous to the buffeting Jesus took for his statement to Caiaphas was the last denial of Peter in the courtyard. Jesus was painfully aware of Peter's loss of faith and nerve, and at this point Luke adds some new information for us. He revealed, "And the Lord turned, and looked upon Peter" (Luke 22:61a).

This look was certainly not a look of condemnation but one of sorrow and grace. We recall Noah's story in a similar vein. God was preparing to pronounce judgment upon the face of the earth due to the wickedness that abounded, yet the Bible says, "But Noah found grace in the eyes of the Lord" (Genesis 6:8).

Indeed, God was preparing to pronounce judgment upon the Messiah for *our* wickedness, yet Peter found grace in his eyes!

Thus the beating our Lord took ended the night trial. The time was in the wee hours of Tuesday the thirteenth of Nisan. It was approximately thirty hours before our Lord was crucified, which was 9:00 a.m., Wednesday the fourteenth. The Jewish leaders had the charge they intended to use in obtaining judgment against Jesus from the governor. But they still had a problem even they in their zeal to kill Jesus understood. They knew that criminals were to be tried in the daytime. Thus Jesus was put in hold, likely in a pit below Caiaphas's house, to await daybreak and the "legal" trial.

The gospels do not indicate this event, but David, as well as the psalmist Heman, gives us multiple prophetic pictures of this incarceration in Psalms 57:6, 69:15, 142:7 and 88:1–7.

> O Lord God of my salvation, I have cried day and night before thee: Let my prayer come before thee: Incline thine ear unto my cry: For my soul is full of troubles: And my life draweth nigh unto the grave. I am counted with them that go down into the pit: I am as a man that hath no strength:

Free among the dead, like the slain that lie in the grave, whom thou rememberest no more: And they are cut off from thy hand. Thou hast laid me in the lowest pit, in darkness, in the deeps. Thy wrath lieth hard upon me, and thou hast afflicted me with all thy waves.

Psalm 88:1–7

Tradition teaches that this pit was below the site that today is believed to be the home of Caiaphas. It is located upon Mount Zion just outside of the southwest sector of the old city. It is indeed a dark and dank place where Jesus may have hopelessly waited out the night in prayer, all the while laying his heart before the Father.

The Day Trial

After sunrise, Matthew and Mark mention the second trial and Luke gives the details (Matthew 27:1, Mark 15:1, Luke 22:66–71).

And as soon as it was day, the elders of the people and the chief priests and the scribes came together, and led him into their council, saying, Art thou the Christ? Tell us. And he said unto them, If I tell you, ye will not believe: And if I also ask you, ye will not answer me, nor let me go. Hereafter shall the Son of man sit on the right hand of the power of God. Then said they all, Art thou then the Son of God? And he said unto them, Ye say that I am. And they said, What need we any further witness? For we ourselves have heard of his own mouth.

Luke 22:66–71

Jesus, realizing the Jews would not believe his claim as Messiah, the Son of God, nonetheless confessed to his own detriment that he is indeed the Messiah, the Son of Man, the Son of God. Once again he said that he is I AM!

Jesus' First Appearance Before Pilate

Matthew, Mark, and John do not differentiate between the first and second appearance before Pontius Pilate. Only Luke gives us the extra information that Jesus' audience before Herod was sandwiched between his appearances before Pilate. By comparing the narratives of Matthew, Mark, and John with Luke, we can learn what happened at each of these meetings before the procurator Pilate.

> And the whole multitude of them arose, and led him unto Pilate. And they began to accuse him, saying, We found this fellow perverting the nation, and forbidding to give tribute to Caesar, saying that he himself is Christ a King.
>
> Luke 23:1–2

Notice that the leaders did not tell Pilate that Jesus was a blasphemer, that Jesus claimed to be the Messiah. They knew Pilate would not care for such religious matters. The leaders knew that their rhetoric needed to put Jesus between Pilate and Caesar. Thus they used the threat that Jesus wanted to set up a kingdom that could challenge Rome itself. Of course, Pilate knew this wasn't the Jews' real agenda. So he interviewed Jesus himself.

> And Pilate asked him, saying, Art thou the King of the Jews?
>
> Luke 23:3a

Pilate understood immediately what was happening! He asked Jesus if he was "the King of the Jews." He was asking Jesus not if he was a king, but if he was *the* King. He realized this was about a messianic claim!

> And he answered him and said, Thou sayest it. Then said Pilate to the chief priests and to the people, I find no fault in this man.
>
> Luke 23:3b–4

Jesus confirmed to Pilate that he indeed was the Jewish Messiah. This did not seem to fluster or worry Pilate as he told the chief priests that he found no fault in Jesus. Surely, though, Pilate did not understand just how true his statement was. Indeed, this man had no fault!

> And they were the more fierce, saying, He stirreth up the people, teaching throughout all Jewry, beginning from Galilee to this place. When Pilate heard of Galilee, he asked whether the man were a Galilean. And as soon as he knew that he belonged unto Herod's jurisdiction, he sent him to Herod, who himself also was at Jerusalem at that time.
>
> Luke 23:5–7

The Jews were relentless in their desire to condemn Jesus. After their initial arguments were rebuffed by Pilate, they became fierce using a ridiculous argument—one without any meaning—that Jesus must be stopped because he stirred up the common people from Galilee to Jerusalem.

How glad Pilate must have been when he learned that Jesus might not be his problem. Since Herod, the tetrarch of Galilee, was in the city, it seemed expedient to send Jesus and the Jews away, hoping Herod could settle the affair.

But before we look at Jesus' interaction with Herod, there is additional information concerning this first appearance before Pontius Pilate, which the Apostle John describes to us.

> Then led they Jesus from Caiaphas unto the hall of judgment: And it was early; and they themselves went not into

the judgment hall, lest they should be defiled; but that they might eat the Passover.

John 18:28

It is clear from this verse, as well as John 19:31, that the Passover had not yet occurred. The Last Supper was not the Passover meal, despite what tradition has taught. Jesus had shared his last meal with his disciples, but the Jews were still in preparation for the Passover meal.

Because Passover had not yet arrived, they did not want to go into the judgment hall, as their presence inside a Roman governmental site would defile them. What an irony! They wouldn't go into Pilate's court to avoid temporary defilement, but in seeking the death of Jesus, they permanently defiled themselves!

Pilate then went out unto them, and said, What accusation bring ye against this man? They answered and said unto him, If he were not a malefactor, we should not have delivered him up unto thee. Then said Pilate unto them, Take ye him, and judge him according to your law. The Jews therefore said unto him, It is not lawful for us to put any man to death: That the saying of Jesus might be fulfilled, which he spake, signifying what death he should die.

John 18:29–32

Although he didn't have to, Pilate went out to the Jews to listen to their accusations. After listening to the leaders, he told them to deal with Jesus according to their law. He may have even been indicating that he would look the other way should the Jews stone Jesus according to the Law. But it was at that point that the true intention of the Jews came forth. They were looking for Pilate to pronounce the death penalty. They likely feared a backlash from the people if they stoned Jesus yet understood that a Roman execution would be hard for the people to come against them for. Thus they used the Roman prohibition against their administration of capitol punishment to their benefit. They wanted Jesus to suffer the Roman method of execution: crucifixion! They desired for Jesus that terrible method of capital punishment devised by the Romans to terrorize the people of their conquered nations, the method of death that no Roman would have to suffer was what the Jews wanted for one of their own!

Indeed, John points out that Jesus had said that crucifixion would be his fate (John 12:32–33).

> Then Pilate entered into the judgment hall again, and called Jesus, and said unto him, Art thou the King of the Jews? Jesus answered him, Sayest thou this thing of thyself, or did others tell it thee of me? Pilate answered, Am I a Jew? Thine own nation and the chief priests have delivered thee unto me: What hast thou done? Jesus answered, My kingdom is not of this world: If my kingdom were of this world, then would my servants fight, that I should not be delivered to the Jews: But now is my kingdom not from hence. Pilate therefore said unto him, Art thou a king then? Jesus answered, Thou sayest that I am a king. To this end was I born, and for this cause came I into the world, that I should bear witness unto the truth. Every one that is of the truth heareth my voice. Pilate saith unto him, What is truth? And when he had said this, he went out again unto the Jews, and saith unto them, I find in him no fault at all.
>
> John 18:33–38

Jesus not only witnessed the truth, but he told his followers that he *is* the truth (John 14:6) that Pilate was not willing to see or understand.

Nevertheless, at that point, he told the Jews that he had found no fault in Jesus. He may have been willing to turn a blind eye to a Jewish execution, but he was not at this point going to rubber stamp a Roman execution.

Subsequently, according to Luke, Pilate learned from the Jews that Jesus was from Galilee, and thus he sent the Savior to Herod for judgment.

Jesus Before Herod

And when Herod saw Jesus, he was exceeding glad: For he was desirous to see him of a long season, because he had heard many things of him; and he hoped to have seen some miracle done by him.

Luke 23:8

Herod was the grandson of Herod the Great. The later was most remembered for his brutality. The Bible documents his actions in the region of Bethlehem upon learning of the Messiah's birth when he ordered the killing of all the children from two years old and under.

The grandson of Herod the Great, Herod the tetrarch, was cut from the same cloth. They were related to the Jews as sons of Abraham, but they were not sons of Jacob. They were Idumeans. This was the Greek name for the land of Edom. The Herods were children of Esau, the father of Edom!

The Bible has much to say about Esau as well as Israel's relationship with Edom. And not much of it is good! So with this we can now sense the tension in our Lord's heart at standing before Herod, this son of Esau.

You may also remember that Herod had reluctantly beheaded John the Baptist after making an ill-advised oath to his stepdaughter in front of many important men during a drunken celebration. Thus, when Jesus' fame had reached Herod, he openly wondered if Jesus were John risen again from the dead (Matthew 14:1–2). So he was glad to finally meet Jesus as he wanted to see a miracle performed by the man from Galilee.

Then he questioned with him in many words; but he answered him nothing.

Luke 23:9

Once again Jesus was silent. And this time nothing Herod could say would compel our Lord to give him the satisfaction of a word from him. Isaiah describes it prophetically in these terms: "He was oppressed, and he was afflicted, yet he opened not his mouth: He is brought as a lamb to the slaughter, and as a sheep before her shearers is dumb, so he opened not his mouth" (Isaiah 53:7).

> And the chief priests and the scribes stood and vehemently accused him. And Herod with his men of war set him at naught, and mocked him, and arrayed him in a gorgeous robe, and sent him again to Pilate. And the same day Pilate and Herod were made friends together: For before they were at enmity between themselves.
>
> Luke 23:10–12

Once again the Jewish leaders vocally accused Jesus of capital crimes in the fear that Herod may not see the gravity of the situation and let the rabbi free. To their relief, Herod did not do that. Instead, he had his military guard set Jesus at naught. That means they mistreated him. They physically and verbally abused our Lord. They mocked the claim of Jesus as Messiah by adorning him with a robe of a king. Indeed, it may have been one of Herod's robes that was used in this satire! Lastly, Herod and Pilate became friends that day by showing respect toward each other. First, Pilate deferred Jesus to Herod when he learned he was a Galilean. Then Herod returned the favor by deferring final judgment to Pilate as they were on the latter's home turf in Judea. Again, irony is seeping out as the two earthly kings respected each other for the first time while totally disrespecting the King of kings!

With that, it was back to Pilate for Jesus' second and distinctly more torturous appearance before the governor.

Now with the day trial before the Sanhedrin, as well as the first appearance before Pilate and the audience before Herod complete, the day was fast passing by. We must now cover the appearance before the procurator where Jesus was scourged and sentenced. This was an audience where we will see that Pilate appealed three separate times to the Jews for mercy toward Jesus. Even without adding in the traveling time between the stops, it is clear that the day we are studying is not the day Jesus died. We will see that the Lord was crucified at the third hour, or 9:00 a.m., on the fourteenth of Nisan (Mark 15:25). The time in question now is late morning, the thirteenth of Nisan, slightly less than twenty-four hours before Jesus was nailed to the cross and slightly more than twenty-four hours before his death for you and me.

Jesus' Second Appearance Before Pilate

All four authors give details to us of the terrible labor pangs Jesus endured during this second appearance before Pilate (Matthew 27:11–25, Mark 15:2–14, Luke 23:13–23, John 18:39–19:15). Luke reveals that Pilate appealed to the priests and the people three times to accommodate his desire to release Jesus.

"And he said unto them the third time, Why, what evil hath he done? I find no cause of death in him" (Luke 23:22a).

The casual reader may miss that these three statements of Pilate's were at separate settings, but by comparing the narratives, we will see that Pilate interfaced with the people three distinct times over the fate of Jesus.

Matthew gives us the most detail of Pilate's first appeal

to the accusers while all of the writers mention it (Matthew 27:11–18, Mark 15:2–11, Luke 23:13–19, John 18:39–40).

> And Jesus stood before the governor: And the governor asked him, saying, Art thou the King of the Jews? And Jesus said unto him, Thou sayest. And when he was accused of the chief priests and elders, he answered nothing. Then said Pilate unto him, Hearest thou how many things they witness against thee? And he answered him never a word; insomuch that the governor marveled greatly.
>
> Matthew 27:11–14

Pilate, as a judge over the people, was accustomed to guilty men arguing their innocence. But by this he was surprised— an innocent man not fighting for his innocence! Of course, Jesus did not need to claim to Pilate that he was free of guilt. He had already heard the procurator state that fact. Now it was completely up to how much integrity Pilate could muster. Could he stand strong in the face of the political pressures he had come under? Or would he give in to the mob? We know that he couldn't. Jesus was aware of that also!

> Now at the feast the governor was wont to release unto the people a prisoner, whom they would. And they had a notable prisoner, called Barabbas. Therefore when they were gathered together, Pilate said unto them, Whom will ye that I release unto you? Barabbas, or Jesus which is called Christ? For he knew that for envy they had delivered him.
>
> Matthew 27:15–18

Mark and Luke add that Barabbas had committed murder in an insurrection. John notes also that he was a robber. Barabbas was apparently a dangerous man whom Pilate believed the people would not want to see released for fear that he might kill again. Unfortunately, Mark states, "But the chief priests moved the people, that he should rather release Barabbas unto them" (Mark 15:11).

Incredibly, the people chose Barabbas, whose name ironically means "son of the father," instead of Jesus, the true "Son of the Father."

John tells us what happened next, and it was not good.

> But ye have a custom, that I should release unto you one at the Passover: Will ye therefore that I release unto you the King of the Jews? Then cried they all again, saying, Not this man, but Barabbas. Now Barabbas was a robber. Then Pilate therefore took Jesus, and scourged him. And the soldiers platted a crown of thorns, and put on him a purple robe, and said, Hail, King of the Jews! And they smote him with their hands.
>
> John 18:39–19:3

I cannot fathom how bad those last thirty-seven words are! Almost out of the blue, Pilate decided to send this innocent man to be scourged. Somehow through his warped sense of fair play, Pilate must have hoped that a Roman scourging would satisfy the bloodlust of the people! Often though, a person would not even survive the ordeal.

The process was sickening! The victim would be tied naked with his arms outstretched to a pole so that his feet would barely touch the ground. The man's back would thus be stretched so that maximum damage and pain could be delivered. The whip would have pieces of bone, glass, metal, and stone attached to the end of leather straps. A man skilled in its use would then deliver blows in a diagonal direction across the back and buttocks. Deep lacerations would occur with the whip ripping out large chunks of flesh and muscle. Sometimes the injuries would expose the kidneys or rip open arteries. Of course, those latter two injuries would be fatal!

Then after the brutal scourging, the taunting began by the Romans. An incredibly painful crown of thorns was pressed into the scalp of our Lord. The pain of this likely even eclipsed the humiliation that followed. The soldiers then smote Jesus while sarcastically believing the King of the Jews was receiving what a Jewish king deserved. They apparently enjoyed the free reign they had been given to administer torture to a previously popular Jewish figure!

> Pilate therefore went forth again, and said unto them, Behold, I bring him forth to you, that ye may know that I find no fault in him. Then came Jesus forth, wearing the crown of thorns, and the purple robe. And Pilate saith unto them, Behold the man!
>
> John 19:4–5

This picture is beyond words to me! There stood the King of kings beaten to a bloody pulp, wearing not a crown of leaves but one of thorns. Those sharp thorns pierced our Lord's scalp and left dried blood across the now grotesque looking figure. It was a figure that inspired Pilate to utter that memorable remark, that remark which to this day is quoted by those who are not even aware of Jesus' story: Behold the Man! Look what you and I have done to him! He was mocking the Jews in a way, for he knew they were not yet satisfied!

> When the chief priests therefore and officers saw him, they cried out, saying, Crucify him, crucify him. Pilate saith unto them, Take ye him, and crucify him: For I find no fault in him.
>
> The Jews answered him. We have a law, and by our law he ought to die, because he made himself the Son of God. When Pilate therefore heard that saying, he was more afraid.
>
> John 19: 6–8

Now, Pilate was in a terrible bind. He knew Jesus was innocent, yet he wanted to please the Jews and keep the peace. But this latest revelation shocked him to the core. Jesus had already told him that he was a king but that his kingdom was not of this world. Now Pilate learned from the Jews that Jesus claimed to be the Son of God. This was bad for Pilate, and he knew it. He had just had this man brutally scourged. What if Jesus were indeed God's Son? What fear Pilate must have had at that moment. He, as a Roman, was polytheistic. Could it be that the gods were watching in horror? Could it be that he had made the biggest mistake in his life? We know, in retrospect, the answer.

> He went again into the judgment hall, and saith unto Jesus, Whence art thou? But Jesus gave him no answer.
>
> John 19:9

Pilate was ready to explode with anxiety and fear.

> Then saith Pilate unto him, Speakest thou not unto me? Knowest thou not that I have power to crucify thee, and have power to release thee?
>
> John 19:10

Pilate knew Jesus wasn't crazy, yet he was aghast that he was not fighting for his life. Thus one last time he tried to intimidate the Savior into talking. The answer he received was not what he expected.

> Jesus answered, Thou couldest have no power at all against me, except it were given thee from above, therefore he that delivered me unto thee hath the greater sin.
>
> John 19:11

Jesus rejected Pilate's claim to power, spiritualizing the true source of the governor's power. He then confirmed Pilate's guilt. The Lord also stated that he shared that guilt with Caiaphas and the Jews. This, of course, sent Pilate away speechless. Pilate came out now to the Jews for the third time.

> And from thenceforth Pilate sought to release him: But the Jews cried out, saying, If thou let this man go, thou art not Caesar's friend: Whosoever maketh himself a king speaketh against Caesar.
>
> John 19:12

The vice was tightening. Pilate was getting squeezed! On the one hand, he feared what he may be doing to this holy man, but on the other, he feared what the Jews might be able to do to him. He was afraid they would report to Tiberius the actions of this day, actions that could be construed as treason, that of letting a king, a rival of the emperor, go free.

> When Pilate therefore heard that saying, he brought Jesus forth, and sat down in the judgment seat in a place that is called the Pavement, but in Hebrew, Gabbatha.
>
> John 19:13

Pilate brought Jesus out from the judgment hall, that place where the Jews hypocritically would not enter for fear of defiling themselves, to the pavement, the seat of judgment. Pilate was getting ready to pronounce final and irrevocable judgment upon Jesus.

But first, Matthew shares some information that only confused and frightened the procurator all the more.

> When he was set down on the judgment seat, his wife sent unto him, saying, Have thou nothing to do with that just man: For I have suffered many things this day in a dream because of him.
>
> Matthew 27:19

Wow! Just when Pilate was about to explode from the confusion in his mind, his wife dropped a bombshell! Certainly, the gods were watching this decision! What he didn't understand, though, was that the true God was giving him yet another chance to do the right thing!

Matthew continues with the dialogue.

> But the chief priests and elders persuaded the multitude that they should ask Barabbas, and destroy Jesus. The governor answered and said unto them, Whether of the twain will ye that I release unto you? They said, Barabbas. Pilate saith unto them, What shall I do then with Jesus which is called Christ? They all say unto him, Let him be crucified.
>
> Matthew 27:20–23

John adds that they also proclaimed, "We have no king but Caesar" (John 19:15b).

Before Pilate had Jesus scourged, he had asked the mob to choose between Jesus and Barabbas. Now, at the end of tension-filled drama, he once again gave the Jews the choice. They could choose the Son of the Father (Jesus) or the son of the father (Barabbas). They could choose Christ as their king or antichrist as their king: Jesus, the king from Jerusalem or Caesar, the king from Rome.

Moses stated it very eloquently fourteen hundred years earlier.

> I call heaven and earth to record this day against you, that I have set before you life and death, blessing and cursing: Therefore choose life, that both thou and thy seed may live: That thou mayest love the Lord thy God, and that thou mayest obey his voice, and that thou mayest cleave unto him: For he is thy life, and length of thy days: That thou mayest dwell in the land which the Lord sware unto thy fathers, to Abraham, to Isaac, and to Jacob, to give them.
>
> Deuteronomy 30:19–20

The people were at that crossroad. They could choose life. They could choose the Lord, who is life and the length of days, or they could choose death. They had the opportunity to dwell in the land the Lord promised to the patriarchs, or they could choose to be banished. Unfortunately, we know how they chose.

Jeremiah put their choice in these terms.

> The kings of the earth, and all the inhabitants of the world, would not have believed that the adversary and the enemy should have entered into the gates of Jerusalem. For the sins of her prophets, and the iniquities of her priests, that have shed the blood of the just in the midst of her.
>
> Lamentations 4:12–13

Certainly this Old Testament prophecy was being fulfilled at that very moment. The iniquity of the priests in moving the people to choose to shed the blood of the only just one was about to bring Jerusalem to the ground. For we know only a few decades later the Romans did indeed level the city, destroying and dispersing the people.

> When Pilate saw that he could prevail nothing, but that rather a tumult was made, he took water, and washed his hands before the multitude, saying, I am innocent of the blood of this just person: See ye to it.
>
> Matthew 27:24

Of all the actions and words of Pontius Pilate, these are the ones with which people are most familiar. He washed his hands of Jesus' fate and proclaimed that he was innocent in the bloodshed. Is this true? Of course not! Pilate had the power to stop this unjust lynching at any point. Also, he had *already* shed the Teacher's blood earlier that morning in ordering the scourging of Jesus. No, Pilate was guilty, as Jesus had told him only moments before, and no amount of water was going to clean his hands.

It's interesting to me that this saying is often used by people today. One will say, "I'm washing my hands of this matter." Every time I've heard it said, or used it myself, it was in the same light that Pilate used it. The hands really can't be washed when one gets to the point of using this famous verse.

> Then answered all the people, and said, His blood be on us, and on our children.
>
> Matthew 27:25

How quickly people forget what they say. A short time later In Acts 5, the high priest and the Sadducees had the apostles incarcerated for preaching the gospel. But at night the angel of the Lord broke the men out of prison. Again, early the next day, they were found preaching Jesus in the temple. The high priest then made a telling remark. He said, "Did not we straightly command you that ye should not teach in this name? And, behold, ye have filled Jerusalem with your doctrine, and intend to bring this man's blood upon us" (Acts 5:28).

Only a few months earlier they were happy to have Jesus' blood on their hands! Next, John added a postscript, which is very valuable in understanding the true duration of our Lord's labor pains. With it we can see the full length that the Savior suffered before going to the cross. For indeed we are saved by the blood of the Lamb, and it is by his stripes we are healed. He was to enter a time of torture, a time of stripes, a time that is generally not recognized by the Church today.

> And it was the preparation of the Passover, and about the sixth hour: And he saith unto the Jews, Behold your King!
>
> John 19:14

John clearly reveals that the final judgment upon Jesus by Pontius Pilate occurred about the sixth hour. Scholars agree that this type of time reckoning is based upon the sun and the number of hours it is visible in the sky. Sunrise was approximately 6:00 a.m., making the sixth hour noontime. Now we know from Mark 15:25 that it was the third hour, or 9:00 a.m., when Jesus was crucified. Thus, this day of trial and judgment *cannot* be the same day as the day our Lord died upon the cross! It's not! It was the day before. It was the thirteenth of Nisan. It was the preparation of the Passover. The day before!

It's curious to me that this verse seems to have been disregarded in the modern passion story. The few who have taken it on state that the sixth hour is 6:00 a.m. This, of course, invalidates Mark's time reckoning. If one believes that interpretation, then the third hour that Jesus was crucified must have been 3:00 a.m. No, Jesus was about to spend approximately twenty-one hours of further abuse and degradation laboring for our salvation. Matthew and Mark give us the details nearly identically (Matthew 27:26–31, Mark 15:15–20).

The Praetorium

Then released he Barabbas unto them: And when he had scourged Jesus, he delivered him to be crucified.

Matthew 27:26

And so Pilate, willing to content the people, released Barabbas unto them, and delivered Jesus, when he had scourged him, to be crucified.

Mark 15:15

As we have seen previously, John told us that Jesus was brutally scourged by Pilate in an attempt to satisfy the Jews lust for blood. He was hoping that he could still release Jesus and please the people. Matthew and Mark tell us a different version, don't they? Which is it? Was Jesus scourged before he was judged? Or after? Only one can be right. Not only that, but we have the little problem of the Scripture having an error in it!

Well, there is no error. They are both right because Jesus was scourged twice! Our Lord took a second beating for our healing at this point.

The number two in the Bible is an exclamation point by God. When God repeats himself or repeats an event, it is an exclamation point from our Creator. God is establishing and emphasizing the point he is making (Genesis 41:32). Jesus was whipped twice because the Father wanted us to know beyond a shadow of a doubt that by his Son's stripes we were healed!

This isn't the only time that tradition has Jesus doing one thing while a close study of the gospels reveals Jesus repeating an event in a similar fashion twice in order to establish its importance and meaning. For those so inclined, look at all four gospel accounts of the triumphant entry into Jerusalem on Palm Sunday, the withering of the fig tree, and the temple cleansing. You will see that these events occurred twice over two successive days.

The critical reader will see that on the first of two days during the passion week, Jesus rode into Jerusalem upon a colt, he went into the temple and looked around only, and later that day he cursed a fig tree which did not wither away immediately. On the very next day, Jesus again entered gloriously into Jerusalem, but this time only riding an ass accompanied with a colt. He went into the temple and overthrew the moneychangers on that occasion, and later that day he and the disciples walked by the tree that was withered from the curse the day prior. The teacher used that miracle to teach about the power of faith. Shortly thereafter, they came to a second fig tree, which again had no figs. Jesus cursed this second tree, and it withered immediately! Again Jesus demonstrated believing to his disciples, establishing its importance to our lives!

John ended his gospel with these words:

> And there are also many other things which Jesus did, the which, if they should be written every one, I suppose that even the world itself could not contain the books that should be written. Amen.
>
> John 21:25

God did not intend for any of the gospel accounts to stand by themselves as the complete narrative of Jesus' life, ministry, death, and resurrection. Realizing this very fact allows the concept of Scripture buildup to enliven the gospels in a way that tradition has obscured.

Hang on; we will see yet another example of Scripture buildup in comparing the narratives concerning the criminals crucified with Jesus.

> And the soldiers led him away into the hall, called Praetorium; and they call together the whole band. And they clothed him with purple, and platted a crown of thorns, and

put it about his head. And began to salute him, Hail, King of the Jews! And they smote him on the head with a reed, and did spit upon him, and bowing their knees worshipped him. And when they had mocked him, they took off the purple from him, and put his own clothes on him, and led him out to crucify him.

Mark 15:16–20

Again, this all sounds similar to John's account, John 19:1–5, but a close reading, in context, reveals in cannot be the same event. In John's account, Jesus was scourged before Barabbas was released, he was still being judged, and he reappeared in front of Pilate wearing a purple robe. Obviously in this account, Barabbas had been released, the judgment had occurred with Jesus no longer going before Pilate, and the purple robe had been removed.

Once again we see that in the Praetorium, Jesus was mocked, adorned with a crown of thorns, and spat upon. All of these things happening for the second time on that dreadful day of Tuesday the thirteenth of Nisan.

Lastly, did the soldiers let Jesus rest overnight before they led him out the next morning to his execution? We don't know. The Bible doesn't say. All of the accounts pick up the story the next morning. The morning our Lord was led out like a lamb to the slaughter.

Jesus' Death March

Again the four gospels complement each other with additional information given in each account (Matthew 27:32–34, Mark 15:20–23, Luke 23:26–32, John 19:16–17).

And as they led him away, they laid hold upon one Simon, a
Cyrenian, coming out of the country, and on him they laid
the cross, that he might bear if after Jesus.

Luke 23:26

We can understand that Jesus is in a weakened physical
state. He had a sleepless night during the trials in front of
the Sanhedrin two nights earlier. Then he was scourged and
mocked twice the day prior as part of his dealings with Pilate
and the Romans. Thus, our Lord was likely in the throes of
death from the wounds he had already received. Certainly,
Jesus was in no condition to carry the heavy cross. It was a
cross that likely weighed over two hundred pounds. He was
to carry it out from Jerusalem to Calvary—a march that was
approximately one quarter to one half mile.

Unfortunately for Simon of Cyrene, who was coming into
Jerusalem for the Passover feast, the Romans forced him to
carry the cross of Jesus. This verse is watered down for us two
thousand years later. But to a Jew seeing this, he would have
been aghast at what happened to Simon. The closest example
I can think of to illustrate how bad this was for Simon is this:
Imagine you have two tickets to the Super Bowl, and your
team is in the game. You've traveled far with much expense to
get to the game. But just as you enter the stadium, two secu-
rity agents grab you up and tell you that you are to come with
them. There you are made to serve on a jury to decide the fate
of a homeless man who trespassed in a church. You miss the
game, feeling that fate had betrayed you. This is how Simon
felt. He was coming into Jerusalem to worship the Lord. He
had traveled from Cyrene, a locale in north-central Africa. It
was the fourteenth of Nisan, and he had made it into the city
just in time for the celebration. But then the unexpected happened. The Romans grabbed him and forced him to carry a
condemned man's cross to the place of the Skull! "Okay," you
say. "Just get that over with and get back into Jerusalem for
the celebration. After all, it's only 9:00 a.m." Well, it's not

that simple. As a devout Jew, Simon had prepared himself for the feast. This involvement with Jesus had disqualified him from partaking in the celebration. He was defiled. He was an outcast.

Things could not have been any worse for Simon of Cyrene. Or could they?

Mark adds that Simon was the father of Alexander and Rufus (Mark 15:21).

This is wonderful! Simon's children were known to Mark and the disciples several years later at the time Mark penned these words. Could it be that, like Malchus, the servant of the high priest, Simon too became a believer in Jesus as Messiah as he witnessed the events of that fateful day? How else can we explain that Simon's children were known by the early readers of the gospel? Indeed, something Satan meant for evil—defiling Simon for the feast—God turned to good. Simon was introduced to the Savior.

Spiritualizing this event is also important. Simon carried Jesus' cross. It was something he did not want to do. It was a burden, and only later he learned what blessing and honor he received for all eternity as the man who bore our Lord's cross.

We too are told to take up the cross. The difference is we get a choice. Look at Luke 9:23b: "If any man will come after me, let him deny himself, and take up his cross daily, and follow me."

We have a choice to make daily. Will I deny myself and follow Jesus? Will I take his agenda, his will, and make it my goal, or will I follow after my own agenda, my own thing, and miss out on the blessing that will always follow any pain when I take up the cross? There always is a resurrection after taking up the cross.

> And there followed him a great company of people, and of woman, which also bewailed and lamented him.
>
> Luke 23:27

How terrible this must have been for these people. Both men and women bewailed and lamented Jesus' fate. Earlier, it had appeared that all had forsaken him, but here we see a remnant of true believers who are broken as they stand by observing the cruel and apparent end of the man they called Lord. The women are specifically singled out.

> But Jesus turning unto them said, Daughters of Jerusalem, weep not for me, but weep for yourselves, and your children. For, behold, the days are coming, in the which they shall say, Blessed are the barren, and the wombs that never bare, and the paps which never gave suck.
>
> Luke 23:28–29

Think about what this says to a Jewish woman. For in that day, motherhood was considered a great blessing from God. Unlike today, where women have many hats to wear, the daughters of Jerusalem were one-dimensional. From infancy, to be a wife and mother was the only direction they were pointed toward. In fact, the woman who was barren was considered to be involved in a grievous sin and cursed by God (Leviticus 20:20–21). Thus, for a woman to say, "Blessed are the barren, Blessed are those who never bore a child or nursed a baby," things would have to be terrible. Only the worst kind of disaster would cause the daughters of Jerusalem to say this. But as we know, that's indeed what happened.

> Then shall they begin to say to the mountains, Fall on us; and to the hills, Cover us. For if they do these things in a green tree, what shall be done in the dry?
>
> Luke 23:30–31

Woe to the daughters of Jerusalem for the King from heaven was in their very presence, yet he was killed by their leaders. What could they expect when he was gone? The day was bright and warm, yet they abused the Light of the World; what could they hope for from the future?

And there were also two other, malefactors, led with him to be put to death.

Luke 23:32

This little verse is important to the story and will be developed shortly. For now, notice that these men were two in number, they were malefactors (*kakourgos* in the Greek), and most importantly, they were led out to be crucified *with* Jesus. They were led out at the same time.

And when the were come to *the place,* which is called Calvary,

Luke 23:33a (emphasis mine)

Jesus was taken to *the place.* This place called Calvary was foreshadowed in the Old Testament.

And it came to pass after these things, that God did tempt (test or prove) Abraham, and said unto him, Abraham: And he said, Behold, here I am. And he said, Take now thy son, thine only son Isaac, whom thou lovest, and get the to the land of Moriah; and offer him there for a burnt offering upon one of the mountains which I will tell thee of. And Abraham rose up early in the morning, and saddled his ass, and took two of his young men with him, and Isaac his son, and clave the wood for the burnt offering, and rose up, and went unto *the place* of which God had told him.

Genesis 22:1–3 (emphasis mine)

Abraham's sacrifice of his beloved son, Isaac, was a illustration for the Jews of what God had planned to do in sacrificing his Son. The place that God told Abraham to offer up his son is the exact same hill, Mount Moriah, where God did sacrifice his Son for the sins of the world.

Mark adds some information about this moment.

And they bring him unto the place Golgotha, which is, being interpreted, The place of a skull.

Mark 15:22

I've seen Golgotha. Indeed, even to this day, the face of the hill looks like a skull. It's a rounded granite formation with small caves for the eyes and the mouth, which strikingly resemble a human skull.

Not only was it an eerily perfect setting for the Roman's to use for executions, but it was also the perfect place. It was north of the city gates, on the only side of Jerusalem where travelers did not have to climb a steep incline to enter. Thus, it was well traveled and was an excellent place to display Roman justice.

The Romans may have preferred Golgotha for those reasons, but God pictured this northern spot hundreds of years earlier when he instructed Moses and the children of Israel about the burnt offering, that offering that pictures what Jesus did for you and me.

> If any man of you bring an offering unto the Lord ... If his offering be a burnt sacrifice of the herd, let him offer a male without blemish ... and it shall be accepted for him to make atonement for him ... And he shall kill it on the side of the altar northward before the Lord.
>
> Leviticus 1:2b-3a, 4b, 11a

The Old Testament is full of allusions of this moment. Mark continues:

> And they gave him to drink wine mingled with myrrh: But he received it not.
>
> Mark 15:23

Matthew, speaking of the same event,

> They gave him vinegar to drink mingled with gall: And when he had tasted thereof, he would not drink.
>
> Matthew 27:34

This concoction was meant to be a painkiller in preparation for the excruciating pain that one would experience from the spikes that were driven through the condemned one's hands and feet. Jesus refused the medicine!

This verse is found in the Old Testament. The first half of Psalm 69 is recognized by scholars as prophetic toward the events of this day. Seven quotations from that psalm are found in the New Testament. Specifically, we see in verse 21: "They gave me gall for my meat; and in my thirst they gave me vinegar to drink."

With that, Jesus arrived at the cross.

The Crucifixion of the Christ

Obviously this dark day is documented by all four gospel writers. The brevity is notable, though, as the story is told in only thirty-nine verses (Matthew 27:35–45, Mark 15:24–33, Luke 23:33–44, John 19:18–27). I have chosen to follow Matthew's narrative and will bring in additional information when given by the other writers. Later, we will also look at a few of the many prophecies given in the Old Testament about this time of our Lord's labor for our birth.

And they crucified him...

Matthew 27:35a

Talk about understating one of the most significant events in human history! Four little words! Mark uses the same four words, adding as we have seen, that it was the third hour, or 9:00 a.m. (Mark 15:25).

Possibly, early readers of the gospels did not need this event embellished, as, unfortunately, they were quite familiar with this brutal method of execution. But for us in our day, these four words can speed quickly by as we read the passion story.

Let's not let that happen. Thus we must stop for a moment and talk about this form of capital punishment.

First, the cross was laid upon the ground and the victim was stretched out over it. One or two men would grab each forearm simultaneously and would forcibly pull the arms out wide while another executioner pounded large sharp metal stakes through the condemned man's wrists. The pain at that moment would be indescribable! Next, the soldiers would move to the legs. They would hold one foot on top of the other and pound one nail through both feet into the wooden cross. Often, ropes were tied around the arms in order to stabilize the pinned victim while the cross was lifted up.

The next moment, I am told, is the most painful of all! The soldiers would lift the cross from off the ground to past vertical and then drop the cross into a prefitted hole. The transfer of the victim's weight from the cross to the spikes was a labor pain of incredible intensity. When I think of how bad that must have felt and then remember that Jesus was the only truly innocent man who ever lived, it makes me look at sin in a different light.

After the doomed man was hung in the upright position, time began to take its brutal toll. This was a very slow way to die. The hopeless man would push up off the painful spikes in his feet in order to inhale air. Relaxing back down would let air escape passively. Since the drive for air is such a strong reflex, the pathetic victim would continue this painful process for hours and even days before fatigue, dehydration, and slow asphyxiation would finally lead to the welcome of death.

As if that were not enough, the thirst that ensued was mind-boggling. Birds were free to land upon the victim, as well as insects. Sweat would fill the eyes, and any urge to scratch would obviously go unheeded. Lastly, the condemned was naked. That's right—no clothes.

Luke adds Jesus' first statement from the cross as the Savior was being pinned upon the tree. "Then said Jesus, Father, forgive them; for they know not what they do" (Luke 23:34a).

This, of course, is yet another facet of Jesus which makes him so different from me. Here at this most painful moment of his human life, he is praying for his torturers! I know I would not be doing that. Jesus is just so *other!*

Now, this statement does not mean that Jesus' executioners were automatically forgiven, for we know that forgiveness unto life eternal is dependent upon belief in Jesus as a person's savior. But Jesus was praying for that very belief to take root. He was pleading with the Father for the souls of the men who were crucifying him.

We shall see later that this prayer was answered, when upon our Lord's death, the centurion proclaimed, "Truly this man was the Son of God!" (Luke 23:39b).

He became a believer because of all the wonders he saw but also, in no small part, because of Jesus' prayer. Later, thousands of people became believers. Many, no doubt, had taken part in the travesty of this day and were rescued by our Lord's prayer.

This sobers me to think of the potent power of prayer. It can turn those who seemingly are my enemies into friends. No wonder Jesus told us to love our enemies and pray for those who despitefully use us (Matthew 5:44). Prayer changes everything!

> And parted his garments, casting lots: That it might be fulfilled which was spoken by the prophet, They parted my garments among them, and upon my vesture did they cast lots.
>
> Matthew 27:35b

This scripture is found, among others that speak of the crucifixion, in that famous psalm of David, Psalm 22.

John adds a new piece of information at this point. He tells us that the reason the soldiers cast lots for the coat was that it was seamless. It had been woven from the top throughout. After dividing the other clothes into four parts, they decided not to rend the vesture. Instead, they each took a lot, hoping to get the valuable coat (John 19:23–24).

> And sitting down they watched him there ...
>
> Matthew 27:36

Jesus was alive on the cross for six hours. After the initial activity in raising the cross of Jesus, as well as those of the malefactors who were led to Calvary with him, there was a period of waiting for the soldiers. It was guard duty, if you will. They were responsible to guard the site lest anyone come and rescue the condemned men.

> And set up over his head his accusation written, *This Is Jesus The King Of The Jews.*
>
> Matthew 27:37

With Roman justice being what it was, the Romans wanted all to know the reason a man deserved this method of execution.

Interestingly, all four narratives tell of a slightly different superscription.

Mark reports, "*The King Of The Jews*" (Mark 15:26).

Luke reports, "*This Is The King Of The Jews*" (Luke 23:38).

And John states that the writing said, "*Jesus Of Nazareth The King Of The Jews*" (John 19:19b).

John and Luke also point out that the accusation was written in Hebrew, Greek, and Latin. That explains why the four narratives come across slightly different in English.

John also reveals why there is an interval of time after Jesus was crucified before the soldiers set up the accusation over our Lord's head. He reports that Pilate himself gave instructions for the title as an insult to the Jewish leaders for pushing him into a corner with Jesus' fate.

John also faithfully tells us that, as expected, the chief priests were upset. They went back to Pilate and said, "Write not, The King of the Jews; but that he said, I am the King of the Jews."

Pilate had the last laugh though, as he said, "What I have written, I have written" (John 19:21–22).

Pilate had had enough of the Jews this day, and he was not about to change the superscription.

> Then were there two thieves (*lestes* in Greek) crucified with
> him, one on the right hand, and another on the left.
>
> Matthew 27:38

Matthew apparently is making the point that the two other men who were crucified that day were brought out to Calvary at a point in time after Jesus was hung on his cross.

But a close reading of Luke and John tell that the malefactors were led out at the same time with Jesus, not later. Lastly, the timing of the other men's crucifixion is not clear from looking at Mark's gospel.

So do we have an error here?

Certainly the God-breathed Word is not in error. What we have is an error in our understanding. I will comment shortly upon two possible scenarios that may help answer this problem.

> And they that passed by reviled him, wagging their heads,
> and saying, Thou that destroyest the temple, and buildest it
> in three days, save thyself. If thou be the Son of God, come
> down from the cross.
>
> Matthew 27:39–40

As mentioned, Jesus was murdered in a heavily traveled place. Scores of people had seen him over the previous week, as well as many more who had heard of his fame. And it would seem that the saying of Jesus concerning his rebuilding the temple had also been circulated widely. Of course, it was misunderstood, as the people were not seeing with spiritual eyes.

As the many passersby wagged their heads, I would think that some must have thought that this crazy man was indeed receiving the reward of a fool.

But their last statement is frightening when they called upon Jesus to save himself and come down from the cross. What if he had done it? He certainly had the power and the right to do the very thing they were asking. But we know that the atonement was not yet complete. He had not yet uttered those wonderful words, *It is finished.* We would still be in our sins if Jesus had responded. You and I would be doomed if Jesus once again had not used his incredible restraint.

> Likewise also the chief priests mocking him, with the scribes and elders, said, He saved others; himself he cannot save. If he be the King of Israel, let him come down from the cross, and we will believe him. He trusted in God; let him deliver him now, if he will have him: For he said, I am the Son of God.
>
> Matthew 27:41–43

Those that passed by were wondering, but the leaders, those priests, scribes, and elders were mocking. Luke adds that the soldiers were also involved in the taunting (Luke 23:36).

It's interesting to me that the Jewish leaders said what it would take for them to believe. Coming down from the cross! Well, three days later, Jesus did something even more remarkable. He rose from the dead! But true to form, many of those same leaders reneged on their words, choosing not to see Jesus as Messiah.

Also, in looking at their taunt from their point of view, can you imagine how incredibly stunned they would have been if Jesus had done just what they were calling for? What they were doing was like a man going into the lion's cage at the circus and daring the lion to bite. This would be comical if it weren't so terrible.

The thieves also, which were crucified with him, cast the same in his teeth.

Matthew 27:44

This verse has always been a problem for me, probably for you too. To top if off, Mark reports it the same way (Mark 15:32). Both thieves reviled Jesus.

The reason we don't like these two verses is because of Luke's more famous rendition of the men crucified with the Savior. For those who have not ever noticed, let's just say they don't jive well together.

And one of the malefactors which were hanged railed on him, saying, If thou be Christ, save thyself and us. But the other answering rebuked him, saying, Dost not thou fear God, seeing thou art in the same condemnation? And we indeed justly; for we receive the due reward of our deeds: But this man hath done nothing amiss. And he said to Jesus, Lord, remember me when thou comest into thy kingdom. And Jesus said unto him, verily I say unto thee, today shalt thou be with me in paradise.

Luke 23:39–43

We all love Luke's version! Jesus is seeing the first fruit of his labor. How heartening that must have been for him to be able to see saving faith in the one malefactor. What a wonderful moment in the midst of the tragedy!

But what about Matthew's and Mark's accounts? Once again surrounding the criminals crucified with Jesus, we have an apparent schism in the different gospels. Matthew has thieves crucified after Jesus and both casting insults at him while Luke brings the malefactors out with Jesus and only one doubts who he really is.

Well, I promised you two different scenarios to help rectify this glaring inconsistency. They are mutually exclusive. I'll let you be the judge of which one you like better. Of course, it may not be either one of these but some other explanation.

Scenario number one: Scholars have suggested that the timing of the events in the passion story were not of prime importance to the gospel writers. This is how they explain the difference in the arrival of the two other men crucified with Jesus. They point out another example of this from the Gospel of John. In that narrative, John places the parting of the garments of our Lord later in the story than the other writers. One will note that in John, the parting of the garments was after the posting of the superscription over Jesus' head while it was before that event in the other three accounts.

The second point to scenario number one is that Matthew and Mark report how the thieves viewed Jesus in the early moments of the crucifixion. They railed upon him. It is said that later, one of the malefactors changed his mind about Jesus. He repented and called Jesus Lord.

Thus, in scenario number one, the timing is not critical to the writers, and one of the men repented after initially viewing Jesus with derision.

Scenario number two: There were *four* men crucified alongside Jesus!

This one, on the surface, is very hard to believe because none of the writers come out and say that there were four.

Proponents of this scenario point out what we have just said but with a different twist. They say that the timing *is* important, as well as their names: malefactors versus thieves. Also, they go to the Gospel of John for some indirect support. They comment upon John 19:32–33 as making little sense unless there are four men crucified with Jesus, two on each side.

Let's read it together. "Then came the soldiers, and brake the legs of the first, and of the other which was crucified with him. But when they came to Jesus, and saw that he was dead already, they brake not his legs."

Since the Passover was fast approaching, the Jews sought

permission from Pilate to expedite the death of the men so as to not have them on the cross during Passover. Pilate gave the order, and the soldiers were to break the legs of the crucified men. Thus, they no longer would be able to push up for air and would rapidly die.

So picture what John is saying here. The soldiers needed to brutally take a mallet or some other type of heavy blunt instrument and take turns smashing the legs of the hapless men so they would die quickly. If there are only two other criminals with Jesus, then according to logic, they broke the first man's legs, walked around Jesus to break the second man's legs, and then noticed that Jesus was already dead in the middle. Doesn't really make sense, they say. They also make a stand with their scenario by pointing out that John makes a point of saying, "They brake the legs of the first, and of the *other* which was crucified *with* him." They say that that wording flows with the difference in timing between the other narratives.

Lastly, believers in scenario number two point out that in very early Christian art there have been crucifixion scenes with five crosses.

So which is it? Scenario number one or scenario number two?

I don't know!

What I did want to do, though, in taking some time with this is to show that when we think we see a contradiction in the Word of God, we need to step back and remember that we are puny and God is huge! There is always an explanation. We just don't always see it!

The next event that occurred is the third statement of Jesus from the cross. They are truly beautiful words and are found only in John's gospel. It will quickly become clear to the reader why John is the only one reporting these words of our Lord, as they are very personal to him.

Now there stood by the cross of Jesus his mother, and his mother's sister, Mary the wife of Cleophas, and Mary Magdalene. When Jesus therefore saw his mother, and the disciple standing by, whom he loved, he saith unto his mother, Woman, behold thy son! Then saith he to the disciple, Behold thy mother! And from that hour that disciple took her unto his own home.

John 19:25–27

At the foot of the cross were four broken women. Included was Jesus' own mother! How heart wrenching for both he and Mary must this hour have been. Yet both of them knew that this moment was inevitable, for three decades earlier, at the time of Jesus' dedication as a baby, a prophet named Simeon told Mary and Joseph, as he held Jesus in his arms, that he was looking upon the salvation prepared for all people. He was looking upon a light to lighten the Gentiles and the glory of Israel. He also said to Mary individually that this child was set for the fall and rising again of many in Israel and that a figurative sword would pierce through her own soul (Luke 2:22–35).

But think how bad from a human point of view Jesus must have felt. Here before him was the woman his Father chose to carry him as a baby. This was the woman who nursed him and, along with his stepfather, Joseph, had raised him according the Law of Moses to the best of their ability. How bad he must have felt as he was pinned naked to the tree in front of his own mother.

Yet instead of feeling sorrow for himself, Jesus was going to bless his mother in a unique way as John informs us. Just as Hannah before had given Samuel to Eli (1 Samuel 1:24–28), Jesus gave Mary to John. He told Mary that John was now her son, and to John he said that Mary was now his mother. What an awesome privilege for John to be given charge of the mother of his Lord! Think of the wonderful insights he inevitably gained over the remaining course of Mary's life as she recalled for him facets of Jesus' time on earth that were known only to her.

Truly, John, in humility, called himself the disciple that

Jesus loved. For his entire life, he just couldn't fathom the abundance of blessings he had received from his Lord.

> Now from the sixth hour there was darkness over all the land unto the ninth hour.
>
> Matthew 27:45

From high noon unto 3:00 p.m., the land was dark. This was no ordinary darkness. This was blinding, grouping-around-with-your-hands kind of darkness. No wonder the centurion realized that Jesus was the Son of God. This was too unreal!

In the Bible, darkness typifies God's judgment. Jesus, who knew no sin, became sin for us that we might be made the righteousness of God in him (2 Corinthians 5:21). God was judging sin, and it, thus, become frightfully dark.

The Death of the Christ

As I have mentioned, this moment, the death of the Christ, corresponds with our birth. For out of his side came forth blood and water.

And once again the Holy Spirit is brief in his description of this most sacred event, as only twenty-five verses are used by the four gospel writers to inform us of the details (Matthew 27:46–55, Mark 15:33–40, Luke 23:44–47, John 19:28–30). I have chosen to follow Matthew's account for this section of our Lord's passion. I will also bring in new information, which Luke and John provide to complete our understanding of this time.

> And about the ninth hour Jesus cried with a loud voice, say-
> ing, Eli, Eli, lama sabachthani? That is to say, My God, my
> God, why hast thou forsaken me?
>
> Matthew 27:46

Of course, this fourth and very famous statement that Jesus cried from the cross is found in the crucifixion psalm, Psalm 22:1a. The time is about the ninth hour, or 3:00 p.m., as Matthew, Mark, and Luke report. As we will see, our Lord is only moments away from his death.

The question, of course, is why would God the Father forsake his only begotten Son? We understand that this fulfills prophecy, so we accept it, but it still makes one wonder. Jesus himself had previously said that the Father was always with him (John 16:32). He had explained his relationship to the Father in another way by saying that he is in the Father and the Father is in him (John 10:38). So I ask again, how is it that our Savior would come to the point of proclaiming this seemingly dark statement?

Well, as alluded to earlier, Paul gives us the answer in 2 Corinthians: "For he (God) hath made him (Jesus) *to be sin* for us, who knew no sin; that we might be made the righteousness of God in him" (2 Corinthians 5:21, emphasis mine).

Jesus became sin during those dark hours on the cross. The Father was judging sin and turned his back on the Son. The Bible clearly teaches that the wages of sin is death (Romans 6:23a)—death physically but also death spiritually. When you think about it, separation from God is the absolute definition of death! Jesus was separated from his Father as he became sin.

This is the doctrine of substitution. Jesus became sin for us that we would become the righteousness of God in him. He got what we deserve (death, which is separation from God), and we get what we he deserves (life everlasting). Amazing!

Unfortunately for those of us who like to have things fit well, to be neat and tidy, this verse presents a problem, for there is another explanation to its meaning, which, once again, is mutually exclusive to what I have just reviewed. It is an interpretation that is held in the Eastern Christian worldview. I will present the information while trying not to bias you one way or the other.

Bibles printed that are destined for many Asian locales translate this famous verse as, "My God, My God, for this purpose was I reserved." It is said by some scholars that the Aramaic word *lama* means purpose or reason and that *sabach-thani* means to reserve. Of course, it should not be surprising that these words might be difficult to translate. The Bible was written in Hebrew and Greek. But these words are in Aramaic. Certainly, it's reasonable to think that translating Aramaic to English might not be a strong suit of our early translators of the Bible into English. They were scholars of Hebrew and Greek, not Aramaic.

Nonetheless, the spiritual significance of translating these words of Jesus in this light is also beautiful. When Jesus cried out that for this reason, for this moment where he paid for the sins of the whole world, he was reserved; he was saying that this was the reason he came into the world. He came to die for us, and he was announcing for all mankind that this was the ultimate purpose of his first coming. Not to be the king from heaven, setting up an earthly reign—for that would be later— but he came to be the suffering servant, which is described so graphically in Isaiah 53.

No, proponents of this interpretation say that God would never leave his Son, and they get mad when other equally convinced scholars stand alongside the first explanation. They say God was there all along and that judgment of sin did not include being forsaken by the Father. Implicit to this point of view is that these words have no relationship to Psalm 22:1a. They say that these words are not mentioned by the gospel writers as being the fulfillment of Scripture like some of the other statements of Jesus are so prefaced.

So which is it?

Once again, I don't know.

My calling is just to show you the different points of view. We will all learn the correct meaning in that day not too far away. It is good to realize though from time to time that the more we learn about Jesus, the more we realize that we don't know much. It keeps us humble.

Almost immediately after proclaiming, "*Eli, Eli, lama sabach-thani,*" Jesus uttered his fifth statement from the cross as reported by the Apostle John.

> After this, Jesus knowing that all things were now accomplished, that the scripture might be fulfilled, saith, I thirst. Now there was set a vessel full of vinegar: And they filled a sponge with vinegar, and put it upon hyssop, and put it to his mouth.
>
> John 19:28–29

The thirst that a man would endure while dying on the cross was mind-boggling. But the irony of Jesus being thirsty is another one of those paradoxes that we see in the passion story, for Jesus is the fountain of living water. He told the Samaritan woman at Jacob's well that he had water that would quench her thirst forever (John 14:4). He cried out in that most holy moment at the Feast of Tabernacles that all who would come to him would have rivers of living water flow forth from their hearts (John 7:37–38). In the Old Testament, it is well understood that Jesus is the Rock that gushed forth water (Exodus 17:3, 6). So for Jesus to thirst can only be that doctrine of substitution once again. He was thirsty so we could be filled!

Lastly, we should comment upon the hyssop, which was used to offer the drink to Jesus. It is another gem in this prophetic story. In the Old Testament Law, the sacrifice for a cleansed leper (leprosy pictures sin) included taking cedar wood (the cross), scarlet (analogous to blood), and hyssop and offering them over a killed bird while letting a second bird fly away (Leviticus 14:1–7). Of course, this sacrifice symbolizes Jesus' death and resurrection, so we should not be surprised that hyssop shows up in the passion story as well.

Oh, the majesty of God's Word! It's so simple a child can understand, yet so deep that even the most mature in the Lord can continually learn and be amazed!

> Some of them of them that stood there, when they heard that, said, This man calleth for Elias (Greek for Elijah). And straightway one of them ran, and took a sponge, and filled it with vinegar, and put it on a reed (hyssop), and gave him to drink. The rest said, Let be, let's see whether Elias will come to save him.
>
> Matthew 27:47–49

It's clear when studying John and Matthew that these two statements were given in immediate proximity to each other. Without Jesus' remark of his thirst, the response of the person getting the vinegar to drink for Jesus after his statement of *"Eli, Eli, lama sabachthani"* makes no sense. But when seen given together, they fit like a hand in a glove!

Interesting is the simultaneous response the people spoke forth while the person was getting a drink for our Lord. They thought Jesus was calling for Elijah. *Eli* and *Elijah* are very closely related words. *Eli* means *Yahweh is exalted,* and *Elijah* means *Yahweh is my God.* This, of course, shows that even people who spoke Aramaic did not understand what Jesus was saying. It certainly adds to the argument that in AD 1611 when the Bible was translated into English that the translators might have not completely understood the statement also.

We should not be surprised, though, that the people thought Jesus was calling for Elijah, for Elijah was that powerful prophet of the Old Testament who was taken up to heaven in a whirlwind, along with the horses and a chariot of fire (2 Kings 2:11). It had been prophesized that he would come back before Messiah.

"Behold, I will send you Elijah the prophet before the coming of the great and dreadful day of the Lord" (Malachi 4:5).

We understand that the "day of the Lord" speaks of the time around his coming in glory and power, the time centered around the second coming and the kingdom rule. Yet those at the cross were wondering if this was the day, for indeed it was a dreadful day. Could it be that moments before Jesus' death, Elijah would appear and rescue him? Can you imagine if he did?

> Jesus, when he had cried again with a loud voice, yielded up the ghost.
>
> Matthew 27:50

Jesus actually cried out two very important statements, which once again need to be understood using the concepts of Scripture buildup. They are each found separately, one in John and the other in Luke.

> When Jesus therefore had received the vinegar, he said, It is finished: And he bowed his head, and gave up the ghost.
>
> John 19:30

> And when Jesus had cried with a loud voice, he said, Father, into thy hands I commend my spirit: And having said thus, he gave up the ghost.
>
> Luke 23:46

John ended his gospel reporting that the world itself could not contain in written form all the things Jesus did. It should not be surprising then that each gospel writer includes only in part what Jesus said in his last moment. But isn't it enlightening to see them together?

First, Matthew reveals that Jesus cried again loudly. Remember he had just cried out, "*Eli, Eli lama sabachthani*" and then whispered, "I thirst." Next, he cried, "It is finished," as reported in John. Secondly, Luke adds that after proclaiming it is finished, he said, "Father, into thy hands I commend my spirit."

These are the sixth and seventh statements made by our Lord from the cross.

First, let me comment upon the statement "It is finished." What was finished?

Not only was Jesus talking about the terrible ordeal he had just labored through over the past forty hours, but he was also speaking to the fact that the work of salvation was now complete. The Old Testament prophecies had been fulfilled. The Old Testament Law itself was now passé, as we shall soon discover. Jesus had completed the work his Father had sent him to accomplish. The atonement was finished. The baby had finally arrived!

Jesus then commended his *Spirit* back to the *Father.* This statement is loaded. This is the unfathomable trinity. We see all three components coming together as one in this verse. They are one, yet they are separate. I can't even come close to understanding this concept.

On another level, two famous yet simple verses come to mind when I look upon this statement concretely: "Trust in the Lord with all thine heart: and lean not unto thine own understanding. In all thy ways acknowledge him, and he shall direct thy paths" (Proverbs 3:5–6).

Jesus was ever trusting in the Lord. It is my prayer that in death that will be my last conscious thought also.

Lastly, all four writers (I haven't mentioned Mark in this section as his report is the same as Matthew's) tell us that Jesus yielded or gave up the ghost. Jesus let go. He died under his own timing and terms. No one could kill Jesus. He gave it up. He yielded his life at the time when all was finished.

Remember, Jesus is the Passover sacrifice. He died at the same time the Passover lamb was being sacrificed in Jerusalem. It was not for Jesus to die at any other time.

In contrast to this, we can think back to other examples in Jesus' life where attempts were made to kill him. First, in his own hometown of Nazareth, the Jews wanted to cast him over the cliff on the edge of the city. This was after he had proclaimed the fulfillment of Scripture from the book of Isaiah in his reading. Remember how comical it was when he just walked away through their midst (Luke 4:14–30).

Later, the Jews took up stones to kill him after he had told them that he was before Abraham. He once again escaped away from their grasp (John 8:58–59).

But the most revealing thing of all, demonstrating Jesus' control over his destiny, comes from a statement made by the Jewish leaders themselves. When plotting to kill the Rabbi, they said that it should *not* be done during the time of the feast so as to not cause an uproar of the people (Matthew 26:5, Mark 14:2). As we know, their plan did not unfold as they had envisioned but was according to God's. It *was* over the feast, and to say there was an uproar would be a gross understatement!

> And, behold, the veil of the temple was rent in twain from the top to the bottom.
>
> Matthew 27:51a

This is incredible! At the moment of Christ's death, the veil in the temple was miraculously split in two from the top down. I cannot even imagine the hardness of heart that the nonbelieving priests demonstrated in refusing to see this sign for what it was.

The veil was that thick curtain that separated the holy place in the temple from the holy of holies. The holy place housed the table of showbread, the altar of incense, and the golden candlestick. In the holy of holies resided the ark of the covenant, which was covered by the mercy seat. It was there God met the people during the Old Testament administration. The high priest was the only one allowed into the holy of holies. That was only once per year on the Day of Atonement, known today as Yom Kippur.

The high priest was to purify himself prior to entering, lest he be found unclean and die in the presence of God. There, he would offer sacrifice to cover the sins of the people from the preceding year. This was to be done on a year-to-year basis as the nation's sins were only covered; they were not washed away permanently.

So for the veil to be torn from the top down was hugely symbolic. It revealed to all Israel that the way to God's presence had now been opened by the sacrifice of the true Lamb of God, Jesus Christ. Now any man, woman, boy, or girl could enter the holy of holies into the presence of the Father.

The author of Hebrews states it this way: "Let us therefore come boldly unto the throne of grace, that we may obtain mercy, and find grace to help in time of need" (Hebrews 4:16).

Hebrews also proclaims:

> Now where remission of these is, there is no more offering for sin. Having therefore, brethren, boldness to enter the holiest by the blood of Jesus, by a new and living way, which he hath consecrated for us, through the veil, that is to say, his flesh.
>
> Hebrews 10:18–20

His flesh was the veil that was broken and was seen in the literal veil being torn by God from the top down. There was nothing man could or can do to improve on the sacrifice of Jesus. As I mentioned, the Old Testament rules and regulations were now passé. They pictured and showed the way to Jesus. That job was now complete. As Paul stated, the Law was our schoolmaster to lead us to Christ (Galatians 3:24).

> And the earth did quake, and the rocks rent.
>
> Matthew 27:51b

Isaiah spoke that "it is he that sits upon the circle of the earth" (Isaiah 40:22).

So it is not surprising that the earth would quake upon the death of the one who holds all things together by the power of his Word. What is more surprising to me, though, is that the earthly groanings weren't any more destructive than mentioned here. It's only by God's grace and mercy that the whole world didn't explode into space at that terrible moment!

> And the graves were opened; and many bodies of the saints which slept arose, and came out of the graves *after* his resurrection, and went into the holy city, and appeared unto many.
> Matthew 27:52–53 (emphasis mine)

This is very interesting to me. The Bible typifies the two harvests of Israel as representative of the harvest of souls to God—that of the barley harvest in the spring and the wheat harvest in the fall. The barley harvest was a smaller harvest compared to the wheat harvest at the end of the season.

Analogous to that, the Bible calls Jesus the firstfruits. He's the barley harvest. But along with him, apparently there were a limited number of other believers that arose after his resurrection, as this verse describes. They are also part of the firstfruits. In type, they also are part of the barley harvest. We other Christians since that time will be included in the wheat harvest, the harvest still to come!

Paul, in speaking of the resurrection, states it clearly: "But now is Christ risen from the dead, and become the firstfruits of them that slept … But every man in his own order: Christ the firstfruits; afterward they that are Christ's at his coming" (1 Corinthians 15:20–23).

Notice also that this verse we are discussing tells that the graves opened at the time of the earthquake, but the saints did not come up out their graves until after Jesus arose from the dead. This, of course, makes perfect sense as the Bible states that Jesus is the firstborn from the dead (Colossians 1:18). His resurrection is what made the other saints' resurrection possible.

Also of interest, this verse states that they went into the holy city. I don't know about you, but after what we've just been reading, I wouldn't call Jerusalem holy. Nonetheless, God calls it holy, as it is the city of the great king (Psalm 48:1–2).

Lastly, what became of those resurrected saints? Did they live to die again, or did they ascend into heaven to be with the Lord after his ascension?

I don't know!

The Bible doesn't tell us! But I would like to think that the picture is better if they, too, ascended up to heaven rather than dying again at some later date.

> Now when the centurion, and they that were with him, watching Jesus, saw the earthquake, and those things that were done, they feared greatly, saying, truly this was the Son of God.
>
> Matthew 27:54

Have you ever done something bad and caught yourself saying to witnesses, "May lightning strike me if God agrees what I have done is bad"? Imagine how you would feel if it did strike. That's how the centurion and the other soldiers felt.

In another classic understatement, the Bible says that "they feared greatly." That's putting it mildly. They were terrified! They had over the past day and a half brutally whipped, mocked, and nailed to the cross this man who they now concluded was the Son of God! Remember, they were not Jews; they did not understand the concept of one God, for they had many gods in their Roman religion. And most of those gods were vindictive. They were now convinced that they had done these things to the son of a god. They now understood that their future was not very bright.

On another level, though, when we compare this verse with Luke, we note that the centurion "glorified God, saying, Certainly this was a righteous man" (Luke 23:47).

As noted previously, Jesus prayed for the Father to forgive his executioners. This seed of saving faith apparently blossomed from the mighty things of nature, the three hours of darkness followed by the earthquake, that he had just witnessed.

Blood and Water

John adds the postscript to Jesus' death, which bears repeating as it symbolically reminds us of the labor and delivery our Lord underwent for us while also miraculously fulfilling prophecy.

> The Jews therefore, because it was the preparation, that the bodies should not remain upon the cross on the Sabbath day, (for that Sabbath day was an high day,) besought Pilate that their legs might be broken, and that they might be taken away.
>
> John 19:31

Remember, the Jews did not want those cursed men hanging on the tree over the Sabbath. As we have discussed, John reveals that this was the "high Sabbath" or Passover, not necessarily a Friday before the regular Saturday Sabbath. So the leaders asked for permission to have the soldiers break the legs of the condemned men to hasten their death. But this would have been a problem prophetically, as John is about to point out.

> Then came the soldiers, and brake the legs of the first, and of the other which was crucified with him. But when they came to Jesus, they saw that he was dead already, they brake not his legs: But one of the soldiers with a spear pierced his side, and forthwith came there out blood and water. And he that saw it bare record, and his record is true, that ye might believe. For these things were done that the scripture should be fulfilled,
>
> John 19:32–36a

John is saying, "I saw all of this, and I want you to know this is true. I want you to believe! Everything Jesus did here was to fulfill Scripture." As you study the Old Testament, scripture speaks of this moment!

Then he gave two examples to make his point.

A bone of him shall not be broken. And again another scripture saith, They shall look on him whom they pierced.

John 19:36b–37

Moses stated more than once in speaking of the Passover lamb that not a bone of it was to be broken (Exodus 12:46, Numbers 9:12). John makes the connection. He understood, like his predecessor John the Baptist, who said, "Behold, the Lamb of God who taketh away the sins of the world." Jesus *is* the Passover lamb!

The prophet Zechariah, in speaking of Judah and Jerusalem during the tribulation period, prophesied:

And they will look upon me whom they have pierced, and they shall mourn for him, as one mourneth for his only son.

Zechariah 12:10

Instead of breaking Jesus' bones, they pierced his side. They pierced his hands and feet. They tore open his back. In that day still to come, the Jews will mourn their collective unbelief as a father mourns the death of his only son. They will be beside themselves with grief when they realize what they did to him as well as for the centuries of continued refusal to be grateful for what he did for them!

Conclusions: Humility Before Honor

In these pages, I have given at times a longwinded commentary on the description of Jesus' passion, as given by the four gospel writers.

Now, at this point, I have a request for you, the reader. Begin at the scene of the garden arrest and read only the gospel verses of the passion, given in order here from the four writers. Skip over the commentary sections to see the true flow of our Savior's labor for our new birth. You will be blessed!

Now that you have hopefully reread the passion's flow, I would like for us to look at a few Old Testament passages which speak of Jesus' labor and delivery for our sins.

> Preserve me, O God: For in thee do I put my trust … For thou wilt not leave my soul in hell (Hades), neither wilt thou suffer thine Holy One to see corruption.
>
> Psalms 16:1, 10

> My God, my God, why hast thou forsaken me? … But I am a worm, and no man; a reproach of men, and despised of the people. All they that see me laugh me to scorn: They shoot out the lip, they shake the head, saying, He trusted on the Lord that he would deliver him: Let him deliver him, seeing he delighted in him. I am poured out like water, and all my bones are out of joint: My heart is like wax; it is melted in the midst of my bowels. My strength is dried up like a potsherd: And my tongue cleaveth to my jaws; They pierced my hands and my feet. They part my garments among them, and cast lots upon my vesture.
>
> Psalm 22:1, 6–8, 14–15, 16, 18

> For the zeal of thine house hath eaten me up; and the reproaches of them that reproached thee are fallen upon me … Deliver me out of the mire, and let me not sink: Reproach hath broken my heart; and I looked for some to take pity, but there was none; and for comforters, but I found none. They gave me gall for my meat; and in my thirst they gave me vinegar to drink.
>
> Psalms 69: 9, 14, 20–21

Who hath believed our report? And to whom is the arm of the Lord revealed? For he shall grow up before him as a tender plant, and as a root out of a dry ground: He hath no form nor comeliness; and when we shall see him, there is no beauty that we should desire him. He is despised and rejected of men; a man of sorrows, and acquainted with grief: And we hid as it were our faces from him; he was despised, and we esteemed him not. Surely he hath born our griefs, and carried our sorrows: Yet we did esteem him stricken, smitten of God, and afflicted. But he was wounded for our transgressions, he was bruised for our iniquities: And the chastisement of our peace was upon him; and with his stripes we are healed. All we like sheep have gone astray; we have turned everyone to his own way; and the Lord hath laid on him the iniquity of us all. He was oppressed and he was afflicted, yet he opened not his mouth: He is brought as a lamb to the slaughter, and as a sheep before her shearers is dumb, so he opened not his mouth. He was taken from prison and from judgment: And who shall declare his generation? For he was cut off out of the land of the living: For the transgression of my people was he stricken. And he made his grave with the wicked, and the rich in his death; because he had done no violence, neither was any deceit in his mouth. Yet it pleased the Lord to bruise him; he hath put him to grief: When thou shalt make his soul an offering for sin, he shall see his seed, he shall prolong his days, and the pleasure of the Lord shall prosper in his hand. He shall see the travail of his soul, and shall be satisfied: By his knowledge shall my righteous servant justify many; for he shall bear their iniquities. Therefore will I divide him a portion with the great, and he shall divide the spoil with the strong; because he hath poured out his soul unto death: And he was numbered with the transgressors; and he bare the sin of many, and made intercession for the transgressors.

Isaiah 53:1–12

Jesus of Nazareth, Jesus the Christ, is the fulfillment of Scripture. The Bible in its entirety speaks in illustrations, as well as directly, of what he has done and will do. As has been said, history truly is *his* story.

In closing, we see in the Bible a continuing theme concerning the relationship of suffering to glory: the relationship of humility to honor. That is, suffering always comes before glory; humility always comes before honor. Before the advent of C-sections, we would say obstetrically, that labor comes before birth. In today's vernacular, we might say, "No pain, no gain!"

Paul demonstrates the specifics of this concept well in urging us to emulate the Master.

> Let this mind be in you which was also in Christ Jesus: Who, being in the form of God, thought it not robbery to be equal with God: But made himself of no reputation, and took upon him the form of a servant, and was made in the likeness of men: And being found in fashion as a man, he humbled himself, and became obedient unto death, even the death of the cross. Wherefore God also hath highly exalted him, and given him a name which is above every name: That at the name of Jesus every knee should bow, of things in heaven, and things in earth, and things under the earth; And that every tongue should confess that Jesus Christ is Lord, to the glory of God the Father.
>
> Philippians 2:5–11

Jesus humbled himself. He was obedient. He suffered.

Humility, obedience, and suffering. These are three attributes that my flesh does not like. But they are choices I can make every day. Will I be obedient to God's Word and his prompting? Will I walk in humility, seeing importance in others, or will I let my pride put me first at the expense of others?

Will I put my fleshy needs above everything? Will I suffer loss of status or position, or will I seek to elevate myself above everyone else?

Obviously, Jesus took the road of humility and obedience, and we see the ending. Yours and mine will also be glorious as we walk in humility, being obedient to the Father. As we suffer for a season, we will always reap a harvest in another season. It's a great paradox. The more I try to elevate myself, the lower I will go. But the less I seek fame and honor, the more I will receive!

Speaking of sufferings, trials, and tribulations, which we, like the Lord, undergo, Peter stated this concept wonderfully. "Beloved, think it not strange concerning the fiery trial which is to try you, as though some strange thing happened unto you" (1 Peter 4:12). Peter is saying, "Don't despair when trials come as if God has abandoned you."

"But rejoice, inasmuch as ye are partakers of Christ's sufferings; that, when his glory shall be revealed, ye may be glad also with exceeding joy" (1 Peter 4:13).

Like Jesus, sometimes the joy and glory doesn't even come until after this life. Sometimes it's sooner.

God, though, through the author of Hebrews, gives us our marching orders well. And he tells us how to walk successfully and effectively in this life.

> Wherefore seeing we also are compassed about with so great a cloud of witnesses, let us lay aside every weight, and sin which doth so easily beset us, and let us run with patience the race that is set before us,
>
> Hebrews 12:1

He is saying, "People have gone before you; it's not just about you and your problems." So get rid of the weight that's holding you down, stop sinning habitually, and patiently, yet aggressively, move forward in the calling God has given you.

But how do we do that?

Looking unto Jesus the author and finisher of our faith; who for the joy that was set before him endured the cross, despising the shame, and is set down at the right hand of the throne of God.

Hebrews 12:2

Look to Jesus. Trust in Jesus. See how he did it. He fixed his eyes on the joy set before him. What was that joy? Seeing you and me justified and sanctified before the Father. He kept his focus on the big picture. He was looking toward eternity and not living only for today. That's the secret. Live for eternity, and you'll have a great day today!

God bless you as we remember what Jesus did to give us life.

BOOK SEVEN

The Valley Between the Mountains:
The Postpartum Blues

Introduction

Verily, verily, I say unto you, That ye shall weep and lament, but the world shall rejoice: And ye shall be sorrowful, but your sorrow shall be turned to joy. A woman when she is in travail hath sorrow, because her hour is come: But as soon as she is delivered of the child, she remembereth no more the anguish, for joy that a man is born into the world. And ye now therefore have sorrow: But I will see you again, and your heart shall rejoice, and your joy no man taketh from you.

John 16:20–22

God is in the business of resurrection as was noted in book three, entitled "Sorrow to Joy." Jesus compared the trial that his disciples were to soon experience upon his passion to the travail of a laboring woman. But he also promised them that they would experience the joy that a new mother feels at the moment of her delivery when he returned to see them again. This principle of sorrow to joy, which we have seen illustrated previously, is a principle of life, and it is a recurring theme in God's Word. But there is another principle in life, as well as in the Bible, which is its antonym. And that is the standard that often after a victory will come a trial. Often after a mountain-top experience, one will enter a valley of temptation. Often after delivering a baby, a woman will get the blues.

This should not be surprising, for in the Bible, that God-authored book that details life for you and me, we see count-less examples of this phenomenon.

Jesus, after hearing his Father proclaim to the crowd wit-nessing his baptism that he was his beloved Son, was driven by the Spirit into the wilderness (desert) where he hungered for forty days and forty nights. (You may remember that forty is the number associated with a trial in the Bible.) During our Lord's time of testing, he was attacked mercilessly by the devil in a preview of his upcoming time of literal travail that he would experience three years later upon the completion of his first earthly calling.

Moses, after being rescued from death in the Nile River as a baby, rose to a position of prominence and prestige in the court of Pharaoh. He had it all it would seem! But God, of course, was not through with him. He was driven, like Jesus, to the desert, that dry and lonely place of depression, for forty years while not knowing that his greatest days were still before him.

Abraham, the father of faith, waited fourteen years after receiving the joyous promise from God that he would be a father through his wife Sarah, until he realized the arrival of Isaac, the promised child. During that time, his faith was tested and wavered. Sarah convinced him that God must have meant that he was to father a child through her handmaid, Hagar, as time went by and the fulfillment of God's Word seemed not to be. Those must have been days of sadness and despair as they questioned God's Word in their lives and his power over their lives!

Imagine the feeling David experienced upon defeating the giant Goliath. He was a true hero in Israel. Women were even singing songs to and about him of his potency and prowess. But then the other shoe fell! Saul, the king of the nation, became enraged with jealousy toward David and attempted to assassinate the champion on numerous occasions. Once again, the wilderness—that place picturing spiritual dryness—was the destination to which David was driven.

Paul the apostle must have felt incredible joy and relief upon leading the storm-tossed ship of 280 men to safety upon the rocky shores of Malta only to be attacked by a serpent (a biblical picture of the devil) while he was helping the group by collecting sticks for the fire on that cold and wet day.

Yes, truly, often after a victory in life will come a trial, a temptation, an attack. Often after the emotional high of delivering the baby will come the despair and depression of the postpartum blues.

Trial after victory—that's what this book is about. Specifically, I am going to address postpartum depression in detail, but just about everything I will say can be applied to any moment of despair and depression, any time of attack, and any time of trial that will come your way.

So let's look at the baby blues.

The wonderful joy that a woman experiences upon the birth of a baby is accompanied by the elevation of the female hormones, estrogen and progesterone, to levels that are only reached during pregnancy. These two very important hormones are made by the placenta as the ovaries are quiescent during gestation. But as you probably know, soon after the baby is birthed, the placenta will follow. Now the half-life of these two steroid hormones made by the placenta is about one day; therefore, in two to three days after giving birth, a woman's chemical balance will be altered radically. Indeed the female hormones, which were heretofore at record levels for months, will now come crashing down to levels seen only before the onset of puberty or to later be experienced after the arrival of menopause. And please note this is not a gradual change like those other two times in a woman's life. This is nearly an instantaneous and precipitous drop in the feminine hormones. This is falling off a cliff!

Thus we should not be surprised that women suffer a significant physical challenge after their deliveries. Actually, what surprises me is that severe postpartum depression doesn't manifest itself in every woman. Along with the hormonal fluctuations, we must not forget the physical pain and injuries that most women experience from the delivery process, as well as the many sleepless nights they experience as they worry about and extend themselves wholly toward the welfare of their newborns.

I think it is fair to say that due to these many factors, all women will note some difficulties after delivery. But doctors tell us that 7 percent of women suffer from what would be considered severe postpartum depression. By that they mean depression to the degree that a woman would seriously consider either taking her own life or the life of her baby. Another 30 percent report moderate depression. This can be manifested by some combination of significant and recurrent emotional labiality, irritability, anger, hostility, anxiety, obsessiveness, lack of energy, or extreme fatigue.

Fortunately, God in his Word has given us counsel for all of these symptoms. He has given us promises that his daughter must claim and cling to in order to overcome the trial.

Let's look at a few of God's words that may help when postpartum depression arrives and, for that matter, when any type of despair presents itself.

Suicide. Have you felt like dying? Do you sometime just wish it could all end? Don't feel alone. So did Paul and Elijah!

> For we would not, brethren, have you ignorant of our trouble which came to us in Asia, that we were pressed out of measure, above strength, insomuch that we despaired even of life.
>
> 2 Corinthians 1:8

Paul, writing about himself in the third person, admits that due to the intense persecution hurled his way in Turkey that he felt pressed out of measure and above strength. He despaired even of life itself.

We would say that he didn't even think he could go on. He didn't want to wake up in the morning. He didn't want to eat; he just wanted to die.

Have you ever felt that way? Sometimes women experience those feelings a few weeks after bringing their babies home.

Paul was able to pull himself out of his mental tailspin, though, by remembering God's promise of eternal glory that was still ahead.

> For which cause we faint not; but though our outward man perish, yet the inward man is renewed day by day. For our light affliction, which is but for a moment, worketh for us a far more exceeding and eternal weight of glory; While we look not at the things which are seen, but at the things which are not seen: For the things which are seen are temporal; but the things which are not seen are eternal.
>
> 2 Corinthians 4:16–18

Paul is reminding us of the obvious. Even though we feel like dying, even though our outward man (woman) is perishing, the inward man (woman) is renewed daily. That is, even though we feel like dying, we are actually growing closer to God.

He goes on to say in the next verse that afflictions in life actually work on a spiritual level to produce a future infinite and everlasting weight of glory!

Therefore, Paul tells you and me in the third verse that we must take our eyes off our present despair and place them upon the future reality of glorious joy.

Elijah also felt suicidal. After seeing the four hundred prophets of Baal defeated as fire rained down upon the altar he built to the Lord upon Mount Carmel, Elijah was intimidated by a message he received from the evil Queen Jezebel. She promised that she would have him assassinated by noon of the next day, causing this great man of power and faith to flee to the desert.

There we learn:

> But he (Elijah) went a day's journey into the wilderness, and came and sat down under a juniper tree: And he requested for himself that he might die; and said, It is enough; now, O Lord, take away my life;
>
> 1 Kings 19:4a

The suicidal prophet did the right thing in dialoging with his Maker while he was in his personal cave of depression. Reading the rest of the story gives insight to me for another way out of the suicidal thought pattern, for God didn't speak to Elijah in the wind or the earthquake or the fire. God doesn't shout deliverance to you and me. No, God spoke to Elijah in *a still, small voice* (1 Kings 19:12). Elijah heard the quiet voice of the Spirit, and he comprehended God's rhetorical question of "what the heck are you doing here in this cave, Elijah?" Then the Almighty graciously commissioned the prophet to get back into the game and reminded him that he wasn't alone. Yahweh told Elijah to go to Damascus and anoint Hazel to be king over Syria and that there were still seven thousand in Israel who had not bowed the knee to Baal.

That's how the Lord will deliver you and me in our day also when we find ourselves wanting to die. He will speak to us if we will listen to the still, small voice. But we must quiet our hearts, as the noise of the world will drown it out if we surround ourselves with its chatter. It may be godly words from another person, or it may be holy words directly from the book he has given us. In the latter case, though, we must open it if we want to hear that voice.

Emotional liability. Crying can be good for the soul. But in moderation, please! Sometimes postpartum women can find themselves crying over a literal glass of spilt milk.

This is the classic symptom of postpartum depression and is the direct result of the chemical imbalance occurring in the brain.

But first I must share Jesus' words of comfort to the weeper.

Blessed are the poor in spirit: For theirs is the kingdom of heaven. Blessed are they that mourn: For they shall be comforted.

Matthew 5:3–4

Also, we remember that he shares our pain. The Bible tells us in Isaiah 53 that he was a man of sorrows. It adds that he has borne our griefs and carried our sorrows. The shortest verse in the Bible, found in John's gospel, states that Jesus wept after he shared in the mourners' anguish at the gravesite of Lazarus. Truly our Lord wants to comfort us in our time of despair. Somehow, on a level I don't understand, yet I do believe, he actually shares in our sadness. And like Lazarus, the Healer is going to resurrect us in his time!

Irritability, anger, and hostility. These unfortunate symptoms of depression, in general, and the baby blues in specific, of course are not isolated to these conditions. They are the direct result of what the Bible calls the "carnal man" ruling. Anger bubbles up when we focus upon ourselves. It comes about when we live in the "me first" mode. Unfortunately, that's much of the time! Of course, when the flesh is compromised by the hormonal imbalance of the postpartum time frame, well, the fuse just gets shorter, doesn't it?

For the postpartum sufferer of irritability, anger, and hostility, realize these symptoms for what they are—they are sin! Confess them and move on.

> If we say that we have no sin, we deceive ourselves, and the truth is not in us. If we confess our sins, he is faithful and just to forgive us our sins, and to cleanse us from all unrighteousness.
>
> 1 John 1:8–9

Oh! And stop dwelling upon yourself. If you must, you will continue to battle your anger.

Anxiety and obsessiveness. These gruesome symptoms of depression will steal your peace and choke out your joy! Of course, they are not limited to the baby blues and to depression in general, but certainly it can be amplified during those times. Anxiety is the state of mind that will turn a good day into a bad one, for anxiety attempts to control the future, but it does so by worrying about it in a negative sense. Anxiety is married to fear while their opposites—peace and believing—are also bed partners.

You see, God knows the future, but we don't. When we start to worry about our upcoming days, what we're really doing is demonstrating our lack of faith in his ability or willingness to provide and care for the very same things with which we concern ourselves. That's silly when you think about it. When we presume that the God of love will "drop the ball" on the details of our lives, we're really just living outside of the realm of faith as we walk in fear, unbelief, and negativity. That's not what we want!

Happily, God's Word is chock-full of counsel for the worrier.

My favorite section that has helped me the most in my times of hopeless anxiety is found in Philippians. I recommend you underline this one in your Bible. No, better yet, this one should be memorized, as in a powerful way it takes down the devil and his henchmen when they attack!

> Be careful (Old English for anxious) for nothing: but in every thing by prayer and supplication with thanksgiving let your requests be made known unto God.
>
> Philippians 4:6

Paul, through the Spirit, states that we are to *not* worry about anything! Why, that's not possible unless we remember to *do* the rest of the verse. That is, in *everything* that might want to make us anxious, we must tell God about our needs through prayer and supplication with thanksgiving. Now it's not as though God doesn't know what we need, but he wants us to tell him about the problem as part of the antidote.

The usages of the three action verbs are beautiful, as I understand them. *Prayer* is adoration toward God's power, beauty, and authority. It's once again moving my mind off of myself! *Supplication* places the emphasis on my specific need or worry, on the very thing I am anxious about. *Thanksgiving* is the acknowledgment that I appreciate what he will do and understand that he is truly in control. It also confesses that what he does in my life will ultimately be the best for me. Prayer, supplication, and thanksgiving—it's a winning combination.

Now look at the result of God's anti-anxiety formula.

And the peace of God, which passeth all understanding, shall keep your hearts and minds through Christ Jesus.
Philippians 4:7

If I desire peace instead of worry and fear, then I must remember these words of God. When I praise him, pray to him, and thank him, I will have peace that I don't even understand. It will be like a river that flows by and off into the distance, so far that I can't even see its end! And I won't understand the peace because I don't know the future. But the very thing I am anxious about will now flee away because I have given my worries over to the one who not only knows the future but *holds* the future!

Okay, this is great! Look at the next two verses, for they give not only the treatment for anxiety, but they give the cure.

Finally, brethren, whatsoever things are true, whatsoever things are honest, whatsoever things are just, whatsoever things are pure, whatsoever things are lovely, whatsoever things are of good report; if there be any virtue, and if there be any praise, think on these things. Those things, which ye have both learned, and received, and heard, and seen in me, *do:* And the God of peace shall be with you.
Philippians 4:8–9 (emphasis mine)

It's a truth in life. I become what I think about, especially if I *do* what I think about. If I think negative thoughts, if I worry about tomorrow, then guess what? What I fear will likely come to pass to my detriment. But if I think about things that are true, honest, just, pure, lovely, of good report, virtuous, and praiseworthy, and especially as I do what I'm thinking about, then the peace of God, that state of mind of undisturbed believing, shall be with me.

Now track with me for a moment. What are the only two entities that are clothed with the eight attributes listed above? Why, the Lord and his Word. As I think upon Jesus and the Word, I will become more like him and the peace will just roll in. So put your mind upon things above, dear anxious or obsessive person. Do the things he tells you, and you will have peaceful believing that you never imagined you could experience this side of eternity.

Fatigue. Oh how I hate this one! If anxiety steals my joy, then fatigue takes my life, for I miss life as I sleep it away in a cloud of incomprehension. In fact, as I've mentioned before, in God's eyes, sleep and death are just about the same. When I arise every morning, I am living a spiritual illustration of the resurrection. Truly, on that day, Jesus will awake the sleepers. So, as I miss life in the fog of fatigue, well, I'm really missing life!

So what does the Word say to the postpartum sufferer about this symptom?

> Come to me, all ye that labor and are heavy laden, and I will give you rest. Take my yoke upon you, and learn of me; for I am meek and lowly in heart: And ye shall find rest unto your souls. For my yoke is easy, and my burden is light.
>
> Matthew 11:28–30

It's Jesus, our Redeemer, our Savior who brings rest.

He tells us to take his yoke. What is a yoke? Well it's the wooden harness that was used to join two oxen together so they could work in unison. In our Lord's day, farmers would yoke a strong and a weak ox together to maximize their proficiency. Also, historians believe that Joseph and Jesus' carpentry trade in Nazareth consisted of building yokes for this very purpose. So, for Jesus to tell us to take his yoke means that he is telling us to let him help us. "Travel with me" is what he is saying.

"Learn of me." Now that's a statement that can be expounded upon! "Watch me; see what I'm doing" would be another way of putting it.

Well, what was Jesus about?

First of all, he lived in the present. He lived for today. That's what we need to do. Slow down and lighten up are other ways to think about what Jesus is saying to do if we want rest for our souls. And be thankful. Jesus thanked his Father for everything. So must we.

Thus, as one suffers the symptoms of depression, that of wanting to end it all or of being too emotional or of living with anger, hostility, anxiety, and/or fatigue, remember that God's Word contains treatment options. Realize that godly men preceding us have also been to that cave of depression. Recall that Jesus has sorrowed as we have. Confess the sin of anger and hostility that wells up, and get your mind off of self and onto others. Claim Philippians 4:6–8, and let your requests be made known unto God when anxiety knocks upon the door. And lastly, learn of Jesus, follow Jesus, walk with Jesus, and you will find rest for your soul.

Spiritual Treatments for Depression

Exercise: It is understood that physical exercise is good for the mind & body. That is, for the new mother, getting one's heart rate up, getting the blood pumping, is good for the soul. Likewise, the physical treatment of exercise to defeat depression also has a spiritual counterpart. It's called "doing good to others!" I love the line I've heard Pastor Jon teach several times. It goes like this:

There are ten ways to overcome depression.

Number one is to do something nice for someone else.

Numbers two through ten: repeat step number one!

And that's really true. As I do good to others, I take my mind off of myself and become more like Jesus. The Bible teaches that even though he was a man of sorrows in regard to my salvation, it also says that he was anointed with the oil of gladness above his fellows (Hebrews 1:9b). Jesus was always happy—happier than other men—because he always went about doing good. And like exercise, going out of my way to bless others can initially feel hard, but after the proverbial five minutes, my endorphins will kick in, and I'll get my second wind.

So, do good to others; bless other people. You're the one who will be healed in the process!

Bright Light: Truly we humans crave the sunshine. As you probably know, many cultures, some even in our day, have and do worship the sun. I'm thankful for the sun, and in the physical sense, we inhabitants of planet earth are totally dependent upon the sun. Sunshine is a wonderful reliever of some of the depression that can accompany the days after childbirth.

Spiritually, God has placed the sun in the sky to remind us of his Son! In actuality, it's God in which we are totally dependent upon. The sun is just his physical agent to teach us that. You see, God is light and in him is no darkness at all (1 John 1:5b). The endorphin release I receive from my daily dose of sunshine is also received when I look at my Maker.

How do I do that? Well, look at Jesus. The one of our affection told Phillip that the person who has seen him has seen the Father (John 14:9). We know that Jesus is the exact representation of the Father, given to us in a way that we can begin to comprehend (Hebrews 1:3). Thus, as I look at Jesus, as I think about Jesus, as I spend time with Jesus on a daily basis, it's the spiritual equivalent of enjoying the sunshine day after day.

Also, Jesus is the Word made flesh (John 1:14). When I look at the Word of God, I also get to read with the bright-light effect. Look at Psalm 119 soon. It is 176 verses long and each one of them speaks of God's Word. Contained in this psalm are promises that the sunshine of the Word delivers to my soul: joy, peace, comfort, and rest to name a few. Truly, God's Word is a lamp unto my feet and a light unto my path (Psalm 119:105).

Sometimes at night I will wake up around 4:00 a.m. and find it difficult to fall back to sleep. What will often help is to move to a different bed and read a bit in the Bible. Many times, after just five or ten minutes of reading, I will find myself getting sleepy again. I love it! From reading in the Word, my serotonin level has risen, and it's off to sleep I go! So again I want to remind you, Jesus promised if we come to him, we will find rest for our souls (Matthew 11:28–29).

Music: God is so good! As I reflect upon the many good gifts our Maker has given us, the joy derived from music is very high on the list. The Lord has wired our brains in such a way that we derive intense pleasure in listening to music. The particular melody may be different from person to person, but the effect is the same. The endorphins go up and the depression goes down. Indeed, for the sufferer of the baby blues, music is a God-send!

Marketers understand this. The next time you go to the mall, listen. What do you hear? In nearly every store, there will be music playing, which is targeted toward the customers. If the store is looking for young people to spend money, the music will sound different than what is playing in the art gallery. This is a good tip for you spouses also. If you want to get your husband or wife to agree to something you would like to have or do, ask your mate while listening to music that he or she enjoys. To hear a no to that request is almost an impossibility.

Spiritually, God has given music to me in the form of worship of him. As I sing of his beauty, grandeur, greatness, and love, it is music to my soul. Sometimes, though, I fall into the trap of thinking subconsciously that God must be awfully insecure in that he tells me to worship him. But it's not because he needs my worship, but because I need to worship him! That is, worshiping my Maker in song is one of the best cures for depression I know.

Let's look at God's Word to see how this plays out.

> Speaking to yourselves in psalms and hymns and spiritual songs, singing and making melody in your heart to the Lord.
>
> Ephesians 5:19

Chapter 5 of Ephesians is one of the marriage sections found in the Bible. In it I learn that I can have an intimate relationship with Jesus spiritually, just like I do in the physical sense with my wife! Paul teaches that marriage is a great mystery in that it pictures our relationship with Christ! Thus, if I want to get close to my Lord, then a real key is to sing to him. As I make a melody in my heart to him, I can get close to him!

So sing to Jesus often, especially when you are alone. You don't have to worry about what other people will think of your voice, and you won't be distracted by other people and their bad singing. In church, I like to close my eyes, as I know my puny brain will wander as I observe other worshipers if I have my eyes open. Sometimes I will go to the very back of the church too. That way, I don't have to worry about people watching me as I worship. You see, a key for me in worship is to get my mind off of myself. That should be a strategy in worship for you too!

David was a worshiper. Just read the Psalms. The Bible teaches that David was a man after God's own heart. I'm sure that his worshiping nature was instrumental (excuse the pun) in that divine proclamation.

> My praise shall be of thee in the great congregation: I will pay my vows (Vows is Old English for praise.) before them that fear him. The meek shall eat and be satisfied: They shall praise the Lord that seek him: Your heart shall live forever.
> Psalm 22:25–26

Truly, your heart will live in the fullest sense as you praise the Lord!

That's what I want. I want to clap like David. I want to dance like David. I want to sing like David!

One of the most famous messianic sections of the Bible is found in Isaiah 61. In it we learn of the Deliverer's ministry to Zion.

Look at verse 3 with me.

> The Spirit of the Lord God is upon me ... to comfort all that mourn; To appoint unto them that mourn in Zion, to give them beauty for ashes, the oil of joy for mourning, the garment of praise for the spirit of heaviness ...
> Isaiah 61:1a, 2b–3a

Do you want the spirit of heaviness to flee? Then grab this promise! Put on praise like a garment, and your depression will go away. But you must wear it in that time of the blues. It's not a dress you try on at the store in the changing room to see if you like it. You must wear it all day, and then watch and see if this promise will not come to pass. Indeed, depression will leave during that time of praise. So praise him often!

Laughter: Oh, the joy of a good laugh. And the harder the laugh, the better! A gut laugh is the best. You know, that funny thing that just cracks you up and keeps tickling you for a time afterward. That will knock back depression in a big way.

Wonderfully, for the new mother, when her newborn starts smiling, and especially when the baby starts to laugh, well, the baby blues just fly away! How wonderful it is to hear a baby laugh. That's because God has wired us to release an intense amount of endorphins upon hearing a baby laugh or seeing a baby smile. Just thinking about it is making me happy right now!

So the baby's laugh is curative for mom. How brilliant is that?

But when you think about it, laughter is something that you do with other people. Even a comedian doesn't laugh in private at his own jokes!

The spiritual equivalent to the physical pleasure of laughter is fellowship with other believers around Jesus. You see, in the Old Testament, one of the most profound pictures or types of our Lord is found in the story of Isaac. His name means *laughter!* And it is joy to my heart as I enjoy the greater than Isaac, Jesus Christ, with other believers. Paul teaches that we are to not neglect to assemble with other believers. I feel it is so we can have spiritual laughter with each other as we consider how good the Lord has been to us.

> When the Lord turned again the captivity of Zion, we were like them that dream. Then our mouth was filled with laughter, and our tongue with singing: Then said they among the heathen, The Lord hath done great things for them. The Lord hath done great things for us; whereof we are glad.
>
> Psalm 126:1–3

Food: Like music before, the joy of eating a tasty meal is God-given! The chocolate industry has certainly figured this out! You know, the Creator did not have to make eating pleasurable. Imagine for a moment how boring it would be if eating a good steak were no more enjoyable than breathing. Both are necessary, but eating brings pleasure.

Thus, it doesn't really surprise me as I consider Jesus and his ministry to us that eating food plays a huge role. The Savior loved to share a meal with his friends. And he told me to remember and to celebrate him at the table of communion. As I eat the bread and drink the wine, my soul is refreshed and revived. Later, when we meet him in the air and go to be with him in heaven, we again will feast at a great banquet he has prepared!

> And when one of them that sat at meat with him heard these things, he said unto him, Blessed is he that shall eat bread in the kingdom of God.
>
> Luke 14:15

Truly, Jesus is the feast. He is our food. He is our daily bread!

Horizons: I'm so thankful that God has graced me with a home on top of a mountain east of Medford, Oregon. In an arc of 270 degrees, I can look out and see the undulating horizon of the mountains against the sky, and it brings pleasure to my soul. For the new mother, a nice walk can bring some relief. As she looks upon the horizon, certain brain waves are produced which are quite enjoyable.

In a spiritual sense, I can go up into the mountains every time I come to the Lord in prayer! For talking with God, communing with the Lord, will give me the spiritual equivalent of standing upon the mountain.

You see, it's on the mountain that I can see clearly. I can look down and get my bearings for life. On that mountaintop of prayer, I get direction on where to go and on what to do. But when my prayer life is in the valley, when I'm not talking things over with my Lord, well then I just don't see where to go next. I get lost in the forest of life, and that's not what I want.

So climb that mountain of prayer. At times, like climbing a literal mountain, it can be hard. But the view along the way is great!

Medications: Certain over-the-counter and prescription remedies are available to help with depression. Likewise, faith and hope are tied together spiritually in a way that is a medicine for my soul.

> Now faith is the substance of things hoped for, the evidence of things not seen.
>
> Hebrews 11:1

Faith—that is, the state of believing—is the building block of hope. Thus, without faith, I don't have any hope. You know this is true in everyday life. As I look toward that vacation, as I hope for it, I believe it will come to pass. If something happens at work that causes me to believe that my vacation will be cancelled, well, then I've just lost my hope for that time off. I may still get the week off if circumstances work out, but ahead of time, I missed out upon looking forward to it!

Spiritually, faith works the same way. As I take in God's word by faith—for faith comes by hearing, and hearing by the word of God (Romans 10:17)—then I will have hope, hope for today, hope for tomorrow, and hope for eternity.

And my ultimate hope? Why, that's an easy one. I have *the hope* of the return of Christ.

So there you have it. My list of spiritual treatments for depression.

Let me remind you of them again all together.

First, we have spiritual exercise. That's doing good to others. Why, that's *love!*

Next, we have the bright light of the *Word of God.* We remember that Jesus is the Word made flesh, and, of course, we recall that God is Light!

Thirdly, we have the melodious music of *worship* followed by the laughter of *fellowship.*

After these, we have the food of *communion* and the horizon of *prayer.*

And lastly, we have the medication of *faith* and *hope.* These two go together and are pleasing to God (Hebrews 11:6).

Conclusions and Applications from Depression

It's obvious to me as I reflect upon these things, trying to listen to God's spirit as I write, that this book is not really written to the man or the woman who superficially believes in Jesus, but to the depressed person who is or has walked with him, for nearly all of the spiritual applications of the physical treatments for depression come in to play as we spend time with him. Think with me on this. Except for the exercise of love, the unbeliever and the carnal Christian who is depressed will have a very difficult time getting benefit from the other spiritual remedies. The bright light of the Word, the music of worship, the laughter of fellowship, the food of communion, the horizons of prayer, and the medications of faith and hope really can't be assimilated if I don't know Jesus and am close to him.

Thus, the ultimate treatment for depression is to really get to know the Lord in my heart. It's not the mental assent of him in my mind, for the mind is fickle and will be wiped out by many things including depression, but it's a personal relationship with him in my heart.

That if thou shalt confess with thy mouth the Lord Jesus, and shalt believe in thine heart that God hath raised him from the dead, thou shalt be saved. For with the heart man believeth unto righteousness; and with the mouth confession is made unto salvation.

Romans 10:9–10

I would like to emphasize that these two very important verses clearly mention that it's the heart of a man or woman that must believe in order to be saved. And that's not only saved eternally, but wonderfully, it means to be saved *now!* It means that as I believe in the Lord in my heart, I can and will be saved in all aspects of my life today! To bring home the point, Jesus told his listeners that even the devils believe in God; they just don't have a "heart" relationship with him.

So this is why it's so important for the lover of Jesus not to fall behind to the back of the pack. As Moses cautioned the children of Israel in recalling what Amelek did to the people who lagged behind, how he picked off the weak and the slow, this is what can happen to me as my flesh attacks in life. When I'm depressed due to illness, darkness, stress, or circumstances, and in addition, when you ladies are overcome with the hormonal changes of the monthly cycle, the postpartum, or the menopause, it's a lot easier to "snap out or it" if we're not lagging behind. We can navigate life and its difficulties a lot easier, and we can take advantage of the spiritual treatments for depression, when we are camping out in the presence of the Lord!

I see this often as a medical doctor in practice. Depressed women who don't know the Lord or who are far away from him will still benefit from the physical treatments we have mentioned, but the spiritual corollaries can't be taken in. Sometimes, though, in the case of the carnal Christian woman, the one who has at one time been close to the Lord but has fallen back, she will benefit from taking Prozac or Lexapro to jumpstart her mind to the place that she can begin to come back to the Lord. I've seen this happen, and it's not a sin for the Christian woman to take antidepressants despite what I've heard many well-meaning preachers state from the pulpit. It's one of those gray-zone areas in spiritual life. For one person it may not be the best, while for another, it can help bring her back into the love of God (Jude 21).

With that said, we should now consider if this state of mental anguish is really good for anything.

Of course, when I consider God's Word, I see that it is. The dark and lonely times of the soul often are used to refine the man or the woman who is walking with the Lord. It's the potter and the clay analogy that God has given to us in both the Old and the New Testaments. God will mold and shape us into the vessels he desires to make by applying pressure and heat. I can be mad at him for this painful process until I remember to look at the hands he is using to mold me, for those hands have scars from the nails that were brutally driven through them to atone for my sin and stupidity! When I remember the events of the passion of the Christ, then the heat of life, including the dark times, have a lot more meaning.

Look at nearly every main character in the Bible. Almost without exception there were dark days included in their stories. The names of Adam, Job, Abraham, Jacob, Leah, Joseph, Moses, David, Elijah, Isaiah, Jeremiah, Hosea, John the Baptist, Peter, John, Paul, and Jesus all jump into my mind as I consider their dark days and how God was using those days to bring them to the place of perfection. It is a true statement that on that day when we begin to see the big picture, we too, like the angel in chapter 16 of Revelation, will say, "Even so, Lord God Almighty, true and righteous are thy judgments" (Revelation 16:7b).

I could end this book right here, but I won't. There is still a bit more to say.

James, the Lord's half brother, shares some very important and life-changing truth on this topic at the very outset of his epistle.

> Knowing this, *(Pay attention, this is what you must know!)* that the trying of your faith worketh patience. But let patience have her perfect work, that ye may be perfect *("perfect" is the Old English word for* mature.*)* and entire, wanting nothing.
>
> James 1:3–4

This is huge! You see, trials are perfecting me, they mature me, they are completing me, and they are making it so I lack nothing.

Did you get that? The trials of life are what God is using to make me into the man I really want to be. They are making you into the woman you really want to be. I know you want to be mature and complete. I know you want to be entire and wanting of nothing.

And not only are the dark days making me into the man I want to be, but they are making me into the man *God* wants me to be. This is so great!

Thirdly, besides making me into the man I want to be and the man he wants me to be, trials and tribulation make me relatable to others. Look with me at Paul's opening salutation in his second letter to the Corinthians.

> Blessed be God, even the Father of our Lord Jesus Christ, the Father of mercies, and the God of all comfort; Who comforteth us in all our tribulation, that we may be able to comfort them which are in any trouble, by the comfort wherewith we ourselves are comforted of God.
>
> 2 Corinthians 1:3–4

Trials enable me to give comfort to others who are in tribulation. And it doesn't have to be the same trial. I can comfort women who are experiencing postpartum depression even though I've never been through that one because I've been tested in other areas. Areas that have developed the gifts of mercy and encouragement that the Lord has worked in me! This promise shows me that he does the same thing for you too!

I love the book of Romans! Talk about a mountaintop!

In it, I learn the principle doctrine that I am saved from the penalty, the power, and the preoccupation of sin by the cross, for I have been crucified with Christ. I also learn that even with the theology down I still need the person. For without relying upon Jesus, I will still continue to live in the flesh, as chapter 7 so poignantly describes when Paul asks, "Oh who shall deliver me from this body of death." I note that Paul asks *who*, not *how*, shall I be delivered from this dead body that I inhabit.

And the wonderful truth found so clearly in Romans is that I died with Christ, thus, I'm no longer married to my first husband, the Law, also known as Mr. Perfect. After that, I was resurrected with Christ and became his wife. He is known as Mr. Love. (Romans 7:4). That is, I traded Mr. Perfect for Mr. Love!

Thus, after learning these truths in the first seven chapters of Romans, I come to chapter 8. I come to Mount Everest, so to speak, for in chapter 8, I see three promises from God which I can claim that absolutely throw water upon the fires of depression.

Number one: "There is therefore now no condemnation to them which are in Christ Jesus" (Romans 8:1a).

What condemns me? Why, my past, of course. The mistakes, the sins, the wasted time of my past can depress me deeply. But God says no longer am I condemned for my past. No longer do I need to be depressed for the past. I can move on now!

Number two: "And we know that all things work together for good to them that love God" (Romans 8:28a).

Do you love God? If you do, then *all* things in your life are working out. You don't have to be depressed about any circumstance or feeling you have because it all is working out for good. This is so large that indeed it's hard to get my head around! But God said it, so I'm going to believe it. I need not be depressed about anything in the present.

Number three speaks of the future:

> For I am persuaded, that neither death, nor life, nor angels, nor principalities, nor powers, nor things present, nor things to come, nor height, nor depth, nor any other creature shall be able to separate us from the love of God, which is in Christ Jesus our Lord.
>
> Romans 8:38–39

There you have it! *Nothing* can break up my relationship with Jesus. Dying won't. Devils can't. The future will not take me out. No, nothing forever can come between us! Talk about good news. When I remember this it's hard to be depressed about the future!

So chapter 8 indeed gives the antidote for depression: depression from the past: there is no condemnation. Depression in the present: all things work for the good. And depression in the future: nothing can separate us from the love of God.

So we have come full circle. By that I mean that often there is a valley to enter after coming down from the mountain. Often, depression comes after the joy of the birth. But the great news is in the title of this book. The valley *between* the mountains! For after we have traveled into the valley, just like after those heroes of faith mentioned previously were in their valleys of depression, trial and travail, we, like they, will get to go up to the next mountain. The depression and despair will have an end. We can expect to someday leave the valley and climb back up to that mountaintop place of joy that our Maker had in mind for us all along!

Now as we end this book, I must again remind you and me that holiness equals happiness. Even though I am no longer married to the Law, it is clear that the Law is good and perfect. As I follow the precepts of the Law, I will be happy. As I trip up, then I will be unhappy as the repercussions of my mistakes come back upon me.

So with the Master's help, follow after holiness. You will be much happier.

Oh, and one more thing!

Believe God as much as possible. For in doing that you will have *all joy and peace!*

> Now the God of hope fill you with all joy and peace in believing
>
> Romans 15:13a

BOOK EIGHT

She Shall Be Saved in Childbearing

> In like manner also, that women adorn themselves in modest apparel, with shamefacedness and sobriety: Not with broided hair, or gold, or pearls, or costly array: But (which becometh women professing godliness) with good works. Let women learn in silence with all subjection. But I suffer not a woman to teach, not to usurp authority over a man, but to be in silence. For Adam was first formed, then Eve. And Adam was not deceived, but the woman being deceived was in transgression. Notwithstanding she shall be saved in childbearing, if they continue in faith and charity and holiness with sobriety.
>
> 1 Timothy 2:9–15

I don't know about you, but I've always had more than a little problem with these verses. I mean, come on, Paul! Aren't you being just bit chauvinistic?

But I believe with my whole heart that the Bible is the inspired word of God. Thus, even these seemingly difficult verses must be "God breathed." Over time, I have filed these verses away in my mind as ones that I don't fully understand and just try to move on to areas in the Bible that my puny little brain *can* understand.

But unfortunately, this is a book about women and childbearing, so I feel compelled to tackle these verses. It is my prayer that this little book will bless you and let you, the reader, see God as the loving Father that he is, not as some female-suppressing God, which some have wrongly made him out to be because of these verses.

> In like manner also, that women adorn themselves in modest apparel, with shamefacedness and sobriety: Not with broided hair, or gold, or pearls, or costly array.
>
> 1 Timothy 2:9

Some have said that women should not wear makeup and nice clothes based on this verse. I don't believe that is what is being said here. The Greek word for *modest* is *kosmios*. It is used only two times in the Bible, once translated *good behavior* and here in verse 9 as *modest*. It's easy to understand that the word *cosmetics* is derived from this word.

No, I don't think God is saying through Paul that women should not look nice, have nice clothes, and wear makeup. What I believe the Lord is saying, though, is that a woman should not dress in a distracting manner, in a manner that draws inappropriate attention to the beauty that he has bestowed upon her, the beauty for which the Creator meant only her husband to fully share.

You see, God made the male to be responsive to the female form. But he knows also that women can have an effect upon men by their dress, which can lead men to sin, which can take men out, which can break up marriages and hurt families. Thus he wants to spare his children this temptation by giving us this advice. Women actually are being considerate to their "weaker" brothers when they heed this instruction.

Before leaving this verse, I would like to comment upon the word *shamefacedness*. This means to have the ability to blush. A woman wants to keep in mind this power she has over a man and actually blush over it. Paul is saying it's not good for a woman to forget this effect she produces in her man and in men in general.

> But (which becometh women professing godliness) with good works.
>
> 1 Timothy 2:10

Godly women are the most beautiful! They glow and radiate Jesus Christ in a way that is only seen in this group of people. I agree with Paul. Godly women are the ones I want to look upon!

> Let the woman learn in silence with all subjection. But I suffer not a woman to teach, nor usurp authority over the man, but to be in silence.
>
> 1 Timothy 2:11–12

Sounds pretty harsh ... until we break this down. The word for silence in these two verses is *hesychia*. It's important to note that earlier in this chapter Paul exhorts Timothy, and you and me by extension, to pray for those in authority. This is so that we may lead peaceable lives. The word for peaceable is *hesychios*, which is just another tense of the same word.

Women are to be at peace in the church. This doesn't mean they cannot talk and contribute in the church body.

As these two verses are proscribing women from teaching men, they do not prohibit women from teaching other women. In fact, in the book of Titus, Paul writes to Titus that the mature women of the congregation *should* teach the less mature ladies (Titus 2:3–4).

Why does God not want women to be teachers for the entire group of men and women? The next two verses give the answer.

> For Adam was first formed, then Eve. And Adam was not deceived, but the woman being deceived was in transgression.
> 1 Timothy 2:13–14

The book of Genesis describes how God created man. He created Adam in his own image (Genesis 1:27). Adam was complete. Like God, he had both masculine and feminine characteristics. But in Genesis 2:18, we learn that God felt that it was not good for man to be alone. Thus he took a rib from Adam's side and made woman. He took part of Adam, the feminine part, and made his beautiful woman, Eve. Adam was no longer complete, and God told Adam to take the woman as his wife to complete him.

Adam declared, "This is now bone of my bones, and flesh of my flesh" (Genesis 2:23a).

They were complete in each other, and to this day this continues to be a primary role of marriage: to complete a man, to complete a woman!

As a digression, many relationships I observe in my role

as a women's health care provider suffer needlessly because a husband and a wife don't understand God's role for each of them in the relationship. The husband doesn't want to be a man or the wife does. How happy the couple is when they get it, when they understand they are to complement each other, when they recognize it's not a contest.

God made women to be much more sensitive, much more spiritual, if you will, than men. Women long for a close and intense relationship with God. In fact, I envy this trait that I see in women!

But it is this very trait that can get a woman into trouble. It's this very trait that Satan used to fool Eve, for the serpent lied to her about the forbidden fruit: "For God doth know that in the day ye eat thereof, then your eyes shall be opened, and ye shall be as gods, knowing good and evil" (Genesis 3:5).

Understand that women are more intuitive and less detail-oriented than men. Thus they are able to follow hard after the Lord, but they also can fall hard after the pseudospiritual, after the counterfeit.

That is why God wants men to lead the church. He knows that the traits he gave to Adam and his gender are better able to promote stability in the church, especially in doctrinal issues. You see, these verses are not a slam on women but simply recognize the innate differences between men and women.

> Notwithstanding she shall be saved in childbearing, if they continue in faith and charity and holiness with sobriety.
> 1 Timothy 2:15

She shall be saved in childbearing!

Now you've really gone over the edge, Paul! So women are just supposed to be one big baby-making machine? If they want to do God's will, then they just have to submit and birth a bunch of kids?

This is *not* how God intends this verse to be understood. The word *saved* is the Greek word *sozo*. It's not talking about salvation from sin here or even salvation from the difficulties of childbirth. It's talking about receiving a blessing. It's speaking of women being fulfilled, of receiving the full gamut of God's blessing for their lives. Paul is stating that in raising a family, a woman will be most blessed.

You know this is true! Look around. Every "on fire" woman that I know—and that's more than a few—who are working the job and raising a family always put the family first. And when things get out of kilter, they feel incredibly guilty. Don't believe for a second that men are the same. A man will sink into his job and almost forget the family. Not so with women. Paul is stating the obvious here. Women, you will be most blessed in life in raising your family. Period. End of sentence.

Now you men who may be reading this chapter may be thinking this isn't for you. Hold on, for it may be more important that you understand this than for your wife. You see, we all are the bride of Christ. We are all women! For the Lord is our husband and we are his wife! This entire concept of being a woman seems foreign to men. Indeed, I suspect that our role as the bride of Christ may come easier for a woman to grasp than a man for this very reason.

Think with me; everything I have said in this chapter about women and their roles also applies to men in their relationship with Jesus. We are not to grab the glory away from the Lord by our appearance, as verse 9 teaches. We are not to be distracting. But we are to strive with good work, as verse 10 states. We are to be at peace in the Lord's presence and recognize that we can be easily deceived by the adversary. Lastly, we too will be saved in childbearing. That is, we will be most fulfilled in raising a family. I'm speaking of our spiritual family. As the bride of Christ, we will be most blessed, most fulfilled, in bringing up kids in God's family, in witnessing and undershepherding children into the kingdom!

So there we have it, *A Woman's Silent Testimony: How Pregnancy Enlivens Biblical Truths*. We have come to the end of this book. In it, we have seen that God has used the intense and dramatic time of pregnancy to enliven and magnify spiritual truths. I love it. My favorite people in the entire world—pregnant women—and the trials and joys they encounter are used so beautifully to bring warmth and color to sections of God's Word.

I hope you have enjoyed traveling with me on this journey. And remember, we all are married to our wonderful Lord and Savior, Jesus Christ. As his wife, we get to hold hands with him and travel with him in ways that are only dimly seen this side of eternity.

I hope that in considering the words of this book that you can begin to see his plan for our future even a bit more clearly.

> For now we see through a glass darkly; but then face to face: Now I know in part; but then shall I know even as also I am known.
>
> 1 Corinthians 13:12

God bless you in the name and nature of Jesus Christ.

By His Grace Alone,

Dr. Dan Tomlinson
Medford, Oregon

listen|imagine|view|experience

AUDIO BOOK DOWNLOAD INCLUDED WITH THIS BOOK!

In your hands you hold a complete digital entertainment package. In addition to the paper version, you receive a free download of the audio version of this book. Simply use the code listed below when visiting our website. Once downloaded to your computer, you can listen to the book through your computer's speakers, burn it to an audio CD or save the file to your portable music device (such as Apple's popular iPod) and listen on the go!

How to get your free audio book digital download:

1. Visit www.tatepublishing.com and click on the e|LIVE logo on the home page.
2. Enter the following coupon code:
   1ee2-ee46-72f4-2926-a7d4-f394-480f-2fd0
3. Download the audio book from your e|LIVE digital locker and begin enjoying your new digital entertainment package today!